FAMILY CASE STUDIES

FAMILY CASE STUDIES

A Sociological Perspective

Edited by
Ralph LaRossa

THE FREE PRESS
A Division of Macmillan, Inc.
NEW YORK
Collier Macmillan Publishers
LONDON

HQ
536
F364
1984

The Free Press
A Division of Macmillan, Inc.
866 Third Avenue, New York, N.Y. 10022

Collier Macmillan Canada, Inc.

Printed in the United States of America

printing number

1 2 3 4 5 6 7 8 9 10

Library of Congress Cataloging in Publication Data
Main entry under title:

Family case studies.

  Bibliography: p.
  Includes indexes.
  1. Family—United States—Case studies. I. LaRossa, Ralph.
HQ536.F364 1984   306.8′5′0973   83-48641
ISBN 0-02-918010-4

For my father and mother

Contents

Preface

I REMEMBER FEELING NUMB at the end of both *Kramer vs. Kramer* and *Ordinary People*, two films that did more to communicate the complexity of family life than many of the family textbooks currently on the market. There was a certain amount of jealousy on my part, I must admit. Why, I asked, could my courses not have the same effect on my students as these two films had had on me?

It occurred to me that the difference between these films and my courses was not simply that the films were visual while my courses were verbal. The key difference was that the films used case studies to communicate their points, while my courses relied primarily on large-scale surveys. What the films lacked in breadth, they gained in depth (and vice versa, as far as my courses were concerned). But in their willingness to focus on a particular case, the films had accomplished something that my courses had not: they had forced the audience to become emotionally involved in the discovery of how families work. As a teacher, I knew that any learning device that operated on a visceral level and that encouraged people to see the forest, as well as the trees, was obviously powerful.

This book is, quite simply, an outgrowth of that insight. Based on the same educational principles used in films like *Kramer vs. Kramer* and *Ordinary People*, it presents and analyzes fourteen case studies to involve you, the student, in the discovery of how families work.

The way the cases are presented and analyzed is worth noting. First, there is an introductory chapter that will help you to understand some of the more subtle aspects of the cases. Then, before each case, there is a brief section that provides background material (e.g., why the case study was initially written), as well as key concepts and propositions specific to that case. Finally, at the end of each case, there is a series of questions that are meant to stir your imagination and sharpen your analytical skills.

I think you will find that the various parts of the book—the introductory chapter, the forewords to the cases, the study questions, and the cases themselves—go together nicely and that the book as a whole is not only informative but also fun to read. In fact, this is probably one of the few texts that you may want to share with your family and friends.

A number of individuals have helped me with this book, and I would like to express my gratitude to each of them.

Students in my family courses over the past few years have given me valuable suggestions both on the case study approach to teaching and on selected cases. The opportunity to experiment on them no doubt has made this a better book.

Joyce Seltzer, senior editor at The Free Press, has been a part of this project almost since its inception. She was one of the first to see the value of a family casebook, and she has worked closely with me throughout.

Individuals who reviewed the prospectus and gave me encouragement, perhaps when I needed it the most, include Richard Gelles, Chris Guzzardo, Barry Klein, and David Petersen. There were also five anonymous reviewers whose comments on the prospectus were especially helpful.

Several people examined one section of the book or another. For their willingness to lend a hand to a friend in need, I would like to thank Craig Allen, Bruce Brown, James Kochalka, Tony McCormick, George Magakis, Donald Reitzes, Joseph Stevens, Murray Straus, and Frank Whittington.

Special recognition is due to David Klein and two anonymous reviewers who read the entire book in draft and provided me with detailed written critiques.

Two co-workers who are probably as happy as I am to see this venture come to a close are Joyce Johnson, who typed the manuscript, and Jacquelyn Rosemond, who typed the project's correspondence. Their patience and good humor certainly made my job easier.

Finally, I would like to acknowledge a debt to my wife and colleague, Maureen Mulligan LaRossa, who offered both substantive feedback and moral support. I could not have done it without her, nor would I have likely tried. Thanks Maur.

Guidelines for Instructors

FAMILY CASE STUDIES CAN BE USED as the principal (perhaps only) textbook in a family course, but it was designed to be used as a secondary text. In other words, it is intended to serve as a supplement to other family texts, especially those that review and summarize the major research in the field.

In my own undergraduate and graduate family courses, I have discovered that I can better communicate the significance of a particular research finding or the essentials of an abstract idea if I rely on the cases in this book. For instance, when I want to talk about what it is like to get married, I use the Dick and Gail case (Chapter 1); when I want to talk about the process of deciding to become a parent and the transition to parenthood, I rely on the Ginny and Rick case (Chapter 2), the Sterling case (Chapter 3), and the Bernard case (Chapter 4). Dick and Gail's and Ginny and Rick's cases also provide an opportunity to discuss gender roles, and the Sterling case is essential if you devote any time to interracial marriage. The Breel case (Chapter 5) is an excellent supplement to a lecture on physical violence in the home, and the Gram case (Chapter 14) provides a graphic illustration of the kinds of nonphysical violence that can be directed at elderly family members. The structure and function of family ties in the black community are described in the Hines case (Chapter 7) and in the Ward case (Chapter 9). The former is also a nice illustration of social mobility in the United States, while the latter—along with the Neumeyer case (Chapter 8)—deals directly with boundary ambiguity in families with adult children. The processes of separation, divorce, death, and remarriage are vividly portrayed in the cases of Lynn (Chapter 11), Harry (Chapter 12), and Ruth (Chapter 13). Harry's case is especially interesting because it focuses on the pros and cons of joint custody, which is a controversial approach to parenting after divorce. If you are a therapist or like to raise questions in your course about the practice and ethics of family therapy, you will probably find the S. family case (Chapter 6) useful. And if you think that a lecture or two on communal families is a good way to uncover taken-for-granted assumptions about what families are and should be, then you will be interested in the Cliveden House case (Chapter 10).

As you can see, a variety of issues are covered in the book. In fact, you will discover when you begin to scan the cases that this brief review of topics barely scratches the surface. Furthermore, although the cases are arranged in a sequence that roughly corresponds to the family life cycle, each case is basically independent. Thus, you should feel free to ask your students to read the cases in whatever order works for you. The advantage here, of course, is that you can continue to use the same text or anthology and basically the same syllabus that you have been using all along, only now you can assign a series of cases that will complement—and make more comprehensible—your current book and lectures.

Why are case studies so effective in the classroom? Ever since I started using case studies, I have been trying to answer this question. In the beginning, I did not understand why I was having more fun with my students or why the grades in my courses started to improve. All I knew was that my case study courses flowed much more than did my other courses. Looking back over the past few years, however, I think that I may have finally figured out what case studies do to a class. First, case studies increase the clarity of written and oral presentations. They require instructors to be more precise, and they provide concrete referents that students can latch on to, identify with, and remember. Second, and more important, case studies establish a much needed bridge between instructors and students. They force instructors to keep one foot in the proverbial real world and, at the same time, because students want to know why families behave one way and not another, they lure students into discovering the scientist's world of research and theory.

Over the years I have learned a few things about using case studies in the classroom, and there are several techniques with which I have experimented. First of all, I recommend that you ask your students to answer the questions at the end of each case before you discuss the case itself.

This insures not only that everyone has read the case but also that everyone has seriously thought about it and is committed to a point of view. You may also want to supplement my questions or perhaps substitute your own. Whatever system you prefer, make sure it guarantees that your students are familiar with the cases beforehand.

On the day you are discussing a case, you may be surprised to find that you have all you can do to keep everyone from talking at the same time. A good case study should serve as a stimulus to interaction, and for some students the adrenaline will really be flowing, especially if they identify with the people described. When this happens, your job is to bring the students' comments to bear on the subject at hand (e.g., gender roles, parenthood, divorce). Do not worry about your apparent loss of control. With a little experience, you will soon be guiding your class through the material much as a conductor guides an orchestra through a symphony.

Taking into account the level of your course, you may want to ask your students to write their own case studies. Two of the cases in this book—the Hines case and the Gram case—were based on undergraduate papers, and two others—the Bernard case and the Ward case—were based on doctoral dissertations. If you are thinking about requiring family histories or genealogies, I suggest you read *Your Family History* (Lichtman, 1978) or *Tracing Your Ancestry* (Helmbold, 1976). If you are thinking about requiring an analysis of a current family group, I suggest you review "The Case Study: The Family" (Wiseman and Aron, 1970) and "Sociological Family Analysis" (Lehtinen, 1977).

Again, taking into account the level of your course, you may want to spend some time on case study methodology. If so, I recommend "The Theory of Case Studies" (Foreman, 1948), "Alternative Approaches in the Study of Complex Situations" (Weiss, 1966), and "Ethnographic Case Studies" (Rosenblatt, 1981). If you are interested specifically in case study ethics, see "Ethical Dilemmas in Qualitative Family Research" (LaRossa, Bennett, and Gelles, 1981).

Finally, there are two books that you should probably consult: *Dating, Mating, and Marriage: A Documentary-Case Approach* (Bernard, Buchanan, and Smith, 1958) and *Family Insights through the Short Story: A Guide for Teachers and Workshop Leaders* (Somerville, 1964). The first book is a bit dated, and the second deals with the use of fiction in the classroom, but each does an excellent job of outlining the advantages of relying on case materials in family courses. I particularly like Bernard, Buchanan, and Smith's characterization of a case study approach: "Whether or not the teacher is experienced, class discussion and analysis built around student reaction to cases is an almost failure proof technique" (p. xiv). Extreme? Perhaps. But I think that when you begin using this book, you will come to realize that basically they are right.

Introduction:
A Family Is a Social Group

IF YOU WERE TO GO on a jungle safari, you would ask a guide to escort you, to tell you where to go (and where not to go), and to point out places and things of interest. The fact is that while you may not be conscious of it most of the time, you are *always* using guides of one sort or another to take you through experiences. Your favorite movie or music critic, for example, helps you decide where to spend your money. Your closest friends help you interpret your innermost feelings. Indeed, the very act of perceiving something is a guiding process, as you pay attention to, or focus on, some items and ignore others.

The reason I mention this is that if you were presented with the fourteen case studies in this book and nothing else, I could not say with confidence that reading this book would increase your understanding of family dynamics. You see, the case studies can be interpreted in more ways than one. Some of you might see in them confirmation of the Judeo-Christian ethic. Others might see evidence for biologically based theories of human behavior. And still others might conclude that personality factors loom large in family life. Any one of these interpretations could be said to be correct; a lot depends on the criteria used to judge. The purpose of this book, however, is not to pit one explanation against the other, to use the case studies as a critical test, as it were. My goals are much more modest: I simply want to introduce you to one way of looking at families and to impress you with the usefulness of this vision. The way of looking that I am referring to is called a *sociological perspective,* and the object of this introductory chapter is to outline the essential features of that perspective.

What is a sociological perspective? It is not, as you might think, a perspective that sociologists alone use. Although sociologists probably have used this perspective more than other observers of the human condition have done, many anthropologists, psychologists, psychiatrists, social workers, home economists, historians, novelists, playrights, and journalists also have very effectively employed a sociological view.

The key ingredients of a sociological perspective are, first, a focus on groups rather than on individuals and, second, a belief that what goes on in groups and between groups is related to large-scale social forces, such as economic or political change. *Thus, the most important assumption in family sociology is that a family is a social group.*

Now, sociology is a comparatively new field of inquiry; consequently, it is not uncommon for a concept like social group to be defined in more ways than one. But, despite the variations from one textbook to the next, most sociologists would be comfortable with the following: a *social group* is a collection of two or more people who (1) share a set of goals, values, beliefs, and norms; (2) exhibit a pattern of interaction; (3) are structurally tied to each other; and (4) have a sense of identity with one another. Allow me to show you how these four elements can be applied to families.

Family Culture

What is the purpose behind your family? To pool resources? To justify sexual relations? To make babies? To socialize children? You could easily answer yes to every question and probably add several more reasons. These particular *goals* (aims, functions, etc.) are especially important, however, because they constitute the four goals that some social scientists believe are fundamental to the definition of a family group.

Of course, you might reject this view, and you would not be alone. Many scholars question both the validity and the utility of defining the so-called normal or ideal family on the basis of these four goals because, for one thing, to insist that families must somehow satisfy these four functions means that a lot of groups would not qualify as families. For example, childless couples would be excluded, as would a number of communes (Reiss, 1980).

But, though it may not be a good idea to rely on these particular goals to distinguish families from other social groups, it is worthwhile to try to determine the goals that in a given society are strongly established and generally accepted. Sociologists would say that these goals have become *institutionalized,* and they would note that institutionalized goals are important for understanding what families are all about.

Take, for instance, child socialization. This is a job that people in the United States generally think should be handled by parents. We are willing to let teachers and other experts have some input, but we still insist that fathers and mothers remain in charge of the task. In the ancient Greek state of Sparta, however, people thought very differently. Since Spartans believed that they should always be prepared to fight, they wanted children who were ready to do battle and comfortable with adversity. Parents supposedly would not be the best trainers because they would be too emotionally involved; they would "spoil their kids," to use a popular modern phrase. Thus, in Sparta child socialization was principally the responsibility of the state (Sommerville, 1982).

The institutionalization of family goals (and work goals, recreational goals, etc.) serves a very important purpose in human society. Human beings occupy a unique position in the animal kingdom in that our instincts are much less developed than those of other animals. Consequently, we lack an internal guidance system to give us direction. To make up for our instinctual deficiencies, we have developed the ability to construct an external guidance system, which sociologists call *culture*. Institutionalized goals are only one component of culture and their purpose, like that of the other components, is to help us chart a course through life (Berger and Luckmann, 1966).

What else, besides goals, would be subsumed under culture? Essentially all those elements that constitute our collective conscience and consciousness (Durkheim, 1950)—namely, shared *values* (what we like and dislike), shared *beliefs* (what we think is true and what we think is false), and shared *norms* (what we consider correct behavior and what we consider incorrect behavior). Also, generally speaking, the various components of culture influence and support each other. For example, Spartan norms for child socialization were based in part on Spartan beliefs and values.

A family is perhaps the group par excellence in which to observe social processes on a small scale (Kuhn, 1974). Therefore, considering what has been said up to now about culture at the societal level, we would expect to find that each family group has its own set of goals, values, beliefs, and norms—that is, its own culture. We would also expect that each family's culture would be related, in some way, to the surrounding culture.

The case studies certainly provide evidence of these assumptions. Consider, for instance, the Hines case, the story of an upwardly mobile, middle-class, black family. Because the Hines family is committed to moving up in this society, it has constructed a group culture that fits with the larger culture, a group culture in which personal achievement is accorded a high priority. By the same token, however, because the Hines family is a black family, it also has constructed a group culture that fits with the black community, a group culture in which the importance of racial equality is stressed. Understanding the Hines family thus requires an understanding of the family's culture, which is a combination of goals, values, beliefs, and norms drawn from at least two different social spheres.

The importance of a family's culture should not be underestimated. A family's culture influences not only how the members of a family interact with one another but also how the family as a whole interacts with its environment. And how a family interacts with its environment determines, to some extent, how successful it will be in dealing with that environment (Reiss, 1981). The Hines family, for example, is able to deal with what in many respects is an alien environment because its group culture defines interaction with that environment as a game that can be mastered and won.

Family Interaction

I said that families have the ability to construct goals, values, beliefs, and norms, which are used to guide their behavior, but I did not say how this construction process takes place. How, then, is culture created? The answer is that culture is formed through social interaction.

In sociology, *social interaction* is said to occur whenever people attach meaning to their own behavior or to the behavior of others. Thus, to say that culture is formed through social interaction is to suggest that institutionalized goals, values, beliefs, and norms arise from human conduct (Berger and Luckmann, 1966).

The behavior, or conduct, that gives rise to culture can be either verbal or nonverbal. *Verbal behavior* would include speaking and writing, while *nonverbal behavior* would include such things as posture, facial expression, voice inflection, clothing, scenery, locale, and timing (Watzlawick, Beavin, and Jackson, 1967). The more important kind of human behavior in the culture construction process is verbal. And the more important kind of verbal behavior is speech or, more accurately, conversation. Hence, it is essentially through conversation that culture is passed on from one person to another and from one generation to the next.

If you learn anything from reading and analyzing the cases in this book, it will probably be the significant part that conversation plays in the social construction of family cultures. Case studies demonstrate perhaps better than any other medium (e.g., statistical tables, graphs, charts) the complex connection between what people *think* and what they *say*. But you should be aware that the connection is sometimes implicit, often subject to controversy, and almost always indirect.

A conversation, for example, can operate on a number of levels such that a word may mean one thing at one level and a different thing at another (Ruesch and Bateson, 1951). In the Neumeyer story, for instance, the father tells his son, who has moved out of the house against his parents' wishes and who is visiting for the Christmas holidays, that he must put on a shirt for supper because that is the rule. On one level, the father has done nothing more than remind his son of the family's customary way of eating. On another and more important level, however, the father is creating an impression. The father is letting his son know that although he has gone out on his own, he is still a child as far as his father is concerned and thus is not in a position to rewrite the family's table norms.

Family members also disagree over the meaning that should be attached to conversations. Indeed, disagreement and conflict seem to be inherent to family life (Sprey, 1969, 1979). For instance, as far as Mr. Neumeyer is concerned, his son Richard's Christmas visit is really a sign of defeat—a return of the prodigal son. But, in Richard's mind, the visit is a favor to his parents, especially to his mother. Thus, as you might expect, the meaning that the two men attach to the shirt conversation is not only different but contradictory. Add to this the fact that each of them has a vested interest in promoting his own definition of the situation and you can understand why some sociologists contend that conversations in families can be seen as negotiations or manipulations as well as transmissions of information (Scanzoni and Szinovacz, 1980).

Finally, the fact that family conversations are multidirectional rather than unidirectional can make it difficult to follow the line between what people think and what they say. Dad says something to Mom, which causes Mom to respond, which leads Dad to say something else, and so on. Or, even more complex, Dad says something to Mom, which causes Mom to say something to Sis, which prompts Sis to say something to Junior, which leads Junior to say something to both Dad and Mom, etc. You will see a lot of this in the Neumeyer case study. One can easily understand why figuring out what goes on in families can be real puzzle. By the way, family members will often try to determine the beginning of multidirectional interactions, and they will often disagree among themselves as to who started such an exchange. But, however easy it may seem to name a single person or act as the origin of a string of events, dividing sequences of social interactions is as fruitless as identifying the beginning of a circle (Watzlawick, Beavin, and Jackson, 1967).

Family Structure

Besides having a culture and a pattern of interaction, groups also have a *social structure,* a network of relationships among group members. The *power structure* and *role structure* are the most relevant dimensions of a group's relational network; hence, I will limit my discussion of family structure to these two and will examine each in turn.

When sociologists use the term *power,* they are referring to the probability that a person or a group of people can carry out selected goals despite the resistance of others (Weber, 1946). Although this definition may seem cumbersome, it captures an essential feature of power, namely, that power is not something you have in the same sense that you have a car because power is not an entity; rather, power denotes a specific kind of relationship between people.

What does it mean to say that power denotes a specific kind of relationship between people? Suppose a husband says to his wife that he has the right to make all the decisions in the family because he is the breadwinner. What the husband is doing is trying to exchange his financial duties for decisionmaking rights, and what is implied is that if he were not the breadwinner, he would not expect to be in charge. The husband's claim is based on an *exchange theory of power*—a theory that asserts that power is tied to dependence: the more dependent you are on another person, the more power that person has over you (Emerson, 1962). And the exchange theory of power assumes that an institutionalized *norm of reciprocity* exists—a norm that says that people should reciprocate favors received from others (Gouldner, 1960). Thus, if someone does something for you, you are obliged to reciprocate. And if someone can establish a pattern of giving you things that you value, you not only are in debt to that person but also you can be asked to show your appreciation by doing what the person wants. In other words, indebtedness or dependence can be translated into powerlessness.

Exchange theory and the norm of reciprocity help us to understand how power is not an individual trait but a relational variable. First, exchange theory and the norm of reciprocity emphasize that behavior in a social group is a function of the configuration of relationships among the members in the group. As with a jigsaw puzzle, it makes little sense to look at the pieces apart from each other; one must inspect how the various segments fit together. Thus, a husband's income by itself is not sufficient to tell us how much power he might have over his wife; we would also want to know the wife's income, so that a comparative assessment could be made. And, in fact, if we wanted to fully test the exchange theory of power in a particular marriage, we would want a complete list of the husband and wife's resources, financial and otherwise, *and* a complete list of the couple's alternative sources of resources (e.g., a husband's parents may provide him with so much social approval that he feels he does not need any from his wife). Only by examining the total configuration of dependence and independence in a marriage can we determine who has the power in that marriage (Blau, 1964; Emerson, 1962; Thibaut and Kelley, 1959).

Exchange theory and the norm of reciprocity also help us understand how power denotes a specific kind of relationship between people by implying that people and families can and do change. The birth of a child, the loss of a job, the onset of an illness—common enough happenings—can all affect the pattern of power and dependence and thus radically alter the structure of a family. For example, one of the main reasons the divorce rate has increased during this century is that there has been a dramatic change in the percentage of wives working outside the home: in 1900 only about six percent of all married women were employed, while today that figure is over fifty percent (Scanzoni and Scanzoni, 1981). Wife employment not only affects the division of labor in a marriage, challenging the notion that the husband is *the* breadwinner, but also provides the wife with alternative sources of companionship, self-esteem, social approval, etc. In other words, by working outside the home, wives become less dependent on their husbands for a variety of resources, which means that they become more powerful in their marriages. This is not to say that women now have the same amount of power as men. Men still manage to keep on top in the marital power struggle. But the increased power that some wives have accrued seems to have given them the leverage that they needed to pull away from unsatisfying relationships.

What about family roles; how are they part of a family's social structure? When sociologists use the term *role*, they usually are referring to a set of norms associated with a social position. For example, the norms associated with the parental position constitute the parental role and the norms associated with the child position constitute the child role (bear in mind that not every role is as formal as the parental role and child role; social groups may also include people who play a variety of informal roles, such as complainer, mediator, or scapegoat).

Typically, social positions and their associated roles interlock with other positions and roles: children interlock with parents, husbands interlock with wives, uncles interlock with nieces and nephews, and—in the case of informal position and roles—mediators interlock with combatants (among others), and so on. The reason for this convergence is that social roles generally become meaningful in conjunction with *counterroles:* being a husband makes more sense if one has a wife (Turner,1962). It is not uncommon, however, for people to play roles even in the absence of a counterrole. For instance, in Edward Albee's play *Who's Afraid of Virginia Woolf,* the principal characters take on the role of parents even though they have no child.

Thus, a role analysis of a particular family or of families in a particular society would, at a minimum, include a description of four kinds of roles: formal roles with interlocking counterroles, formal roles without interlocking counterroles, informal roles with interlocking counterroles, and informal roles without interlocking counterroles. The analysis would also have to be broad enough to include those family roles that have become institutionalized; in other words, such roles as the economic provider role, the housekeeper role, the child care role, the child socialization and development role, the sexual role, the recreational role, and the kinship involvement role (Nye, Bahr, Bahr, Carlson, Gecas, McLaughlin, and Slocum, 1976).

The concept of looking at families in terms of the roles that family members adopt might cause you to wonder to what extent family life is analogous to a stage play. Actually, there are some striking similarities between the theater and family life. But there are also some significant differences. In both the theater and the family, people can play a variety of roles, and they can play them either poorly or well. Also, in both situations there are props, costumes, entrances, exits, and front- and backstage behavior. The critical difference between the two, however, is that most scripts in the theater provide fairly detailed instructions as to how actors should perform (actors are given lines), while most scripts in real life are ill defined and open to interpretation. Thus, family life is more like an improvisational skit (or series of skits) than a Shakespearean drama.

Of course, some family roles are more vague and subject to debate than others. The parental role is a good example (LeMasters, 1970). Though at one time people thought that they had a fairly good idea of what it meant to be a parent, today the norms associated with the parental position are vague or, if not vague, conflicting. Parents, in other words, often do not know how to act with their children either because they lack a clear set of guidelines (specific do's and don'ts) or because they are caught between two or more relatively clear but conflicting sets of guidelines (e.g., some experts say that children should be coddled, while others recommend corporal punishment). The first situation focuses on the issue of *role ambiguity;* the second describes what is called *intrarole conflict.*

In addition to having to deal with ambiguous and conflicting sets of roles, family members must also cope with the fact that they occupy a variety of interlocking social positions and that the demands of one position can compete with the demands of another. This predicament is known as *interrole conflict.* For example, a woman may be a wife, a mother, an employee, a friend, a daughter, etc., and be expected by her counterrole partners (her husband, her children, etc.) to do a variety of things to the point that she feels overloaded and/or pulled in five different directions. When this happens, the woman has several options. She can try to do everything that is asked of her but in the process reduce the quality of her performances, or she can appeal to the people who are making demands on her to "give her a break." Alternatively, she can select to do some things but not others. Or she can take what is generally considered an extreme course of action and drop certain roles from her repertoire; she can, for example, get a divorce or quit her job (Goode, 1960; Marks, 1977; Merton, 1957). Whatever action the woman takes, however, is likely to be influenced by how much she values her various roles. Roles that have less value to her are likely to be performed haphazardly or possibly relinquished in order to give more attention to high-priority roles. The institutionalized ranking of roles is something that sociologists consider very significant. It is hardly coincidental that in postindustrial societies, like the United States, the occupational role is often the one that adults are expected to perform well, even at the price of neglecting their family roles. And the fact that in virtually every society women are taught to value motherhood more than men are taught to value fatherhood explains, if only in part, the disproportionate amount of child care that women carry out.

Family Identity

Sociologists use the term *personal identity* to refer to the sense you have about who you are (*I-ness*), and they contend that your personal identity is essentially a product of your interactions with your counterrole partners. Hence, someone who plays the roles of male, teenager, son, brother, student, friend, and football player (to name but a few) would develop a personal identity based upon his interactions with his family, his buddies, his teachers, his coach, etc.

A *group identity*, on the other hand, is the sense of cohesiveness, interdependence, or *we-ness* that you develop from being a member of a social group, and, like your personal identity, it is a product of your interactions with your counterrole partners, especially your interactions with the members of the group with which you identify. Since a family is a social group, its members are prone to build for themselves a group identity, a feeling that they are the Joneses as opposed to the Smiths.

Every social group establishes some balance between personal identity and group identity. Social groups that emphasize personal identity are likely to encourage independence; individual pursuits; time alone or at least apart from the group; and separate spaces, possessions, friends, etc. Social groups that emphasize group identity encourage just the opposite: mutual dependence; group activities; time together; and common space, property, social networks, etc. (Rosenblatt and Titus, 1976).

Groups that affirm personal identity to such a degree that there is little sense of a group identity come very close to not being a group at all. Some therapists say that if this happens in a family, the family members will feel *emotionally divorced* from each other. Groups that affirm a group identity to such a degree that the members of the group feel that they are losing their personal identity—their individuality—would, in principle, operate as an undifferentiated unit. Some therapists say that if this happens in a family, the family members will feel *emotionally fused* with each other (Bowen, 1960). Emotionally divorced and emotionally fused families may need help (psychological or otherwise) to move them closer to the middle—though not necessarily precisely to the midpoint between these two extremes. Most families, however, achieve a reasonably satisfactory (and satisfying) balance between I-ness and we-ness without the aid of a therapist or counselor (Olson, Sprenkle, and Russell, 1979).

I do not want to give the impression that individual families are somehow fixed at one point on the I–we continuum; just the reverse is true. Families are constantly in motion along this continuum, and they are constantly striving to maintain whatever balance they happen to desire. Moreover, there are events that take place in the course of a family's life that can produce an abrupt and often unwanted change in a family's identity. Think of how the addition of a new member (e.g., a new baby or a new daughter-in-law) or the removal of an old member (e.g., the death of a spouse or child) can affect a family's identity. Thus, a family's identity is like an ocean's edge—always shifting and potentially alterable.

It could be argued that "the ways in which a family is a unit and the ways it provides for being a separate person are, in one sense, what every family's life is all about" (Hess and Handel, 1959, p. 1; see also Kantor and Lehr, 1975). Certainly most, if not all, of the case studies in this book can be seen as variations on this theme. But in order to see the cases along these lines, you must know what to look for.

Consider, for instance, the Cliveden House case study, which is about a small Philadelphia commune. The fact that I included a commune in a family casebook may seem odd, but when you read the case you will discover that it tells the story of how eight adults and one child tried to meld into one (big, happy) family. You will also discover that since communal families do not have an institutionalized base like that in traditional families, they must work especially hard to develop a family identity. It is precisely because communes are so deliberate in their identity-constructing efforts that I chose to include the Cliveden House case study. What the members of this commune had to do so consciously and conscientiously, most families do as a matter of course. Hence, the commune enables us to see more clearly the taken-for-granted world of family life and especially the taken-for-granted world of family identity construction and change (cf. Garfinkel, 1967; Schutz, 1967).

Conclusion

You may have decided by now that the four components of a social group—culture, interaction, structure, and identity—are so closely related that it is difficult at times to know where one component ends and the other begins. How is it possible to separate culture from interaction or interaction from identity? The answer is that it is possible only analytically; in reality, the four operate as a system, with each component reinforcing and/or modifying the other.

The sociological perspective is like a prism. Although it is possible to rotate a prism so that you can directly see one side, the other sides can still be seen through the side facing you; in fact, your appreciation of that side is enhanced by the appearance of the other sides in the background. Likewise, although it is possible to analyze one theme at a time, as I have done in this chapter, a full appreciation of that theme ultimately depends on seeing its relationship to the others.

The value of a family casebook is that it encourages you to ask how a family works—not how family culture works or how family power works but *how a whole family, taken together, works* (Weiss, 1966). A casebook does this because when you begin to try to make sense of family situations rather than particular family variables, you cannot help but see that families are more than the sum of their parts. This is not to discount the importance of looking at particular family variables and showing how they, often one by one, correlate with each other (the strategy in most family textbooks). It is, rather, to emphasize that at periodic points in the search for knowledge about families we must try to develop frameworks and theories that capture the contours of family systems.

To assist you in your search, I ask you to think of families as social groups. This introductory chapter is meant to give you the basics. The forewords to the cases are meant to sensitize you to the key sociological issues in the various stories. And the questions that follow each case are meant to force you to consider how each family illustrates, refines, elaborates, and qualifies the major points that were made in this chapter.

I think you will discover, as I have, that no matter how many times you read the cases, there is always something new to ponder, always some phrase or scene that takes on a different meaning the second, third, or fifth time around. For this reason, I encourage you to read the cases more than once and to talk about them with your classmates. Keep track of your feelings about the cases, especially if your feelings change as time goes on. Your reactions (pro or con) to the people and to their situations can tell you a lot about yourself.

And now, on to the cases.

Study Questions

1. Define the following:

social group	power
goals	exchange theory of power
culture	norm of reciprocity
institutionalization	role
values	counterrole
beliefs	role ambiguity
norms	intrarole conflict
social interaction	interrole conflict
verbal behavior	personal identity
nonverbal behavior	group identity
social structure	

2. What do you think Mills (1959) meant when he said, "The sociological imagination . . . is a quality of mind that seems most dramatically to promise an understanding of the intimate realities of ourselves in connection with larger social realities" (p. 15)?

1

Love, Sex, and Getting Married

Cast of Characters

Dick and Gail, newlyweds
Interviewer, Carl R. Rogers

Several years ago I had the opportunity to do a series of in-depth interviews with a number of young married couples (LaRossa, 1977). Looking back on that study, I remember how struck I was by the participants' answers to my question of why they had decided to marry the person they did. More often than not, the question would be met by a blank stare, immediately followed by a you-must-be-kidding reply: "Why, of course, we fell in love!" I guess what surprised me most was how self-assured the couples were. To them, love was not simply a good reason to get married, it was the *only* reason to get married.

The couples' answers reflected how well they had internalized this society's norms on *mate selection* (the term sociologists use to denote the process of choosing a spouse). For while the motivation to marry has varied throughout history and from one society to the next, the predominant norm governing mate selection in America is that couples should marry for love (Garrett, 1982). This is not to say that other factors are disregarded. On the contrary, there are also strong norms dictating that people should choose spouses who are basically like themselves (the same race, religion, social class, age, etc.). But no other nation gives as much prominence as the United States does to the importance of love in

determining who, within the structurally defined pool of eligible partners, is a good choice (Goode, 1982).

Love is not an easy concept to define. Some view it as "the polar case of
intrinsic attraction" (Blau, 1964, p. 76); that is, the extreme form of being
attracted to someone for herself or himself rather than for some extrinsic
benefit, like money or prestige. Others are more specific, contending that
love constitutes the upper limits of three interrelated variables: attachment (the desire to be near the other person), caring (the concern for the
other person's well-being), and intimacy (the desire for close and confi-
dential communications) (Rubin, 1973).

As difficult as love is to define, it is even more difficult to measure
(Rubin, 1970). How do two people know when they are sufficiently in
love to marry each other and what effect, if any, does getting married
have on the quality of their love? All of which brings us to the story of two
young people, Dick and Gail, who found themselves wrestling with such
questions perhaps more than they cared to admit.

The two met while they were in college in California; at the time, Dick
was nineteen and Gail was eighteen. After graduation, they moved to
Boston and decided to share an apartment; several years later, they were
married in a conventional ceremony. Six months afterward, Dick and
Gail were interviewed by a noted psychotherapist, and the case study that
follows is a transcript of several parts of that interview (Rogers, 1972).

The case centers on the character and depth of Dick and Gail's love
for each other. For instance, when they talk about the early stages of their
relationship, Gail confesses that she fell in love with Dick more quickly
than he fell in love with her and that their being out of balance hurt her a
lot. Dick admits that at first he did have trouble deciding how he felt
about Gail but that a two-month separation helped him realize that he
was indeed fond of her.

Interestingly enough, even after they had started to live together,
they deliberately avoided the word *love* in their conversations simply because the word implied a far greater commitment than they were willing
to make. Then, one day, Dick came to the conclusion that they should
break up. As he was walking out the door, presumably for the last time,
he told Gail that he really loved her. Though Dick did leave and, in fact,
began to date someone else, in a matter of weeks he and Gail were back
together again. However, Dick's disclosure had transformed their relationship; the belief that they were in love with each other was now an inte-
gral part of their shared life.

The decision to get married was made in much the same way as the
decision to acknowledge their mutual love had been. In the middle of a
long and heated argument, Dick blurted out a proposal and Gail, much

to her surprise, accepted. But while getting married seemed to remedy whatever was bothering them at the time ("It was obviously a resolution of something critical"), it did not put to rest their perennial doubts about their relationship. In fact, if anything, getting married only made them more self-conscious about their love. Gail, for example, says that she had the "funny" idea that "you didn't have to be in love any more once you got married" but that she has since discovered that marriage is "a lot of work." In his own way, Dick agrees: "Perhaps marriage only expresses an *intention* to resolve . . . things and not an actual resolution of itself."

The different reactions that Dick and Gail have to becoming husband and wife are interesting. Although Dick was the one initially reluctant to tie the knot, he actually feels *freer* now that the decision has been made ("I don't have to go shopping any more. I've made a choice"). Gail, on the other hand, pursued Dick, yet she has found the transition to marriage *stifling* ("I had ceased to be a person"). The fact that, at this point, Dick enjoys married life while Gail does not may have some connection to the rights and duties associated with being a husband and a wife in American society. When one examines the social realities of marriage—especially the division of household tasks and the structure of power and dependence—the evidence suggests that getting married may be a better deal for men than it is for women. Hence, every marital union is actually composed of two (often unequal) marriages—his and hers (Bernard, 1972).

Finally, something should be said about the level of conflict in Dick and Gail's relationship. It may seem odd that two people who are so hostile toward each other should claim to be in love. The truth is, however, that in many marriages conflict and love go hand in hand (Straus and Hotaling, 1980). One well-known study, in fact, found that for some couples conflict not only is a habit but also is a reason for *staying together* (Cuber and Harroff, 1965). Dick and Gail may very well fall into this category.

Dick and Gail

Carl R. Rogers

GAIL: Well, I saw Dick first. I liked him first. I saw him on the first day of school. I thought he was good-looking but I thought he was obnoxious. He wore these dark glasses inside. I found out later he had broken his real glasses and couldn't see without glasses, but he gave this impression of being very snooty. . . . I couldn't *stand* him. His roommate told me he really wasn't so obnoxious, and we started seeing each other. But I liked him almost immediately, after thinking he was just a brat. From the first I was pretty intense. Somewhere along the line I think he talked me into letting go of my feelings and just letting myself fall in love. I can remember making up my mind and saying, "Well, why not? What's it going to hurt?" And I think there were really a lot of hard times 'cause, you know, I was quite willing to keep at it heavily and steadily and Dick was different—he would start to back off. And my feelings were hurt.

ME: The difficult times really came before you started living together, when you were sort of up and down in your relationship?

DICK: Yeah, up and down. I was taking drugs heavily at one point, having gone to San Francisco on Christmas vacation from college, and I went through some *awful* experiences there and decided that that wasn't what I wanted to do. And all this time while I was in San Francisco, which probably wasn't more than two months—it seemed like ages—being away from Gail sort of reinforced my feelings about her. It was easier to make up my mind as to what I felt about her when I wasn't around her. . . .

Living Together
. . .

ME: Did living together make any difference whatsoever, whether for worse or better?

GAIL: We couldn't get away from it so easily. Dick couldn't walk out and disappear and stay gone for a month because, well, he did that when we were dating, but if he did that when we were living together, he would have to find somebody else to feed him. And it forced me to have to talk about it a little bit more, which is still going on. It puts us up against the wall, so to speak, and the big change, I think, was putting theory into practice. You know, when you're dating you can say, "Well, I'll be this way or this would happen when we're living together," but when you're living together, it *happens* and you can't theorize any more.

DICK: We never mentioned love in our relationship. And that's for at least three years. We never committed ourselves to loving one another until well into the fourth year, although I don't know *why*. We'd ask each other if we liked each other and placed a great deal of significance on that, but just as significantly we avoided the word "love," and all I remember about the first time we did mention love was that it was kind of a trauma.

GAIL: I can remember everything. I think we were arguing about us. And Dick was trying to tell me, without telling me, that he was leaving me. You know, saying there's this problem and that it's stale and it's . . . and so on. And I'm all ready to change and work it out and then he just got frustrated and he said, "But I love you and I really care for you," and then he walked out. That I really couldn't understand. You told me you loved me and walked out and left me! I thought, "Well, that's crazy." I thought that was just the nuttiest thing I ever heard. I thought, "Well, does he feel guilty about hurting me and is that why he's saying it?" And if he was all that crazy about me, he wouldn't have been walking out to somebody else! And he didn't tell me, you know, he never told me he had another girlfriend, which bugged me a lot because I thought he could at least do that. And I had to go through this whole painful thing of finding out, when somebody said they saw Dick with this little blonde. And I thought, "Well, if that's true, he's probably at her house," and so I went over there and there they were and Dick was mortified. I was bitchy and I wouldn't go away. I just sat there making small talk—and I know now that I loved every minute of it. And so I really didn't believe it.

DICK: You mean you didn't believe it when I said I loved you. . . .

GAIL: Yeah. But I guess I sort of had it in the back of my mind that we would get back together.

DICK: I was very dissatisfied with this other girl after a very short period of time, and it was interesting, because she outwardly seemed to have everything. I could, you know, I could list off consciously what I wanted and she had it, but it wasn't enough. I think one thing that I was very impressed about was that in comparing the two girls, this girl seemed not to have an independent life of her own. She seemed to be tied to whoever she was with. When we'd be talking with somebody else, she'd voice *my* opinions, and Gail doesn't do that hardly at all. She forms her own opinions and sticks to them. And I found that this really takes a great burden off of me in a relationship. And I don't have to be carrying the emotional stability, or the opinions, for two people. It's really like having a burden lifted off yourself when you're not living with a mirror image of yourself but actually another person. At that point I realized that for me Gail was another individual whom I did care for. . . .

DICK: Here is a problem that still gets to us, I think, and I think it originates with me. I don't . . . I'm not sure how these things arise anyway. But I think that I am *still* hung up about what *should* be and what *is*. It seems that all of a sudden I'll reach a threshold of Gail behaving in such a way that it just seems to me that it's *intolerable*. It should be *otherwise*, I think. But I get so *angry*. I guess that the reason I really love her is that she's her own person and yet because she is her own person there are things which I find *immutable*.

GAIL: I really can't be angry like Dick. I'm afraid to. I'm afraid he's going to beat me up or kill me or something, and he does get *really*, really furious and I get scared and I don't want to do anything that will make him any madder. . . .

The Changes Wrought by Marriage

GAIL: There was a more dramatic change when we got married than when we began to live together. There was to me.

ME: In what way? Why?

GAIL: Well, I don't know where all my ideas came from, but when I got married, I suddenly felt like my life was over. That was the end. I had nothing to do. I might as well lie down and die. There was no place for me to go, nothing for me to do. I had ceased to be a person. I could no longer be an independent human being or do what I wanted, even though when I thought about it, I couldn't tell why there had to be a difference between when we were married and when we were living together. . . .

ME: You felt much less of a person after you were married?

GAIL: Yes. I was really depressed and I am just now trying to pull myself up by the bootstraps. . . .

DICK: I don't know where my ideas came from either. They were just there. I thought, of course, that I wouldn't enjoy marriage and I would be tied down and I couldn't just really leave. My experience would be as Gail describes it. But it actually hasn't been. I am feeling like things are just starting and this is a surprise to me, a *real* surprise, and I can't account for it, you know. I just think that a lot of my attention toward other women as prospects is turned off. I don't have to go shopping any more. I've made a choice. I think the commitment has taken a lot of pressure off of me and left me feeling freer about actually going about the business of living.

ME: (*to* GAIL): What were your expectations *before* you got married?

GAIL: I talked myself into being very romantic about it and how nice it would be, and then other times I didn't want to be attached to someone, and other times I'd talk to myself and say, "Look, there's no *difference* between just living together and marriage—the only thing that changes is your name, and society will accept you," that kind of thing, but it does mean to be more stable.

ME: What were the reasons you got married?

GAIL: Well, I had kind of pushed Dick every once in a while about getting married. I'd say, you're never going to marry me. I'm never going to have any children, blah blah blah, but I wasn't all that serious about it. Then one night we went over to some friend's house and I was being kinda bitchy. I was in a nasty mood. Dick got mad afterwards and he kept getting madder and madder. We fought all the way home from their house, and it was a long drive, and we got ready for bed and we were still arguing and carrying on and then Dick told me to get out.

He said, "You can pack your bags and get out." And I didn't want to and I said, "No, I'm not going to. I live here and I'm not going to go. I don't want to." Then after a moment, he said, "Okay. Then do you want to get married?" And I said, "Okay." It was almost like he said, "We'll get married or you'll get out." And I didn't want to get out. So I said okay. And then I was happy about it. It was nice to make this commitment.

DICK: It seemed to clear the air. It was obviously a resolution of something critical. Marriage did seem to resolve whatever caused this incident. Certainly the proposal of marriage at the time did seem to make a commitment one way or the other— either of dissolving the relationship or solidifying it. Also I think a large factor was to make everybody else happy. I knew immediately that it would clear the tension of our parents, on both sides, you know. . . . It was a legal thing and kind of a public commitment of what was already committed privately, and I had always thought that was what it was. And perhaps under ideal circumstances that's maybe what it is. But certain of these aspects did reverse themselves.

ME (*to* GAIL): Are there any other things that you think of in regard to your life since marriage?

GAIL: I found out that I had a lot of other funny ideas about marriage too. One of them, and I don't know where I got this, is that I thought you didn't have to be in love any more once you got married. And then I wouldn't have to be bothered with Dick and I could ignore the whole thing and go about my merry business. And none of them worked out. I can't go about ignoring Dick all the time and I still care about him, which is another shock. If you expect not to have to be bothered with that and you are bothered with it, it's a lot of work. . . .

Some Problems in the Relationship

DICK: What we've been saying has regard to the marriage and not just living together. Living together was a very smooth transition. Gail met me in Boston and we immediately went about the business of trying to exist, though certainly we had conflicts and stuff. . . . One example, Gail, was when you would have a hard time letting me hold your hand sometimes.

ME: I'm sort of curious about this. When you would have trouble,

Gail, letting him hold your hand, was that because you didn't like the physical aspect of it or was it just giving him a temporary message such as, "I'm not keen about you right now"?

GAIL: Well, it was more. It was, I think, this thing about commitment. It seemed more personal somehow to me to hold hands than just about anything else. You know, more personal somehow than making love. I never have been able to make a commitment without trying to wiggle out of it once it was settled that there *was* a commitment. And that's probably a bit of the reason I feel so upset about being married.

DICK: Getting married, to me, either was a resolution or it wasn't. . . . I tend to want things resolved immediately and without time being a factor, perhaps a simple decision. . . . *(Thoughtful pause)* Perhaps marriage only expresses an *intention* to resolve these things and not an actual resolution of itself. You know, an intention to say it's worth it if the two of us can come to an understanding and live together doing it. I think perhaps that would be a more realistic way of looking at it. It occurs to me right now that I might be able to live with that attitude a little better. An intention isn't a nothing, it's a something, and yet it does admit freely that what you're after isn't to be found right now, immediately, but is a product of something else, maybe work and time. . . .

ME: As you look back are you better at working things out in the relationship than you were in the early days, or is it about the same?

GAIL: Well, I'd say in some ways it's a lot better, but . . . I think it takes a while to recognize that somebody else is a person, for one thing. You know, it just has to be beat into you like learning to talk or something. 'Cause there's no reason for thinking that somebody else is just as human as you are unless you set out to do so. . . . After I started seeing that Dick really was another person with feelings that are just as valid as mine, then it was easier for me to really think about them and not think of him as an ideal, but to make allowances for a person. . . .

Society's Pressures

DICK: Can I digress for a second? About the effect of getting married. . . . All of a sudden I realized there is a price to pay for this social aspect of it, for making everyone happy, and that was that all of a sudden I realized the role that I as a male was supposed to be, and I have been reminded of it in no uncertain terms by the in-laws and my parents. . . . When Gail and I were living together, we were sort of equal partners in making the living, and if we were broke, nobody really took the blame for it; but when we moved back and came into such close proximity with our respective in-laws, all of a sudden it became *my* fault when we weren't making money and *I* was the bum who wasn't going out and looking for work or wasn't doing enough. . . .

GAIL: I know what Dick's talking about. I sort of had expectations like he did, you fall into a role even if you don't want to, which is *so awful,* of a husband is supposed to be this way and a wife is supposed to be this way, which is part of the reason, I guess, that I felt my life was over. . . . Dick is not likely to be a typical breadwinner husband and I'm not likely to want to stay home and clean house. So it put me in a big conflict because I'm thinking, "Well, I've *got* to be like this, I'm married, and I'm supposed to do this". . . .

The Sexual Relationship

ME: Another question I would like to ask is what role has sex satisfaction or dissatisfaction played in any of this? Has it been a very satisfying part of your life or does it go up and down like the other aspects?

DICK: I'll try to answer this. I think it's really important. I think definitely we have had very little sexual . . . it's not as frequent as Gail likes, and somehow there's a frustration that I don't think either of us can put our finger on. I have varicose veins that will act up and really hurt. And too much lovemaking or making love too hard will make it hurt and in the back of my mind this is there. When we first started making love, I had quite a few cases of ah, ah . . . impotence—not being able to perform. And this worked itself out. I don't know what it was. . . . I think there were many different doubts and fears, certainly homosexuality fears, because I was an adolescent, and, ah, perhaps even drugs had something to do with it. It's hard to tell, but the point is that after a while that part of it hasn't been a problem.

GAIL: Ah, I don't know exactly what it is. There are times when I don't have an orgasm, though not very frequently any more. I have a hard time being satisfied, and when I'm not, it's not anything Dick is doing or not doing, it's in me, and I haven't figured out what it is. And also I have a lot of times a fear of pregnancy. Because of special medical problems I can't use the Pill or an IUD, and so I have to use a diaphragm, which is not foolproof, and I don't want to have any children now, and it *is* a problem. I think there is some little evasive problem that I can't really put my finger on and it's not something simple that you can read about. . . .

DICK: It seems like Gail needs and wants more sex than I do. Would you agree that outwardly that's the way it seems? *(She nods)* When Gail doesn't feel satisfied, I feel very sympathetic because I remember when I couldn't perform and I just don't feel any hostility toward her. . . .

GAIL: I don't like this speaking for Dick, but a couple of times I've gotten the feeling that Dick felt like women took advantage of him sexually. That he was being taken advantage of, to be expected to perform. And that makes me a little hesitant because sometimes if he's feeling like this, I don't want to approach him, because I don't want him to think I'm some evil woman who's going to rob him of his virtue or something. It used to hurt my feelings if I'd make advances and he wouldn't respond, but it doesn't so much any more.

DICK: That clarifies something for me. I think you're right on that.

ME: Your sex life evidently hasn't been ideal. There is this elusive something that is not quite figured out, but it impresses me that you don't fight each other on this. You, both of you, sound quite understanding and sympathetic toward the other individual.

DICK: I feel . . . I really try to empathize. I think sex problems . . . I've had 'em and you know, it's a matter of having . . . I wouldn't wish it upon anybody else.

ME: What could have been a matter of "You want too much," or something of that sort, doesn't seem to come out that way at all.

GAIL: One time it did. Remember when you got so mad at me and told me I was twisted?

DICK: Oh, did I?

GAIL: Yes, and that *really* upset me. . . .

A Brief Look at the Future

DICK (*to* GAIL): Since we got married I really see you expressing yourself in different ways. Instead of expressing yourself only one way, and that's getting depressed, you're being hostile, or when you're happier, you're actually happier too, you know. I have a feeling of optimism about it, although Jesus, it could go in any direction but I feel optimistic about you, you know, and your own feelings. . . .

GAIL: You really get tired after a while of making yourself not be depressed or making yourself feel something rather than just be blah. And it's very tiring. It's like exercising muscles that have never been used. . . .

Study Questions

1. The process of getting married and being married transforms a man and a woman—it changes the way they define themselves and the world around them. This transformation takes place in the course of marital conversation; *talking about* the new relationship serves to make the marriage and its accompanying changes more real to the couple (Berger and Kellner, 1964). What connection do you see between the way Dick and Gail talk about their relationship and the relationship itself?

2. Some studies suggest that very early in a marriage a husband and wife may establish a pattern of interaction that lasts for as long as they stay together (e.g., Raush, Barry, Hertel, and Swain, 1974). Do you see any evidence of this happening to Dick and Gail? What do you think might explain the development of such a persistent pattern?

3. "When a man and woman decide their association should be legalized with a marriage ceremony, they pose themselves a problem which will continue through the marriage; now that they are married are they staying together because they wish to or because they must?" (Haley, 1963, p. 119). Do you think this assertion is true? Do you think it might help us to understand some of the dynamics in Dick and Gail's relationship?

2

Kids and/or Careers

CAST OF CHARACTERS

Ginny, former teacher, now law school hopeful; Rick's wife
Rick, attorney; Ginny's husband
Interviewer, Gail Sheehy

GINNY AND RICK BRAINARD have been married for five years, and they have a son who is about three and a half. They were interviewed by Gail Sheehy and included in her best-selling book *Passages* to illustrate the kinds of knots that people often get entangled in as they graduate from their twenties to their thirties. The case focuses on two decisions that for Ginny and Rick seem to be inexorably linked: the decision over whether to have a second child and the decision over whether Ginny should go to law school.

Ginny, who has a teaching certificate, has not worked outside the home since she became engaged. But after being a homemaker and mother for several years, she now feels that the time is ripe to pursue a career and has a hunch that she is better suited to be an attorney than an educator. Since law school is a big commitment—typically involving three years of full-time study—she also does not think that it would be a good idea to have a second child, at least not yet.

Rick disagrees. An attorney himself, he thinks that he knows what it takes to succeed in the legal profession and he does not believe that Ginny would succeed. He thus sees her interest in going to law school as well intentioned but misguided. What is more, he wants very much to have a second and a third child and possibly a fourth, and he suspects that Ginny's schooling would get in the way of her responsibilities as a mother, as he defines them. Finally, since he is now at a point in his career at which he is trying to make a big move, he does not want to cater to both a new baby and a student wife. In fact, if anything, he would like Ginny to take care of him more than she has up to now.

Ginny's reaction? She feels that Rick is being unfair, and she contends that from the start he has done whatever he could to undermine her career aspirations, possibly even tricking her into motherhood ("You made me pregnant to eliminate any possibility of my going to law school").

Rick responds to Ginny's accusations by saying, first, that she had promised before they got married that she would have a lot of (his) children and, second, that deep down she really wants to be a "wife and mother and protector of the family" but that she is afraid to admit it.

At the root of Ginny and Rick's inability to come to terms with each other is the fact that each of them has different expectations about what it means to be a husband and what it means to be a wife. In other words, Ginny and Rick cannot seem to agree on what their marital roles should be. As you will see when you read the case, Rick believes that being a husband means being committed to a career and making a name for oneself and one's family, while being a wife means raising children, cleaning house, doing volunteer work (if the wife does anything outside the home), and catering to the husband's needs. Ginny, on the other hand, says that a husband is someone who should be allowed, even encouraged, to pursue a career, but she does not think that the husband's career should eat into his family time, at least not to the extent that Rick's career evidently does. She also believes that it is perfectly acceptable for a wife to have a career (not simply a job) and does not agree with Rick that the family should be a woman's main source of identity.

It is interesting that Rick's attitude about marital roles is so traditional, perhaps chauvinistic. He does not fit the stereotype of the working-class hero or blue-collar aristocrat (LeMasters, 1975), the kind of character made famous in television shows like *All in the Family*. Rick is an articulate, college-educated, upper-middle-class professional who nevertheless believes that a woman's place is in the home and behind her man.

Does this mean that Rick is more the exception than the rule and that Ginny and Rick's conflicts are rare outside the bottom rungs of society? Hardly. The truth is that this case study may be more typical than we realize or would like to believe. First of all, it is common for men to espouse more traditional family views than do women. For whatever reason, men seem to prefer a sharper division of labor and they tend to be more supportive of the status quo, especially when it comes to questions of who should have a career, who should take care of the children, etc. Second, although socioeconomic status is inversely related to traditionalism (that is, men who have high-status occupations and college educations tend to be less traditional than men who have low-status occupations and no college educations), the differences across the socioeconomic spectrum are not very strong. In other words, lower-class men may be more traditional than middle-class men, but men in both classes still are fairly traditional (Scanzoni and Scanzoni, 1981).

Generally speaking, it is easy for middle-class men to mask their traditional attitudes if they are simply asked to complete a standardized (i.e., multiple-choice) gender-role questionnaire. But when they are forced to elaborate their views—for example, in an in-depth interview—they tend to exhibit a traditional underside. In a study conducted at an Ivy League college, unmarried men were asked whether they thought it appropriate for mothers of preschool children to take a full-time job (Komarovsky, 1973). At first, most of them said yes. But when they were asked to explain why, they began to qualify their original affirmative response, such that in the end only about seven percent could be said to have no reservations.

The fact that middle-class men may be less honest with themselves and others when it comes to marital roles (or less conscious of how they really feel) cannot help but have an effect on the pattern of family interaction in middle-class homes. Thus, Rick says things like "I don't think she'd make a good lawyer" and "Ginny is defensive" instead of telling Ginny that she cannot go to law school because he does not want her to go and he is the boss—a straightforward, traditional response. As sincere as he may be, Rick makes it difficult for Ginny to believe that he is taking her seriously, and he makes it difficult for Ginny to counter his objections. As a result, Ginny finds herself in the position of having to beg ("I'll try to get as much as I can of him, and he'll try to evaluate the legitimacy of my complaints").

We can only guess whether Ginny and Rick ever manage to work out their differences. What do you think?

Ginny and Rick

Gail Sheehy

AND NOW THEY WERE 30. He, an upstanding Wall Street lawyer chafing to work for the public good. She, a diverted case, a lover of politics and veteran of campaigns, but a mother, a clipper of part-time want ads. They had married at 25. And for several years they seemed to be typically eager people enjoying the new experiences of a typical marriage within the professional class. I knew them as friends, but nothing about the quality of threads that bound them as a couple. Except to sense that by now they had their tangles like the rest of us.

There were brief moments to go by, nothing consistent. Rick seated at a luncheon in his parents' summer home, dutifully quiet while the well-known father expounded on how to win a class action suit. Occasionally his father would say, "Rick dug up that citation for me." The rest of the time Rick would press creases in his napkin. Ginny's place would be at that end of the table where the heads barely clear plate height, the children's end, the conversational junkyard. At moments she looked like a little old woman.

But later they would be a young couple frolicking on the beach, different people. Ginny with her pixie hair scrambled and her slender legs cutting up the sand like scissors, playing Frisbee, playing out her girlhood. Rick would hoist their small son to his shoulders and beam with the contentment of carrying the world on his head.

From time to time a comment would suggest the vast inner space of their marriage, the disconnect points in their dream, the shadows of separate demons.

"The concept of being 55 years old and stuck in a monotonous job drives me wild," Rick would say, "not so much the money, but the *claustrophobia.*" Or another man's wife would express the wish to go to law school. "Great idea, those were the best years of my life," Rick would say, rushing into the young woman's wish and invigorating it with advice, contacts, the full weight of his approval.

"Everybody else's wife can go to law school, but not your own." In dropping the remark, Ginny would take apparent pleasure in exposing a contradiction.

Trapped, Rick would make a weak joke. "Ginny's way of expressing herself is to get into a fight."

I talked with Rick Brainard first. The idea of being an attorney was one he'd had since he turned 13. His parents gave him one share of stock in a major league baseball team, and upon receiving his first proxy form, he went to the ball park and told the coach how to run his team. Newspapers ran interviews with this little free-lance reformer. Rick was tickled at stealing for a day the kind of publicity usually focused on his father, a lawyer who had never succumbed to the temptation to run for public office and therefore held his status as a leading independent reformer in their city. As the only son with several sisters, Rick had a powerful model with whom to compete.

Graduating from college with mediocre grades and a political science major he considered useless, Rick took off for some wandering abroad, which he found a strong learning experience. Even before entering law school, though, his direction was further shaped by a professor who didn't flinch from taking unpopular positions but who demanded excellence of written expression. The professor was a master at employing language creatively to support his argument. Rick added this to his aspirations.

"I've always had three goals. I like power. I'd like to have money. I don't think either of these excludes a third, which is, I want to be in a position to work for the public good."

I asked if he consciously thought of himself as "running for president."

"I used to think I wanted to run for government. But it was never a goal; it was a dream I've given up on. My present goal is to get to a position where I can call up the mayor and say, 'Look, I recommend this.' I have a mentor in the law firm who operates this way, and he bedazzles me."

Apart from his professional goals, there are rumblings in Rick's life system at 30 that he couldn't have predicted. For one thing, he is eager to increase his family. "The concept of a home is very meaningful to me. I love my son in a way I couldn't have anticipated. And I want more children. I could never live alone."

Another change is the tension building between him and his wife. "I don't think Ginny anticipated the concern she has about her role. Or the degree of time I put into my work. I've told her that I'd like to be more taken care of. She feels, and intellectually I agree with her, that I should help more with my son. But emotionally, I'd like everything to go away."

Most upsetting to Rick is the change from feeling that there is plenty of time to do it all to the sense of time pressure. Just to be able to try a case and to be thought competent was enough in his twenties. Now he's impatient to branch out.

"I'd say that 85 percent of the time I thoroughly enjoy my work. But when I get a screwball case, I come away from court saying, 'What am I doing here?' It's a *visceral* reaction that I'm wasting my time. I keep saying there's something more. And I'm afraid I might not get the opportunity to find out what, unless I make it."

He is considering leaving the law firm. If he waits much longer, it will be too close to the time of reckoning on whether or not he becomes a partner. "And that's like getting married to the firm."

Had he talked to Ginny about these visceral changes? I asked. "I haven't talked to her about the internal workings of my mind in this because she's not going through it, and she can't go through it. The input will have to come first from other people."

What would he most like from his wife at this point? "I'd like not to be bothered. It sounds cruel, but I'd like not to have to worry about what she's going to do next week. Which is why I've told her several times that I think she ought to go back to school and get a degree in social work or geography or whatever. Hopefully that would fulfill her, and then I wouldn't have to worry about her line of problems. I want her to be decisive about herself."

Ginny's girlhood was far less complacent. For the first eleven years she was an only child, and then her parents began building a second family.

"The first time I saw my mother drunk was right after she bore the first of four more children. It just got worse with each child. It became more obvious and difficult—mother always going out on some pretense of grocery shopping; Dad literally dragging her out of bars. Whenever I was home I had to work, diapering, vacuuming, cooking, being a second mother to my brothers and sisters. I got into a terrible competition with my mother because I was more patient and clever at managing the little ones. She would yell and scream." Ginny felt smug but always guilty; she had replaced her mother in a role on which the mother had defaulted. Nonetheless, she did take over in a difficult situation and seemed to be on her way to becoming a strong individual.

The bright spot was that she had a lively mind and an excellent academic record, which her father avidly fostered. He stayed up late with Ginny after the housework was done and prepared her for tests. She was especially good in math, and he was an engineer. They became intellectual mates. But he was never satisfied if she brought home less than 100 percent on a math test. At 17, Ginny yearned to break free of her tedious family responsibilities, but she was allowed to stray only as far as her own backyard. Her father insisted that she go to the hometown university where he was an employee.

"I was very scared of being a math major. Math was for boys. All the girls in my social group were history majors. But I did so well in my first math course, I began tutoring two boys. Then, I don't know what happened. I flunked the final exam." The teacher insinuated she had cheated to do well in the first course. He said he would give her a C if she promised not to continue in math the next year.

"It was a shock to fail the math exam because I'd always done so well. I decided I wasn't as smart as I thought I was. I'd switch to history and get decent marks and not rock the boat. My father didn't care anymore. I had failed him badly. It was an end to something."

One night when she was combing her hair before a date, her father said he guessed that she was just going to college to have a good time and find a husband. She wailed at him, "How can you say that?" But there was no changing his mind. What registered with Ginny was, "I guess I'm not as smart as he thought I was." And when it came time to deliberate about how to get a scholarship to a graduate school, her father's testy recommendation was: "Be a stewardess."

With little choice of occupation and no further financial support, her only vision was: "No matter what happened, I was going to New York." Making the rounds of employment agencies there, she was told over and over, "You're overeducated, and you can't type." She fell into a master of arts in teaching program and eked out her degree on a stipend. But this led her into a job she found absorbing. She teamed up with a black teacher in a Harlem school, and together they became a model team, committed to making a social contribution through early childhood education.

A year later she met Rick. "To me, it was a choice of Rick or the job. And I wanted to be with Rick." Having left her teaching post guiltily, she grew restless after the first exciting year of married life. She decided to apply to law schools. Rick said, "Well, try it, if you get through the first year, maybe you can find a way to take it part time."

"His one condition—I don't know if I agree with it or not—was that I could only apply to Columbia, Fordham, and NYU. He said, 'If you can't get into one of those three, then you're probably not meant to be a lawyer.' I thought there were others in the acceptable range, but couldn't apply. The fact that I wanted to become a lawyer was minimally important to what he was doing, in terms of impact on his life and his success. He was concerned about the time I'd have left for him.

"I studied vigorously. Everything was coming together for the first time, my continued interest in politics, my analytical mind, my social service bent, and law school became so appropriate. I felt I had a direction, a goal."

The next episode in her life Ginny recalls vividly, even to the dialogue. A month before the results of her boards came back, she visited the doctor with mysterious symptoms. She phoned Rick at his firm.

"I'm pregnant."

"Gin, that's thrilling!"

"But it may not be very convenient. I think we should discuss it."

His voice thinned. "Discuss—what?"

He came home that night well prepared for the defense.

"You're going to make a superb mother, Gin. Don't panic. Your qualms are just based on feelings of inadequacy. Believe me, I have absolutely no doubt—"

She flew at him, crying, raging. "I'm not ready to have a baby! You did this. You're forcing me to choose."

"What are you saying?"

"You made me pregnant to eliminate any possibility of my going to law school."

"That's unfair." He argued the case with that legalistic sleight of hand which assures that nothing is lost sight of except the point. "Isn't it true that you haven't been accepted yet? It's not as though I found out that Columbia accepted you and did something to prevent it. These occurrences that you're anxious about haven't come together yet."

"We could have an abortion," she said.

His face lost all expression. With an almost clinical detachment, his eyes fixed on his wife, carrier of his seed, hysterical vessel.

"We could try again later," she added.

He led her to the living room sofa, his voice firm. "This is a very bad idea. Right now you're a little upset and afraid."

She sobbed on his shoulder, knowing that his refusal to fight would be her defeat. She did not go to law school.

After reconstructing their histories separately, we agreed it would be illuminating to sit down together and talk about the central points of conflict in their marriage. There were several issues on which each had offered me a dramatically different interpretation: children, work, time.

Who really wants children in this family? How badly? And what are you willing to give up?

RICK: I want at least three, if not four. Very badly. Not just for personal satisfaction, but because of how I grew up. Being the only male Brainard of my generation, I do feel pressure. I'd like to have two sons and one or two daughters as well. I don't know what I'm willing to give up. When I was a boy I didn't see much of my father. Once I figured it up and had a confrontation with him. I said I only got to see him seventy-two hours a year. He began taking me away for one weekend every year, just the two of us. I envision something like that for my sons. And daughters. But I'm not willing to give up the kind of commitment I have for my own profession. Obviously, something has to give at some point.

GINNY: I have a much more reserved commitment to having children. I'm being honest with myself and Rick when I say that I want to see how I react to the birth of each child before I have another one. If everything goes fine, then I'm willing to have four. But I have a stronger respect for how family life can deteriorate if you have more children than you can successfully handle.

RICK: Right now we've worked out a satisfactory arrangement around our son's nap schedule. I try to see him for half an hour in the morning and half an hour at night.

GINNY: I find it totally unacceptable that your relationship with your father, or your son, is based on fixed periods. It's saying:

"Here's your chance, and if you don't take it now, that's tough cookies." I think parents have to be there when they're needed.

Who first brought up the subject of children?

GINNY: You did, right?

RICK: The only thing I remember was Ginny and her roommate in college talking about having eleven children each, opposing football teams.

GINNY: It was more than a joke. I imagine it had a lot to do with bragging about our ability to produce. But Rick tells me now that he assumed I was going to maintain this pact, that I've reneged.

Who wanted Ginny to give up the job she had before she married?

RICK: I think Virginia's job took more out of her than practicing law does for me. She had a total commitment. And I felt to some extent that's inconsistent with marriage and raising children.

Were you attracted by the kind of work she did, because it was with children?

RICK: No, what attracted me was that independent woman who had a commitment. I'm in favor of that.

GINNY: Rick still doesn't see the contradiction.

RICK: Well, my understanding was that Ginny quit because there were lots of premarital details to work out. It was also the first time she had any degree of financial ease; she might have enjoyed that.

GINNY: I enjoyed being with you as much as possible. So the choice became either cut back on seeing you or give up teaching. You had also let me know that you didn't think it was possible for me to balance the two commitments.

RICK: I honestly don't recall. It wouldn't surprise me.

How did you feel, Ginny, about being free for once to have fun?

GINNY: I liked that. Very much.

Deep down, did any part of you welcome the chance to pull loose from the responsibilities of being a mother to the schoolchildren, as you had been at home for your brothers and sisters?

GINNY: That's possible. But intellectually, I had enormous disrespect for a woman who did nothing. Rick and I both agreed after the honeymoon that there was nothing admirable about a woman vegetating. He anticipated having an interesting wife who was involved with volunteer activities or some sort of part-time thing. One of the main conflicts is that Rick doesn't see why I have to be paid. I don't get much satisfaction out of volunteer work.

How did each of you see Rick's future when you married? What part would each of you play in it?

RICK: I know I told Ginny I envisioned working long hours and becoming, hopefully, well known. And doing things to make New York better—not necessarily as a politician, but on the periphery of politics.

GINNY: Not on the periphery! When we got married our social life revolved around election parties. People were always talking to me about your future in politics. And you discussed with me yourself whether you might go to the Justice Department. This was the kind of life that being with you represented.

RICK: As I hear it, most of what Ginny focused on was attending parties and being involved in political discussions. I don't think my projection was that I would be the next Senator Kennedy.

GINNY: You were accustomed to having people look to you as someone who would grow up and have an impact, which fascinated me.

RICK: It's true that some of my parents' friends had transferred their desire to get my father to run for public office to encouraging me.

GINNY: Yes, and they started including me in whatever they were projecting for you. All of a sudden it became, What's your's and Rick's future in politics? My vision of myself was being part of campaigning, decision making, issue resolving. I would have something to say on the topic and be listened to.

RICK: That startles me! I can't see how Ginny got that input. I saw a very different kind of participation on her part. More of the hostess role. My goal was similar to what I'm doing now—except that there's not as much time to make a social contribution as I'd like. . . .

Why doesn't Ginny go to law school? Who "won't let" her? Or what is she afraid of?

RICK: I gather I was alleged to have told Virginia to apply only to three top law schools?

GINNY: You don't remember giving the impression that going to a lesser school would have been demeaning?

RICK: I don't deny it. I just don't remember.

Suppose that Ginny were to talk about going to law school now?

RICK: I'd love it. But I'd be frank to say I don't think she'd make a good lawyer. I do recall telling her that. I would not sponsor her as a member of the bar.

What do you think she would be really good at? As opposed to what it would be convenient to have her do?

RICK: Two things I've found she does very well: She interrelates with children, young children, and I'm sure she's a fine teacher; she also seems to have a facility for administration, organization. The reason she wouldn't do well as a lawyer is that she's not skilled at writing.

You talked, Rick, about the professor you patterned yourself after. He instilled the idea that excellence in law went hand in hand with excellence in written expression. Aren't there other useful kinds of lawyers?

RICK: The best lawyers in my firm can turn a paragraph from a hammer into a sledgehammer.

Was it threatening to you to have Ginny want to become what you are?

RICK: I can't say there wasn't a subconscious threat there. She seems to think there was.

GINNY: He all but said at one point that failing might devastate me, so that I should not attempt it at all. He also told me that three years of concentrated effort would not be compatible with being a wife.

RICK: Let me cut into that. I'm sure I did tell her that my experience in law school was of fully devoting oneself. It was like teaching had been for her.

GINNY: At this point our positions are almost institutionalized. I'm the wife and mother now, so it's my expectation to defend my home. To defend the amount of time Rick gives to our son and to me. So I have a right to be his conscience in this area. Oh yes, and to defend his health.

RICK: That's not how I view our differences of opinion. My attitude is colored by the fact that I want to be successful, both financially and in terms of my own self-image. I see nothing wrong with my hours. They're high, but within the norm of our office.

GINNY: I'm not going to let you get away with that. The second year you lawyered, you had by far, by *far* the largest number of billed hours. So much so that a partner had to tell you to take it easy. You should never have told me that because then I could say Aha! See? Your hours are not normal. You can be successful and still not kill yourself.

Meaning, you can be successful without running away from me?

GINNY: Yes.

RICK: Ginny and I don't have as much time together as if I were a teacher, but there are trade-offs. We can travel; Ginny can have someone come in to clean. Our son will be able to go to a good school. Plus the personal satisfaction of knowing that I'm handling more interesting cases. My attitude is, you've got to put in long hours so you get the best work.

Maybe what Ginny is hearing is the last part. That the major reason you work longer is, not to provide her with luxuries, but to elevate yourself to the position where you can handle the more interesting cases.

RICK: You're absolutely right about that connection. Unless I handle difficult cases now, chances are I'll be stuck when I'm older without the expertise or the opportunity.

GINNY: To me, that can also be interpreted as, "I enjoy work more than I enjoy home."

Do you think this matter of whether or not Ginny goes to law school or broadens herself in some way is central to the ongoing conflict about how much time she expects you to spend at home?

RICK: No. I just don't think Ginny would make a good lawyer.

Suppose she were a second-rate lawyer, or a storefront lawyer, or a paraprofessional, but enjoyed it?

RICK: I'm not going to help her out the door without protest. But I'm not going to stand in her way. I don't think our conceiving the baby was my way of stopping her from going to law school.

GINNY: Well, I specifically remember how the baby was conceived. Do you?

RICK: You refused to make love to me earlier in the evening.

GINNY: Right. And the way it finally happened added to my feeling that this was a coercion. Rick had a subconscious interest in creating the situation. But Rick doesn't believe in psychological motivation.

RICK: The motivation there was very simple. I was—

GINNY: Interested in making love at the time! Not for the entire month, but at that particular time of the month. We didn't stop so I could put in the diaphragm, which was rare. And I got pregnant. One shot.

RICK: Very true.

GINNY: Very potent. Right? Do you remember the discussion after we got pregnant? I all but accused you of doing it so we wouldn't have to face my going to law school.

RICK: Wouldn't surprise me.

GINNY: You don't remember sitting on the couch? You had me in your arms, and I was crying.

RICK: Vaguely. All I really remember is going out for dinner afterward to celebrate.

GINNY: Unbelievable! I don't remember the celebration dinner at all. (An uncomfortable silence)

How much of what you feel, Ginny, is envy that Rick has in his work something very involving and exciting to do?

GINNY: A great deal is envy. Especially if he comes home really proud of a case he's won. As a mother I can be proud of my son, but then I'm accused of being vicarious. Why am I taking credit for another human being's development? And yet Rick is always advising *other* wives to become attorneys.

RICK: I don't do it to everybody. I wouldn't encourage somebody who I didn't think should go.

GINNY: Are you implying then that they're smarter than I am?

RICK: You're the one who attaches the words "smart" and "admirable" to being a lawyer. In my concept a lawyer, teacher, housewife—they're all equally good. . . .

GINNY: You could interpret this argument between us as: Without Rick's sanction it would be impossible for me to go out and have a career, therefore, he has co-opted the authority to make that decision.

RICK: You cooperated. You decided you wanted to have the baby.

Do you put it together, Rick, that what you're doing is engrossing, gives you solid goals and a sense of mastery, and that makes Ginny jealous, because she can't find anything like it in part-time or volunteer work to give her self-esteem? And so long as she has to stay back, she will do everything in her power to take back your time and attention?

RICK: I don't think in those terms. Whatever the motivation, the effect is the same. Do you want to know what my perception is? Ginny is defensive of those roles—wife and mother and protector of the family life—because they're *desirable* roles. I don't resent her doing it. There is tension. But there has to be.

GINNY: I've come to look at it as an established tension too. I'll try to get as much as I can of him, and he'll try to evaluate the legitimacy of my complaints. . . .

Where do you see yourselves at 35?

GINNY: I see no job for me in the immediate future. Kind of resigning myself to a given, and not starting over again. I don't feel I have the opportunity to change. Rick, on the other hand, is broadening his goals.

RICK: The odds are good I'll end up as a partner of the law firm. And not doing as much public service work as I'd like.

You both see yourselves in five years, then, trying to resolve the same conflicts you're working on now?

RICK: I don't think I'll ever fully solve them.

GINNY: I think mine are more potentially solvable—once the children start growing up. . . .

Study Questions

1. Rick accuses Ginny of going back on her word. He says that before they were married, she had agreed to have a lot of children and that now she wants to stop at one. Assuming that Ginny was serious about wanting a big family (there's a possibility that she was only joking at the time), do you think that Rick has a right to demand that she maintain the pact? Some of my students have said that this is but another example of how important it is for couples to talk things out *before* they get married. Do you think that full and open communication on all issues before the wedding will guarantee that there will be no problems afterward? What about putting things in writing, perhaps signing a formal contract that specifies in detail what is agreed and not agreed, as some couples have begun to do?

2. Ginny says something that Sheehy unfortunately does not follow up on. Ginny says that when she met Rick, she felt that she had to make a choice *between* Rick and her job—and she chose Rick. This suggests that even before they got married, Ginny was faced with very much the same choice that she now faces. And it suggests that Ginny may need or love Rick more than Rick needs or loves her. This may seem like an odd way of describing this situation, but (all others things being equal) whichever spouse needs or loves the other more is at a disadvantage in the marital power struggle. Why? Because to need or love someone is to be dependent on that someone and the more dependent you are on someone, the more power that person has over you. Sociologists refer to this axiom as the *principle of least interest* (Waller and Hill, 1951). Do you think that Ginny and Rick's unequal love for each other affects their negotiations? How?

3. Sheehy does an excellent job of demonstrating that husbands and wives can misunderstand and talk past each other, that they can live in

the same house and be party to the same conversations (namely their own) yet have different perceptions of themselves and each other (cf. Laing, Phillipson, and Lee, 1966). For example, Ginny says that when she told Rick that she was pregnant, she ended up crying because he refused to consider seriously the possibility of an abortion. Rick says, however, that he "vaguely" remembers her sobbing but that what really stands out in his mind is that they went out to dinner to celebrate. How would you sociologically analyze this episode? Why do you think Ginny and Rick—and husbands and wives in general—tend to have different memories of episodes like this?

3

Transition to Parenthood

Cast of Characters

Casey, rock musician; Doug's wife
Doug, rock musician; Casey's husband
Leora, Casey and Doug's newborn daughter
The Reverend Sterling, Doug's father
Mrs. Sterling, Doug's mother
The Croswell sisters, Casey's stepmother and aunt

THE TRANSITION TO PARENTHOOD is a significant phase in a family's life in that the birth of a child precipitates a number of familial changes (LaRossa and LaRossa, 1981; LeMasters, 1970; Rossi, 1968). Coalitions, for example, are possible in three-person groups; thus, a husband and wife may find that their first child both comes between them and brings them closer together, depending on who is siding with whom at a given time. The transition to parenthood also initiates a multitude of role expansions. While the husband and wife are adding the roles of father and mother to their repertoires, other members of the family are adding the roles of grandfather, grandmother, uncle, aunt, etc., to theirs. As the following case study demonstrates, however, these changes do not always go as smoothly as planned.

Casey and Doug Sterling are awaiting their first child. But though Casey and Doug experience many of the things that other couples do— the coalitions, the role shifts—they are not the average young couple trying to cope with parenthood. For one thing, they are an interracial couple (Casey is black and Doug is white); for another, they are rock musicians who sing and play together, which means that their work schedule and lifestyle are somewhat out of the ordinary.

The case is divided into four parts. The first part provides some background on Casey and Doug's childhoods and on the early years of their marriage, discusses how they made the decision to become parents, and describes the psychosocial aspects of Casey's pregnancy. We learn that both Casey and Doug were physically abused as children and that Doug's parents, disapproving of his marriage to Casey, have not seen their son in over five years. We also learn that, like many other couples, Casey and Doug waited until they felt financially secure before taking on the responsibilities of parenthood and until they had "done everything at least once" before tying themselves down with a child. Perhaps the best sections in this part, however, are those that offer an inside view of the emotions Casey and Doug experience as they rush headlong to the birth of their child.

The second part of the case picks up the story after the baby is born. It gives us a picture of the couple's first month with their new daughter. Casey and Doug are beginning to discover how difficult it is to entertain a human being who is seemingly oblivious to established norms of civility, a person who knows nothing about proper times for sleeping and standards of personal cleanliness. Casey and Doug also discover, when Casey's stepmother and aunt move in for a week, that it is difficult to take orders about how to change and feed your own child, but that taking orders is what some family members expect a young father and mother to do, especially if it is their first child.

The third part reveals what happens nearly six months later, when Doug's parents come to see the baby for the first time. Though it is brief, this segment does a good job of showing how family members can get caught up in a system of interaction that prevents them from sharing their love for each other. It also illustrates how a child can serve as a bridge for communication. The rift that exists between Casey and Doug and the Reverend and Mrs. Sterling is certainly more extreme than most generation gaps. Yet the pattern of interaction that emerges during this visit is not unlike the pattern that develops in many warring families. The birth of a child is too significant an event to be ignored, and it will often precipitate an uneasy truce among combatants.

The fourth and final part of the case describes Casey and Doug's situation nine months after the birth, focusing on the problems Casey has in balancing motherhood and career. What is especially significant about this part is that by this point Casey has become the principal, or front-line, parent while Doug has become Casey's helper. The couple's division of baby care, in other words, is now more mother centered than it was during the early weeks of their transition to parenthood. Casey, rather than Doug, is the one who takes the baby to the recording studio and Casey, rather than Doug, is the one who loses concentration during the taping session (remember that they are both professional musicians in the same band, which means that whenever one is working, the other is, too). This change in their division of baby care is called *traditionalization* (because a mother-centered pattern is considered more traditional than an egalitarian, or sharing, pattern), and the reason it is significant is that studies of the transition to parenthood indicate that traditionalization is a common change made by new parents during the first few months of their baby's life (e.g., Entwisle and Doering, 1981). Why traditionalization occurs is a question that is hotly debated. Some argue that women are biologically disposed to develop a stronger attachment to their infants (Rossi, 1977). Others contend that traditionalization is a function of psychological forces, that girls develop a heightened capacity to nurture at a very early age and that this ability is put into play when they become mothers later on (Chodorow, 1978). Still others believe that fathers essentially foist child care upon their wives because they, the fathers, do not want their leisure time severely restricted (LaRossa and LaRossa, 1981). The likelihood is that all three theories are at least partially correct and that some combination of biological, psychological, and sociological processes is at work when traditionalization takes place.

The Sterling case study is part of a larger project in which several couples were followed from the time they found out the wife was pregnant through the first year of parenthood. The principal investigators in the project, Sandra Sohn Jaffe and Jack Viertel, wanted to capture the emotional side of becoming a parent. It seems that they were successful when they tried to put into words Casey and Doug's experience.

The Sterling Family

Sandra Sohn Jaffe and Jack Viertel

Choosing Pregnancy

CASEY STERLING knew something was changing when she found herself on her knees in the bedroom closet, applying a quick coat of wax to the linoleum beneath the winter clothes. No one had ever before seen this particular piece of the floor. Casey had no business with sponges or shoe boxes; she was a rock and roller. Nonetheless, it just seemed to need doing. Her husband, Doug, came home from Wally Heider Recording Studios at eight o'clock and found her on the floor, rubber gloves and all.

"Aha," he said. "Nesting instinct."

Casey had not recognized it. She had been off the pill for six months and was not yet, as far as she knew, pregnant. But if this sudden binge of domestic drudgery was something as definable as the human equivalent of a nesting instinct, that could be considered a step in the right direction. Aha, indeed. Doug and Casey believed Mother Nature took care of these things; they were letting her handle the pregnancy. She had been in a whimsical mood when she tossed Doug and Casey together seven years earlier in a Toronto television studio.

Casey was black; Doug was white. They could both compose, play the piano, sing, and manage the guitar, when called upon. They had celebrity looks—a tall, thin, fine-boned woman with mahogany skin and oversized eyes, and a too-tall, well-built man with black hair that curled behind his ears and enough of a mustache to signify gentleness. Clothes came to life on both of them, and all they wanted out of life was music. It seemed irrelevant to them that there was not a shred of common ground in their backgrounds. They were escaping where they had come from and had no desire to be reminded.

Casey was from Brooklyn, raised in a family of musicians and performers going back four generations. Doug was Scottish-born,

Sandra Sohn Jaffe and Jack Viertel, "The Second Family: Doug and Casey Sterling and Leora" (here entitled "The Sterling Family") in *Becoming Parents*. Copyright © 1979 Sandra Sohn Jaffe and Jack Viertel. Reprinted with the permission of Atheneum Publishers.

raised in Toronto, the son of a Presbyterian minister who considered John Knox his spiritual ancestor. The day Doug brought
Casey home to meet his parents was the last day he had seen them.
The family hated show business, hated interracial love affairs,
dreaded miscegenation. Doug and Casey made their own way.

They married, moved to Los Angeles (the center of the music
industry), and joined the mass of young, hopeful singer-song-
writer rock and rollers as a duet. Their Canadian reputation got
them work in the small clubs along Sunset Strip, opening the bill
for midpopular groups on the way up to the concert world, or on
the way back down. It was good, hard, mainstream work, and they
found it rewarding. A major record contract bought them the
down payment on a canyon house away from everywhere. Suddenly they had the security of knowing what their steady diet
would be; they had to compose and record twelve songs, and do
nothing else. With this freedom, this unexpected sense of having
entered the real world, came the idea of the baby.

For seven years (five of them in marriage), they had done just
what they had wanted to do. They had done the work and reaped
the benefits. They had been to the parties, to the movies, to the
concerts. They had laughed a lot and slept late. Life had been awfully sweet to them. Children were the natural next step. They had
known through all the work and the pleasure-seeking that the
right time would come, and that they would recognize it. Other
things came first: their careers, a selfishness about their time, their
freedom. They saw family expansion as a total upheaval of their
lives, but they had had seven selfish years, and sometimes it felt as
if they had already done everything at least once. The day they
took possession of the house, Casey ran out of birth-control pills,
and the prescription was not renewed. Six months went by. Casey
did not panic. Her gynecologist told her to wait nine months before calling. It was shortly after she received this counsel that she
registered the irresistible urge to clean everything.

She missed the next period and cautiously began predicting
that someone new was growing inside her. Doug, who was playing
studio piano during the day, called every noon to see if she had begun to bleed, returning ecstatic to work with each negative reply.
She was pregnant. By the time the tests confirmed it, they had already accepted it as an inevitable fact. Some good Colombian grass
had been sifted for the occasion of her test results; the couple got
blissfully stoned and called everyone in Casey's family. There

was no one in Doug's family to call, a point on which he was silent.

Doug Sterling was a minister's son and a proud emblem of the cliché that such children make the very best hell-raisers. He had been at war with his parents for so long that neither side could possibly recall the first shot. Doug had spent his early teens clawing gleefully at every hypocrisy he could dig out of his father's behavior—a reaction, perhaps, to the minister's temperamental use of the belt and hairbrush during the boy's formative years. Reverend Sterling admitted no pleasure from these frequent whippings; he believed them to be God's way. Doug saw them as a challenge to perform even more daring and rapacious feats, threatening his father's reputation in the community whenever possible. His mother, silent and powerless, grew old watching this raucous dance of antagonism.

In a sudden, and even to himself, inexplicable gesture of conciliation, Doug married at twenty-three. The bride was ideal—a local girl, the organist at the Presbyterian church in suburban Toronto. The marriage lasted two pointless years. Doug could not stay away from the music scene. He was consumed. His wife was quietly appalled. A year after his quiet, uncontested divorce, the magnitude of his father's hypocrisy made itself suddenly, stunningly clear. Doug attended his sister's wedding, presided over by his father, and was surprised to see his ex-wife playing the organ. He was even more surprised to find her positioned next to him in the receiving line before dinner. It was a large party, with guests coming from all parts of the United States, Canada, and Scotland to attend. It did not take long to realize that none of them knew about his divorce. His father had engineered the ceremony, reception, and dinner seating so as to reunite the estranged couple for public display. He had told neither his son nor his ex-daughter-in-law of this plan. Both were dumbfounded and went through the entire day anesthetized by the old man's effrontery.

Still, when Casey laughed on the phone to her crazy vaudevillian father in Toronto, Doug could not help but wish that he and his own family had declared a cease-fire. Too late to do anything about it now. It had been a year since the last, brief letter.

Casey's family was fragmented, but they were at peace with her. The only thing her upbringing had in common with Doug's was the frequency of violent beatings, administered, in her case, by her mother. Casey recognized the temper; it was in her as it had been in her mother and her grandmother, whose screech of fury she could still recall. Casey was capable of anything; she had grown up throwing ashtrays across the living room and working nights to pay for broken plate glass. But she was not going to beat her child. Teaching herself not to explode was part of the five years of marriage. The tantrums had not disappeared, but they were rare, one a year now. Usually they were directed at some crooked practitioner in her profession—an agent or club manager. She believed it exorcised her inborn need to have it out in full color and sound, an experience she would never inflict on her child.

Children could not be asked to deal with adult emotions. They had no equipment for it. Casey watched adults respond to the selfish demands of children as if the children were simply small, ill-behaved grown-ups, and she was horrified. These adults were missing the point of parenting. Casey's mother could rarely interact successfully with *adults*. With children she had shown no ability whatever, and simply resorted to the folded belt and the open hand. It had shattered Casey's youth and broken up her parents' marriage. Casey's father moved to Canada, a dreamworld of peace and quiet. When Casey was fifteen, she had fled Brooklyn and joined him there. Gradually, she had rebuilt a strained friendship with her mother, keeping the distance as a protective barrier.

Eight years after her flight from the United States, Casey met Doug. The assistant director at a television station placed them on opposite sides of the same microphone, and they spent fourteen hours staring at each other's lips. Both had escaped to music.

The new album took shape with almost otherworldly speed; pregnancy had unleashed an emotional tide—memories, dreams, hope and awe. These functioned as new materials and were crafted into rhyme and melody. The emotions of pregnancy became functional commodities, and the Sterlings' work reflected the day-to-day movement of their minds. They vowed to continue the pattern. The infant's upbringing would not be cordoned off, but would take place in the mainstream of their activity. The experience of parenting could be mined for inspiration, and their work would nurture the child.

As her belly grew, Casey made several tours of the bookstores, bringing home an occasional choice from the child-care shelf. She wanted to know how everyone did everything, but it was hard to get interested. Bathing and changing—people had done these things for centuries. How hard could they be to learn? She covered some child-development stuff, then put it all in a carton in the garage. The books were spoiling all the surprises for her.

Not every day was a good day. Although Casey never gained a lot of weight with the pregnancy, there were times when she felt the real old Casey had been swallowed up by her widening torso. Her reserves of high-flung energy flagged easily; she found herself seated more often than ever before. She tried to take a new kind of pleasure in her new body, her Mother Earth gait, but there was no pleasure to be had from it. She missed the old, lithe, dancer's limbs and the muscular flexibility of her waist. She missed being sexy for Doug, and she was not pleased when he seemed to mind not at all. Their sex life tapered off somewhere during the eighth month, and they satisfied themselves with long hugs. There were weekend late-morning naps; they wrapped themselves around each other to whatever extent they could and tried to get comfortable. After one pool party, Casey fell silent for several hours. It was the first time in her life she recalled staring enviously at other women's bodies. She wanted hers back.

At the couple's request, Casey's stepmother and aunt arrived in Los Angeles from Canada a week before the baby was due. They were to cook, clean, and take care, moving into the house the day Casey went to the hospital. In the meantime, they hid out, allowing the couple their last free days alone. But the phone began to ring. What kind of pacifier did Casey prefer? Should some formula be laid in, preparatory for a nursing failure? If so, what kind of bottles? What kind of diapers, talcum powder, shampoo, and lotion? Casey and Doug began to come unglued. They were showered with enough helpful concern to sink the entire parenthood, possibly the marriage. Selfishness once again became essential, and diplomacy was sacrificed.

Unhappily, Doug called his step-mother-in-law. Casey got on the phone, and together they explained, never wavering, that they had changed their minds. They needed one uninterrupted week alone with the baby to get their footing. It would have to be arranged. Reluctantly, the two women agreed. Doug and Casey had regrets about the whole thing, but there was never any choice. Politeness was a low priority.

Throughout the pregnancy, they had speculated lavishly on how their child would look. With one white and one black parent, anything was possible. Would it be a golden girl, a dark, pouting mysterious boy, or a lily-white daughter who would run from home cursing her invisible Negro blood? They laughed at these invented scenarios and invented more. Every prospective parent indulges in this game; the Sterlings had more chips to play with than most. But one night it all came to an end with Casey's dream. Casey dreamed her baby had heard its parents' endless conjecture and was good and sick of it. Casey's baby climbed from between her thighs, wearing a rag diaper and a T-shirt. It was a radiant, maple-syrup-brown baby, wide-eyed and gorgeous. The diaper obscured its sex. As Casey watched in amazement, the infant executed a wide circle of cartwheels, showing off every aspect of itself. This was followed by a short toe dance. Satisfied that everyone now knew what it looked like, it hopped up on the bed and climbed back into Casey's womb, never uttering a sound.

Doug awoke abruptly and discovered his wife laughing in her sleep. . . .

At One Month:
Help at Home—Relatives Move In

The Sterlings had Leora to themselves for a week and a half. For the first days her schedule was upside down. . . . Her few wakeful hours came between two and six in the morning. This was less than ideal. Dazed and half-asleep, Doug and Casey forced each other to take turns singing, cooing, and waltzing their daughter around in the dark. An occasional harsh word was spoken. There was a lot of napping during the day. They had crossed off this period anyhow and weren't expecting to get anything accomplished. On the fourth day home, Leora slept a full three hours between feedings all night. Somehow she had gotten the message. For the next seven days, the three Sterlings lived with a peace so pure that it lit the rooms of the house. Doug brought meals into bed. Casey slept and played the piano. They listened to music. There was nothing else to do but watch Leora.

Only Doug's parents were to be fretted over. At about eleven every morning, Doug would tune out of whatever was happening and wait for the mail. He had sent his folks a telegram the morning of Leora's birth. There had been no response of any kind. Doug kept this routine to himself, but Casey knew what he was feeling, and he knew she knew. Leora was short one set of grandparents.

On the eleventh day, when the daily routine of Leora's life had just gotten set, Casey's stepmother and aunt, the Croswell sisters, descended. Doug sensed that it was a bad idea, that there might be trouble, but he could put them off no longer. To some extent he resented their arrival out of pure jealousy.

It was only for a week, but a week can be a long time. The Croswell sisters had been a singing team in their earlier days. They moved as a united front, even though one of them was married to Casey's father. They took Leora from Doug and Casey's room and moved her downstairs to sleep between them—so Doug and Casey would get some rest. They had lots of ideas about child-rearing, and Doug and Casey tried to be tolerant. The Croswell sisters recommended apple juice and sugar-water. They popped a pacifier into the baby's mouth at the first sign of vocalizing. They made things warmer, cooler, brighter, dimmer, on a regular cycling basis: the room and Leora's clothing were monitored like the atmosphere of a capsule in outer space. The Sterlings tried to steer clear. They felt Leora's stability was established, that nothing could affect her.

But immediately she was constipated and a day after that she stopped sleeping. Doug became taciturn. Casey began to feel humiliated. Her aunt and stepmother corrected everything she attempted to do. Little could be said, however; these people had come a long way to help. As the Croswell sisters seemed to want complete control of Leora, Doug and Casey relinquished it. They played with their daughter, let her know they were there, but left the changing and bedding procedures to the two older women. In one stern argument Doug managed to eliminate the fruit juice, but the sugar-water stayed. Casey nursed Leora, cooing to her about the temporary interruption in their family life. Other than that one regular bonding process, she had little to do with her. It was just too difficult.

The Croswell sisters had their cheerier side. They were out of a show business tradition, full of stories and songs, and Doug and Casey felt a kind of generation-gap kinship with them. They were yesterday's entertainers, and they understood the Sterlings' compulsion about making music. Best of all, they embraced the marriage, interracial or not, in true show business fashion. Both of them had a tendency to get slightly drunk at dinners; Doug and Casey could smoke grass in front of them without worrying. So the evenings, while Leora slept, were all right.

As the days dragged on, a more serious effect of the Croswells' presence was felt. Doug and Casey found themselves whispering to each other in bed or conducting serious conversations in quick, hushed tones because one or both of the old women might enter or return at any moment. The flow of communication was wrecked; short, intense speeches of explanation were issued instead of the normal exchange of talk. Doug and Casey found themselves imprisoned in their own home because two women were doing them a favor.

The week ended appropriately. The sisters packed while dictating a list of do's and don'ts to Casey, all of which were headed directly for the fireplace. Doug waited silently for it to be over. The week had seemed like a month. The last few hours seemed like a year. In a burst of ironic justice, Leora claimed the day. Resting comfortably in her mother's arms, she stared the two Croswell sisters out to the garage and then, just as Casey waved good-bye, had a massive attack of diarrhea all over Casey's Danskin. It was her first bowel movement since the sisters had arrived, and certainly a triumph. Casey greeted it with mixed feelings.

Now things had to get going again. The album Doug and Casey had recorded during the early months of pregnancy was about to break. There was publicity to take care of and bookings. For the first time since before Leora was conceived, they would have to perform: live, on tour. This was part of their record contract. In the eight weeks left before their tour debut, they had to put together material for a second album. As soon as they came off the road, they would be slotted into the studio. There were arrangements and musicians to pick and worry about. Between them they had not one idea for a new song. And all the time they had allowed for adjustment, for Leora to dominate, was gone. The leisure days had melted away. Eight weeks seemed like a long time, once. Suddenly it hardly seemed to exist at all.

Three weeks had been set aside for recovery, but Doug and Casey had not recovered. They were physically all right. Emotionally, they had just started. The schedule kept running away with them: they would program their day around Leora's naps, but with each week her naps got shorter. They could never fully concentrate on making music while she was asleep because they knew they'd never hear her if she started to cry. Their work became half-measured, done with one eye and one ear elsewhere. It wasn't first-rate work, and they knew it.

It seemed impossible that they were not ready for the complete upheaval they thought they had prepared themselves for, but that was what had happened. "Complete upheaval" was just a phrase before Leora was born. Now, it was a reality. They didn't know what it could be like until those last eight weeks started bearing down on them. They didn't know quite what to do, so they just went on living, a half-life in a half-world. They did what they could about the record, and they did everything for Leora.

"We were saved by the six years before," Doug said later. "We had those six years to ourselves. Now we knew we'd never have that kind of time again, not while we were young anyhow. And despite everything else we tried to do to make things work, we never tried to recapture that feeling of being only a couple. We were ready to leave that behind, which was lucky, because holding the fort with everything else was all we could do. If we'd had second thoughts about leaving our private days behind, that would have brought the walls down."

Those six private years began to loom larger and larger in their minds as they ate one meal standing over the kitchen sink with a paper towel in one hand and a dripping wedge of pizza in another.

"Those first weeks after my aunt and stepmother left," Casey recalled, "they were like running through a swamp in a rainstorm. You just can't stop 'cause you'll fall behind, but even when you go, you never get anywhere."

Still, the only serious issue was Doug's parents. Leora's needs were met; the songs, for better or worse, got written; the tour was arranged. As they came into the stretch of the first month, Leora began to produce a cockeyed smile, which they took to be recognition, devotion, and appreciation. It was hardly a controlled grin, just a spring upward of the lips and a thrust of toothless little gums, but it kept them going. A few days after the smile appeared, they discovered her rocking more or less in time to the music as they rehearsed numbers from the old album. From then on they kept her with them; she seemed to like every song, and she could sleep through the loudest drum and piano duets if she was tired.

In October, just before the tour began, Doug's uncle sent a postcard. It read:

Stopped by house to pick up
mail. Got your cable. Reverend S.
and your mother are in Europe now
and didn't see it. Congratulations
from me anyhow.

Doug read it over and over, and threw it out.

"That ought to make you feel better," Casey said.

Doug nodded.

"But it doesn't," she added, looking over.

"No," he said. "When I get a piece of mail like that, I want to settle everything. This doesn't answer a single question."

"Like what?"

"Like what would they have done if they *had* gotten word?" . . .

At Six Months: Grandparents

Casey had written the letter before the tour, before the trouble, and she hadn't really expected it to work. It was an impulsive act. One Sunday morning she woke up, thought about both elder Sterlings in church, pious, on bended knee, and it burned her up; so she wrote them a letter. An excerpt follows:

> I don't think God smiles upon racial prejudice, and I think you know this, but it is not my reason for writing. Because, frankly, I don't want you for myself. If you don't like me, or don't want to talk to me, that's something I can live with. I don't have any choice, do I? But this child is your flesh and blood. She's only two-and-a-half-months old, so you can bet she has not done anything sinful, and there is no reason to punish her. Yet she is being punished because she has only one set of grandparents. That's not something she deserves. You are punishing her for something you hold against me, or Doug, and I think it's unfair.

Casey was no fool. She enclosed a picture of her golden girl in the letter and posted it. The picture was her secret weapon. She told Doug about it, but he didn't have anything to do with it.

"I just woke up angry," she said later. "If not, I might never have written it. I think I could see what it was doing to Doug, even though we never mentioned it, but I don't know where it came from really. It just happened. I woke up, I thought about it, and I said, 'This is it.' "

She had hoped for some kind of response—a beginning of negotiations, at best. Instead, there came a postcard. They were arriving. Their first time in the United States in fourteen years. It was terrifying.

Doug was especially confused about what he should do. He hadn't seen them in six years, had gotten formal, if not hostile, communications from them on holidays, and had grown to think of them as strangers. Now the protective wall he had built up was to be tossed away. He didn't know if he could do it. He went to the airport not knowing what he would say, what he would and would not discuss. It was like the beginning of a sporting event. He really didn't know what would happen. When would be the moment to rehash everything? Certainly not at the beginning. But the issues were so plain and so galling, how could anything else be discussed? How could you talk about the weather when the hills were on fire?

Doug learned how from his parents. They came off the plane like grandparents, nice people, too well dressed for Southern California, all smiles and decorous embraces. He shook his father's hand, and received his congratulations. It was the same hand that had terrified him in youth, pointed the way to the door in adolescence, and blessed a thousand parishioners on the same afternoon. Doug looked: it was an old hand now, white and soft. It was not a hand with power. These were tired travelers.

The ride home was through the dark. Doug talked about the baby, about being present at delivery. His mother talked in a sheltered way about her own delivery experiences with Doug. The Reverend Sterling looked out the window and held his tongue. It was a ride imbued with the color of darkness, buoyed up by trivialities. As they began to climb the canyon leading to the house, the three parties fell into silence for an extended moment. Finally, Doug's mother broke it.

"How's Casey?" she asked. It was if she had just singlehandedly pushed over the Empire State Building.

"She's looking forward to seeing you," Doug said. That was all. The barrier had been crossed, at least once.

It was a week-long visit, and throughout that time Doug and Casey kept thinking, how can this be happening? There was never any mention of previous hostility, of the threats and ultimatums that had brought the curtain down on Doug's previous relationship with his parents. The Reverend Sterling wanted to see San Francisco. They all drove up in the car. The grandparents took Leora on their lap, bouncing her, poking her, doing anything in their sedate repertoire to get a laugh out of her. And there was nothing said.

There were no more than polite to Casey, but they *were* polite. They were barely more than that toward their own son. There had never been a scene of demonstrative affection in the Reverend Sterling's house, to anyone's knowledge, and this was what all

Doug's life had been like. More than once, his mouth half-opened with confrontation on the tip of his tongue, an opening phrase kept repeating itself in his head. He never said it.

They walked along Fisherman's Wharf and ate crab cocktail out of little paper cups. Casey and Mrs. Sterling went into boutiques and browsed through the jade collection at Gump's, leaving the men alone, but the men took no opportunity for private conversation.

"She's awfully sweet, that child of yours," Father would say.

"We're glad you could see her," Son would reply. That was the beginning and the end of it.

On the way home Casey opened a corner of the conversation, quite innocently.

"I want you to know," she said, "that it means a lot to us that you came to see us, and Leora. We're glad you changed your mind."

It must have been the last sentence that did it. There was a fifteen-minute silence after she said it.

Every step was tiny, made on quiet, nearly invisible ground; yet there were steps. As the week approached its end, both parents and children knew the ice had melted, although no one would say just how soft it had become.

"Ten years ago," Doug told Casey when the house was quiet at night, "I would have busted them on it. I would have taken him on every point. I don't have to beat him anymore."

"You already beat him," Casey said. "They're here. You don't have to make 'em go and feel bad about it."

Still, Doug was amazed, not at his father, but at himself. His restraint was something new to him. He didn't even want to take his father to the mat anymore. His father was an old, sad man who had missed a lot and was afraid of a lot. He didn't pity him, but he was willing to let him alone. The feeling seemed to be mutual. Doug was an adult now, out of his father's reach, and the Reverend Sterling seemed to know it. He treated Doug like a parishioner he did not exactly approve of, but who was one of God's children nonetheless.

As for mother, Doug knew she was aching somewhere inside. He suspected, although could never confirm, that his mother was the moving force in this reconciliation, that his mother had mourned through the months that Casey was pregnant, because she could not be a part of it. Mrs. Sterling had cast her lot with the minister, and she would be faithful to his wishes, but hers was a lost life from which she had lately recouped a little. She cried when they said good-bye at the airport and held her granddaughter one last time. It would be beyond her ability now to tell Doug that she loved him. She could not bring herself to kiss Casey. There were too many years of ingrained aversion. It was a sad good-bye because it set the limits of the harmony ever to be achieved by these four people. There were still improvements to be made, there was still some warmth that could be kindled, but only so many and only so much.

There were stiff handshakes all around. Only Leora was kissed, and only by her grandmother. Then they were gone. . . .

At Nine Months: Nine Is a Hard Month

. . . Leora had become a clinger. She wanted her mommy all the time and had developed an infuriating whine with which to make clear her demands. The studio gig, which lasted from late morning until well into the night, seemed like the right thing for Casey; it would get her back to work and away from the baby. It would be temporary, give her distance, and make her time with Leora pure and free of resentment. By leaving her milk in bottles in the freezer, Casey could begin a natural weaning process, nursing Leora only in the morning. It was a great theory.

But the first day was a disaster. Work was lost because of Casey's inability to concentrate. She missed entrances, fluffed lyrics she had written herself, and generally drew attention to herself by incompetence. Finally, she went home, leaving Doug and the musicians to lay down some instrumental tracks for the next day's work. She had never had such an unprofessional day.

The next day a new plan was implemented. Casey took Leora to the studio with her. Now her concentration was really ripped apart. Leora had to be restrained from tearing the guts out of a control panel, and Casey could see the commotion in the control room through the plate-glass panel that separated her from her daughter. Still, she was not about to waste two days of expensive studio time, and she put in a better performance than on the first day. Toward evening, when one song had been finalized, Casey and Doug sat in the control room listening to a playback. Leora was on her mother's lap, unpacking her purse in search of chewables. Everything was fine until the Sterlings' voices began to come through the broad, loud monitors in the room. Leora looked up at the speakers, looked around at her parents sitting quietly in the room, and a wild panic of confusion seized her. She began to shriek as if stung; her head spun and she began to hyperventilate. It was a totally unexpected reaction. Casey took her out immediately, but she was inconsolable. The scare kept her crying for almost twenty minutes, longer than she had ever cried before. Casey was a wreck.

They were facing a weekend, and time for recovery. Casey knew this was it, the great neurotic collapse she had been dreaming about. They always came at the most inconvenient times.

There was not much to do about it. Doug was not having the same kinds of worries, and his sympathy wasn't much help. Casey spent the two free days keeping Leora at her side, taking her to the market and to dinner, refusing to be separated from her. On Monday she knew she would have to have this thing licked. Monday came, however, and Casey felt terrible. She dropped Leora with the sitter, and she and Doug rode to the studio in silence.

"This is for her," he said. "You're doing this for her."

This was true. Most of the songs on the album had been written during Leora's infancy, a few during the pregnancy. The album was very much a product of that time; it was a sunny album, a little out of step with the darkening mood of rock and roll, but it was all theirs. Casey tried to concentrate on that; it was Leora's album, so it had to be good. It got her through the day. When they went to pick up Leora that night, Casey burst into tears in front of everybody. Leora hadn't missed her in the slightest, but she was disturbed to see her mother crying. The result was that Doug took the baby while Casey put herself back together.

"I was going through fruitcake time," Casey recalled. "So many things were operating inside me at once that all I *could* do was cry. Part of it was that I *wanted* to be away from her. I *wanted* that freedom, and I didn't want to want it. It made me sick to think I could need my own, old life back. Like I was some kind of a failure as a mother."

There were bad days and entire bad weeks. Sometimes it was reassuring to know that Leora didn't miss her, other times it was depressing.

"The one thing I hate to think about," said Casey, "is that I might need her more than she needs me."

Casey could produce any side of herself without warning. There were days when she felt that the rock-and-roll world had passed her by, that she had become an old woman overnight, left behind by sexier, bolder women with more time to devote to themselves. There were days when the music industry looked like a sick monster, eating away at her family life. Casey felt everything at once and nothing with any certainty.

"It just happened," she said. "This bad wave of depression. It came and, eventually, it went. I started fretting about my body, about whether I was attractive anymore, about whether anything could ever be sexy again after you spent the day with a lot of vomiting and dirty diapers and drooling all over everything. I really got to wondering, I tell you."

She never stopped loving Leora, but the resentment knotted her up inside.

"I just couldn't handle any negative feelings toward her. Any time any downbeat emotion would come to me about her, it would short-circuit my system. I couldn't react to it. I couldn't *believe* it. And I felt guilty in front of her, like she knew."

It receded as the weeks went by. A balance was struck between career and motherhood. Physical adjustments were made to accommodate new needs. The Sterlings couldn't be in the studio as many hours a day as their record company wanted them to be. That adjustment was made. They had to stay home one day of the weekend with Leora. That adjustment was made. It was an annoyance to have to make rules and regulations about their emotional life, but they did it. The object was to move Casey away from her bad feelings. They attacked each one separately, until there were no more left. Certain inadequacies remained because they were unchangeable. But at least they had been acknowledged, confronted, and dismissed. . . .

Study Questions

1. Casey and Doug's "flow of communication was wrecked" when the Croswell sisters moved in to help with the baby. Why does a family's communication pattern change when relatives come to stay? How does it change for the Sterlings? Is it just the presence of outsiders that disturbs a family's communication pattern, or is it the presence of outsiders at *critical times* (e.g., during the transition to parenthood) that bothers family members?

2. Consider these two propositions: (a) the more roles you play, the *more* difficult it will be for you to meet your total role obligations because

the demands of the various roles will end up competing with each other (Merton, 1957); (b) the more roles you play, the *less* difficult it will be for you to meet your total role obligations because the demands of the various roles will complement and support each other (Sieber, 1974). Which of these propositions is correct? Are Casey and Doug experiencing more or less difficulty since they added the parental role to their other roles? Is it possible for both propositions to be true? If so, what does this suggest about the nature and causes of interrole conflict?

3. Imagine that you are a visitor from another galaxy sent by the leaders of your world to record the culture of this world and imagine that one of the first things you come across is this case study of the Sterling family. What would you say are this family's goals, values, beliefs, and norms? The best way to approach this question is first to ask yourself, What do the members of the Sterling family take for granted (Garfinkel, 1967)? That is, what do they assume is true, good, correct, etc.? Doing this will allow you to step out of the *natural attitude*, the attitude we use every day, and to step into the *scientific attitude*, the attitude of the conscientious skeptic (Schutz, 1967; Weigert, 1981).

4

Living with Preschool Children

CAST OF CHARACTERS

Alice, homemaker; Richard's wife
Richard, policeman; Alice's husband
Carrie, Alice and Richard's five-year-old daughter
James, Alice and Richard's three-year-old son
Nicholas, Alice and Richard's two-year-old son
Observer, Chaya S. Piotrkowski

ALICE AND RICHARD BERNARD have been married for seven years and live with their three children in a small rented home on several acres next to a busy highway. Trying their best to keep up with inflation while relying only on Richard's income, they raise chickens and cows to bring in some extra money and to provide fresh meat and eggs for the table.

The Bernards were studied by Chaya S. Piotrkowski for her doctoral dissertation on the interface between work and family life. Piotrkowski spent over seventy hours with the family, talking to them, observing their daily life, and reviewing with them what she had heard and seen. One of the things that Piotrkowski found fascinating about the Bernards was Richard's variable schedule; a police officer, he was often required to work evenings and nights, which meant that there were times when his sleeping schedule would be at odds with his family's. The case study is, in fact, a slice of the family's life during one of these times.

Most of the cases in this book read like novels because the authors first digested their data and then put together summaries of what they had found (cf. Davis, 1974). This case is different. Instead of getting a synopsis of the family, we have the rare opportunity of reviewing a segment of Piotrkowski's field notes for one of the mornings she spent with the Bernards. These field notes are extremely valuable. First, they show just how far case studies in general are from raw data. Second, they give an idea of what the distinction is between casual observations (the kind you and I engage in every day) and research observations; the latter are much more detailed. Finally, the field notes provide a sense of what we would see if we mounted a videotape recorder in a family's home; while we may feel that we are catching a glimpse of how one family lives, we still wonder to what degree the observer's presence is affecting the family's behavior.

On the day represented in the case, Piotrkowski arrives at 7:40 A.M., about ten minutes after the family has woken up, and stays until 11:30 P.M., leaving just before Alice goes to bed. Much of her day is spent just watching, often while seated in a dinette area, where most of the household activity is centered. Her field notes on this day are organized into fifteen-minute intervals and total over 17,000 words. I have selected only a portion of her notes—the first ninety minutes—because even in this relatively brief period of time there is more than enough to illustrate some important group processes. I have also included the floor plan for the Bernard home, prepared by Piotrkowski, because it helps us to understand the family's pattern of interaction.

Maybe more than showing anything else, the Bernard case demonstrates how much *work* is involved in taking care of small children. Alice seems to be constantly telling the kids to get cleaned up or dressed or encouraging them to watch television and leave her alone. If you read the case carefully, you can count the number of times that she directs, orders, manipulates, or threatens her brood (about forty-five times, or once every two minutes). As Piotrkowski remarks, you get the feeling that Alice is nothing more than "a foreman trying to get stubborn and resistant workers to do their job."

The word *resistant* provides a clue as to what it is about caring for infants and toddlers that makes the task so difficult. It is true that children like to test their parents every once in a while in order to see just how far they can go. But it is wrong to assume that all parent–child conflicts are essentially competitive and gamelike. Some conflict (resistance) stems from the fact that children—especially very young children—do not see the world the same way that their parents do. With most adults, for example, you have to speak only once, perhaps twice, to communicate your intentions. But young children often have to be told many times to finish their breakfast or put on their shoes because they have yet to learn the significance of these acts *to adults.* In other words, the relatively smooth way that adult members of a family perform such mundane tasks as passing the salt or lowering the volume on the television is indicative of an adult culture. And while we sometimes forget that adult culture is a product of our own making, if we introduce a foreigner or stranger to the system, we soon come to realize how precarious this culture is. Young children are, in a sense, strangers in their own homes because they are still being socialized into the adult world and they are still being introduced to the reality that is their family.

One of the most important elements of adult culture in Western society is the set of norms pertaining to privacy. Often conceptualized in spatial terms (e.g., people need "personal space"), privacy is also a temporal variable, denoting a period of time during which an individual or group is inaccessible to others: the more inaccessible people are at a given time, the more privacy available to them at that time (Zerubavel, 1979b). In most homes, for example, a closed bathroom door is a signal that someone is inside and not to be disturbed. In many homes, in fact, the bathroom is the only room in which people can truly be inaccessible and hence be guaranteed privacy. Young children, however, often are undeterred by a closed bathroom door and will rush in where others fear to tread. (After all, aren't *their* bathroom habits closely monitored?) Interestingly enough, the Bernards appear to have an open-door bathroom policy for adults and children alike.

Other strategies for creating and maintaining privacy include reading and watching television—two pastimes that constitute much of what goes on in the Bernard home (at least for the ninety minutes we are allowed to observe). There is little doubt that these activities are being used (and recommended to the children) to try to establish some private time in a relatively public household (Rosenblatt and Titus, 1976).

The Bernard Family

Chaya S. Piotrkowski

7:40 A.M.

I arrive ten minutes later than the time Alice and I had agreed upon. It's a cold spring morning; an early spring snowfall covers the ground. Alice had heard my car drive up and she greets me, still sleepy, in her bathrobe. She is still waking up as I put my things away and find a chair in the kitchen to locate myself.

7:45 A.M.

Three-year-old James is the first of the children up. He also has sleep in his eyes. Alice asks what he wants for breakfast and he goes to the cupboard and pulls out a cereal box, chatting to Alice while he does so. Meanwhile Alice is preparing frozen waffles for the other two children.

Soon Nicholas, aged 2, wanders in. After walking into the bathroom he sits at the table, watching me silently. He says nothing, seeming not quite awake. Alice places the children's plates in front of them, and they slowly begin to eat.

8:00 A.M.

Alice goes into the bedroom to wake up Carrie, her oldest child. Carrie had been sleeping with her, as Richard is working the midnight shift. Carrie was up late watching television. She sits down at the table but is barely awake, taking no notice of me. She sits in front of her plate, slumped in her chair. The general energy level of all the children is low—they are still sleepy and don't say much.

Alice goes downstairs to the basement to turn on the washing machine. Then she comes up and works in the kitchen area.

At 8:10 A.M. Richard, in full uniform, comes home. Alice hears him first and James, grinning, announces, "Daddy is home," an

Floor Plan of the Bernard Home[a]

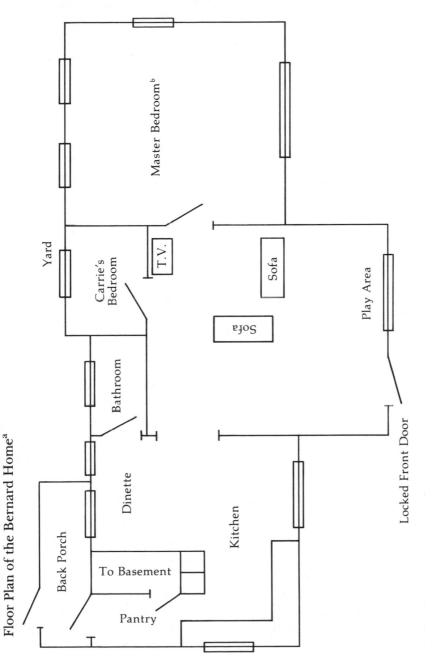

Master Bedroom[b]

Yard

Carrie's Bedroom

T.V.

Sofa

Sofa

Play Area

Bathroom

Dinette

Back Porch

To Basement

Pantry

Kitchen

Locked Front Door

a. The plan is not to exact scale.
b. The boys shared this bedroom with Alice and Richard. Richard had meant to complete an attic room for them, but at the time of the study, this project was not completed.

announcement that is echoed by Nicholas. Richard walks through the kitchen and playfully pulls James's ear, who is pleased and giggles. Richard says hello to Carrie but she seems oblivious to his presence and doesn't respond. James worries out loud that Carrie is not eating her breakfast. Richard walks through the kitchen into the living room.

Alice goes into the bedroom to change the sheets. She complains to me that with the bed being slept in for sixteen hours each day, she has to change them more often. She piles the sheets in the corner of the kitchen near the living room archway, and the two boys, now awake, jump on them. Then they follow Richard into the bedroom where he has gone to change his clothes. Carrie is still at the table, but now she is showing some interest in her food and is beginning to eat.

8:15 A.M.

I can hear the boys chatting to their father as they watch him change his clothes. Alice tells me that this is a daily ritual. I hear Richard's deep voice answering them. They come out of the bedroom together. Richard, now in his farm clothes, goes to the small pantry in the back of the kitchen. The boys begin to play in the sheets again. Alice follows him to the pantry, and I hear them talking about their budget and how much money is left. Alice tells Richard she needs to pick up some clothes from layaway and needs some money.

Alice then goes into the living room to vacuum. She tells me she has to get her vacuuming done when Richard is not sleeping. Richard comes into the kitchen and begins to get out juice for the children, but Alice tells him they've had theirs. Richard then goes into the bathroom, which is just off the kitchen. The boys seem concerned that he has closed the door, and they try to open it. Later I learn that the norm in the house is not to close doors; he is doing so because of my presence. I move into the living room temporarily to give him privacy.

While Alice is vacuuming in the living room, the boys are running around the kitchen. James drapes himself over a chair, and Nicholas lies on the pile of sheets; then they reverse positions. Carrie is still at the table with her juice. She is eating her breakfast very slowly.

Alice comes to the archway of the kitchen and says, "Come on boys, let's watch 'Captain.' " The boys run into the living room. She then says to Carrie, "Come on Carrie, finish up." James turns on the television set. Richard is in the pantry behind the kitchen preparing food for his animals. Alice is cleaning up in the kitchen.

Momentarily, Nicholas comes in to say that "Captain" is over. Alice sends him back to the living room, where Nicholas starts to look for his teddy bear and his blanket. Alice has gone into the bedroom to vacuum and helps Nicholas by finding his blanket for him. The boys now move between the television set in the living room and the bedroom, where Alice is vacuuming. They are interacting with her. Carrie is still quietly languishing at the kitchen table. Finally, the television show catches the boys' full attention; they watch raptly, thumbs in their mouths, holding onto their blankets and teddy bears.

Alice comes out of the bedroom, goes into the kitchen, and talks to Richard. Does he realize his name tag is off his uniform? She had noticed it. I cannot hear the details of his response, but it is short and matter of fact.

8:30 A.M.

For the second time Alice urges Carrie to finish eating. Her patience seems to be wearing thin. She warns her to be finished by the time she has finished changing the sheets on the bed. It is quiet now that the boys are watching television; Alice is now in the bedroom changing the sheets, and noises can be heard from Richard, who is still in the back pantry preparing his animals' food. Quietly, Carrie asks Richard for some more juice; no one hears her. Listlessly and without much energy she repeats her request.

In the living room, James begins to look at his cutout book and interacts with his teddy bear. He's sitting on the sofa. Nicholas is on the floor, and occasionally I can hear him talking to the television characters.

Alice now prepares to dress the children. She takes their clothes out of a dresser in the main bedroom and lays them on the sofa. As she moves through the living room to the kitchen, she asks James curtly to take off his pajamas. She enters the kitchen, where Carrie is still sitting over her breakfast, and irritatedly admonishes her to finish up, as the bed is done. This is Alice's third request to Carrie, who has been sitting over her breakfast, slouching in her chair and playing with her food since 8:00 A.M.

Once again, Alice asks James to take off his pajamas, but he protests that he is not finished "reading." More sternly now, she repeats her request, but he continues to look at his coloring book. Then he wanders over to me to show me his teddy bear. He is using obvious stalling tactics—to him there are more interesting things to do than dressing. Carrie also is still at the kitchen table, passively resisting her mother's admonishments.

Finally, focusing on James, Alice picks him up and starts to undress him, but he protests that he can do it himself. With this show of force, James begins his job. Alice then turns her attention to Nicholas and begins to undress him. As soon as her attention shifts to Nicholas, James asks for help with his shirt. While Alice is dressing Nicholas, he continues to watch television, seemingly oblivious to the fact that his mother is clothing him. He repeats sentences he hears around him.

To no one in particular, since her mother is in the living room and her father is busying himself heating up his animals' food, Carrie asks for some more juice. She repeats herself quietly. Being the only adult in the room, I pour some for her.

Alice tells me that "Captain Kangaroo" and "Sesame Street" really quiet the children down. Without them, she says, "I don't know what I'd do!" While Alice is dressing Nicholas, James asks her for something. Alice is now annoyed and in a quick, irritated voice tells him, "Wait till I finish." James then concerns himself with his Snoopy socks, which he shows me. Nicholas starts to occupy himself with his coloring book.

Alice turns her attention to Carrie, telling her to get dressed. Carrie is still sitting at the table and is making no move to finish. Alice gets a washcloth and brusquely wipes Carrie's mouth.

Alice then moves into the living room to change Nicholas's diaper. Clearly, this is an event he does not like and he begins to protest loudly. In the meantime, Carrie has begun to move. She tells me she'll be 6 soon and takes off her pajamas. In an irritated voice, Alice tells her to dress herself. Carrie and Nicholas discuss their Snoopy items with me. Nicholas is particularly interested in the cap of my pen, to which he points. James is in the living room "reading." The television set momentarily distracts Nicholas and Carrie. Nicholas continues talking with me about my pen. He obviously is interested in my notetaking and my writing. Meanwhile, Alice has gone into the basement to do another load of laundry.

8:45 A.M.

I can hear Alice in the basement putting clothes into the dryer. Richard has gone outside to feed his animals. The children are now in the living room. Carrie and James are watching television; Nicholas is playing near the rocking chair on which his father has draped his uniform.

Alice comes up from the basement and goes into the bedroom to vacuum, warning Nicholas to stay out of "Dad's pockets." I have moved to the living room. Nicholas trips over my feet trying to move toward the television set. He approaches Alice and tells her he hurt his head; she is at the door between bedroom and living room. She gently kisses his head and he seems satisfied.

Alice continues vacuuming in the bedroom. Carrie is dressing while watching television, and Nicholas hovers at the bedroom–living room doorway until Alice emerges with the vacuum cleaner. On the way to the kitchen with the vacuum, she admonishes James to stop sucking his thumb.

Alice begins to vacuum in the kitchen dinette. When she turns on the vacuum cleaner, Carrie turns up the volume on the television set. Carrie and James are watching television; Nicholas is occupying himself in the play area behind the sofa. Carrie and [James] are sitting on the sofas, sucking their thumbs and holding their blankets. Alice announces from the kitchen that they will have to clean up the play area after "Captain" is finished.

Nicholas brings his blocks into the living-room television area. James asks Nicholas if he can "help." Nicholas has already made two trips gathering blocks from the play area and taking them into the living room. (This is after Alice has given them notice that they will have to clean up soon.) Alice notices the block-carrying activity and twice insists that they put them away. James, who has just begun to help Nicholas carry the blocks into the television area, gets admonished as well. Once again, Alice insists to Nicholas that he play in the play area. Nicholas's solution to his dilemma is to play at the boundary between the living-room and the play area. He carries the blocks to the end table marking this boundary and begins to pile the blocks on it, soon incorporating the lamp into his play. James helps him. Alice does not notice this new, forbidden activity.

While the boys are playing with the blocks on the end table, Alice briefly talks to Richard, who has come in from outside and is in the back pantry—at the boundary between outside and inside.

Alice has started the dishes in the kitchen. She does dishes only once a day, she tells me. She then starts to vacuum again, which causes Carrie to turn up the volume on the television again. Alice occasionally stops, throwing a block she has found in the kitchen into the play area. She appears not to notice the block-building activity on the end table. She tells Carrie to bring her the hairbrush so that she can brush Carrie's hair. I get the sense that Alice gives Carrie her instructions before she is actually ready to brush Carrie's hair because getting the brush will take some time. Carrie rises from the sofa at her mother's request but becomes distracted by the television program and then increases the volume when Alice begins vacuuming again. Carrie is now standing motionless in front of the set. Once again Alice tells her to get her hairbrush; Alice sounds tired and irritated now. To deal with Carrie's unwillingness to move, Alice bargains with her by telling her to wait until "the Captain" has finished his explanation and then to get the hairbrush. Meanwhile, the boys have thrown a number of the blocks off the table. Alice goes into the living room, gets the hairbrush herself, turns the volume on the television down, and begins brushing Carrie's hair. Carrie remains in front of the set, captivated by it.

Alice now notices that the table is being used for play and warns James and Nicholas sternly against this forbidden activity. They ignore her. She goes into the kitchen and puts water on to boil. Again she comes to the living-room–kitchen archway and warns Nicholas to clear off the table. James starts to help Nicholas, but she tells him to stop, as she asked Nicholas to do it. Nicholas begins to comply.

Alice goes into the living room and gets her *Reader's Digest* from under the television set. She will try to get some reading done while eating breakfast. As if by signal, James follows her into the kitchen and asks her what she is doing. Alice explains that she hasn't eaten yet. Nicholas gets his blanket from the living room and comes into the kitchen dragging it behind him. In a tired voice, Alice tells him not to drag it on the floor, which isn't clean. The children momentarily return to the living room and "Captain Kangaroo."

9:00 A.M.

The children are in the living room watching "Captain Kangaroo." Alice finally begins to finish preparing her own breakfast—a cup of tea and an instant waffle. She tells me that she and Richard had once thought of a legal separation in order to get welfare because of their financial difficulties. Richard comes in from the yard—he can be heard in the back pantry. Immediately Nicholas comes into the kitchen, followed by Carrie and then James, although they don't overtly acknowledge their father's presence. Alice asks James to put the margarine in the refrigerator, which he does, and then she asks Nicholas to get his shoes. He toddles off to the living room. Carrie starts to play with the vacuum cleaner, which is now in the kitchen. Alice tells her to stop. She is irritated and already tired, it seems. She tells the children the play area has to be picked up, but they make no moves in that direction. Alice does not follow it up, though I am beginning to visualize her as a foreman trying to get stubborn and resistant workers to do their job.

Finally, Alice sits down at the kitchen table with her waffle, tea, and *Reader's Digest.* Immediately, Nicholas and James, who had gone back to the living room, return to the kitchen and hover near her. Carrie again begins to toy with the vacuum cleaner. This time Alice says nothing. Alice puts on Nicholas's shoes, which he had brought to her, and then James starts playing with the vacuum cleaner. Alice tells them to go into the play area. Clearly, she is trying to create some personal space for herself in which to read. Richard comes in, washes up at the sink, and tells Alice he is going to bed. She asks whether he wants to be awakened for lunch. He indicates that he does if the weather's "OK." Richard seems tired; Alice seems tired. Very little passes between them. Carrie and Nicholas have gone into the living room and James announces that they'll be busy, and then he wanders into the play area.

For a moment Alice has quiet, but immediately James returns to complain that Carrie isn't helping to clean up. From the kitchen, Alice admonishes Carrie roughly to help clean up. It almost seems as if there is a conspiracy to prevent Alice from sitting down and resting. Richard comes to Alice's assistance by marching into the living room and sharply reprimanding the children, thereby starting their cleaning effort. It is clear that his presence and booming voice carry authority, for the children are deadly silent when he speaks. Alice comes to the living room–kitchen archway to back Richard up, though she says nothing. When the children start their cleaning effort, she returns to the kitchen for her breakfast and her book. She reads for what seems like only a moment, and then we hear Nicholas asking for her help because Carrie is hitting him. Without getting up, and without taking her eyes from her book, Alice calls sharply to Carrie and commands her to stand in a corner in the kitchen for five minutes. Carrie skulks into the kitchen, goes to the corner and faces outward. Although displeased, Carrie does not seem to take the punishment very seriously. However, when Alice insists that she face the corner, she begins to whimper. Richard, who is near the sink, asks her if she wants a spanking. Looking petulant, she turns toward the corner for the moment.

James then comes into the kitchen and asks for help from Alice in their cleaning effort. Alice indicates she will help them when she is finished. At that point Richard says he is going to sleep, and without further ado walks into the bedroom and closes the door. James asks Alice what Dad is going to do, and in a tired voice that sounds used to such questions, Alice tells him that his father's going to sleep. Not satisfied, James asks why, and Alice perfunctorily tells him, "Dad's tired." She continues to read her book, but I wonder how much reading she is getting done. James asks why Carrie is in the corner. By this time Carrie is sitting on the floor in the corner playing with the vacuum cleaner—she has managed to turn a punishment into a playtime. James is playing in the sheets on the kitchen floor. Alice asks James to leave and give her some peace and quiet—she sounds even more tired, even more drained. James resists this idea but finally goes into the livng room, only to retrieve his blanket to lie down on the kitchen floor near Alice's feet. (Later Alice tells me how much this behavior bothers her, since it indicates to her that the children aren't "coping.") Meanwhile, Carrie is still sitting in the corner playing with the vacuum cleaner; she is now "mouthing" the tube. Alice doesn't seem to notice this and tells her she can leave the corner now (five minutes have not passed). Carrie dallies there. In yet another attempt to create her space, Alice tells Carrie and James to go and play "something" or they won't go outside with her when she goes to the store. At this point Nicholas comes into the kitchen wearing a rain hat and carrying a purse. Alice and I smile at each other. Nicholas asks to sit in Alice's lap, but she says, "Not now." James asks Alice what Nicholas has on his wrist. Alice answers curtly, "It's a watch." Nicholas's entry seems to activate Carrie, who leaves for the living room. She has changed places with Nicholas. Alice still does not have the space she has been trying to create for herself for the last fifteen minutes. . . .

Study Questions

1. "The family, like all other social units, is a power system, resting to some degree on force and its threat" (Goode, 1971, p. 624). How is this axiom illustrated in the Bernard case study?

2. A family's home influences and is influenced by a family's culture, interaction, structure, and identity. Look at the layout of the Bernard home and indicate how this family's living space affects its way of life and vice versa.

3. Families with young children have something in common with medical hospitals and nursing homes. All operate as *continuous coverage systems*, or social organizations in which caring for others (children, patients, etc.) is a round-the-clock responsibility (LaRossa and LaRossa, 1981; Zerubavel, 1979a). Continuous coverage does not mean that parents or nurses or doctors do nothing but care for other people; rather, someone must always be available to lend a hand. Thus, a nurse who is on duty need not be constantly in patients' rooms, but he or she must be ready to respond to call buttons and emergencies. So, too, a father or mother who is alone with a child need not constantly interact with the child, but he or she must be ready to respond to calls for help and to crises. How does Alice try to arrange her activities to be on call rather than constantly interact with her children? Is she successful? Why not? What would you do if you were Alice?

4. One of the difficulties with studying families is that, generally speaking, families cannot be observed *unobtrusively*, that is, without their knowledge or consent. While you can secretly watch how a baseball team or a classroom full of students socially interact, you cannot invade a family's private domain without being noticed. Thus, whatever an outsider sees or hears in a family may be nothing more than behavior orchestrated to create a desired impression (Goffman, 1959). Given the problems with family observation, how much of the Bernard case study, in your opinion, is real and how much of it is illusion? Do you think that Piotrkowski was able really to see how the Bernards live? What should a family observer do to get an accurate picture of family life?

5

Violence in the Home

Cast of Characters

Adelaide, homemaker; Manfred's wife
Manfred, automotive executive; Adelaide's husband
Mordecai, Adelaide and Manfred's twelve-year-old son
Martin, Adelaide and Manfred's nine-year-old son
Andrea, Adelaide and Manfred's baby daughter
Friend/visitor/interviewer, Thomas J. Cottle

THE BREELS are the kind of family that is often held up as the ideal in our society, and at first glance they seem to be ideal, what with Manfred's "more than adequate" salary and Adelaide's commitment to and apparent enthusiasm for homemaking and mothering. But there is more going on in this family than meets the eye. Within the past six months or so, Adelaide and Manfred have gotten into the habit of physically abusing each other, and they are now seriously considering a divorce. Hoping to keep the family together, they have started to see a marriage counselor.

The interviewer is none other than Thomas J. Cottle—sociologist, psychologist, and television personality (a rare combination indeed)—who has made a career of making people feel comfortable when they talk to him about their personal and family lives. There are not many interviewers who can get people to open up as much as Cottle can.

We learn about Adelaide and Manfred's troubles through their older son, Mordecai, and the story he tells of two people "Screaming, hitting. Wrestling each other all over the place," stands in sharp contrast to the picture that Adelaide and Manfred generally project. Actually, the discrepancy should not surprise us: although somewhere between one out of four and one out of three couples have used violence (that is, thrown something at one another; pushed, slapped, or kicked each other; or used a knife or gun on one another), few of us are privy to this darker side of our neighbors, friends, and relatives (Finkelhor, Gelles, Hotaling, and Straus, 1983; Straus, Gelles, and Steinmetz, 1980).

Apropos of this case, one of the first systematic studies of violence in the home was based on children's reports. Some years ago, Straus (1974) asked his undergraduate students to complete a questionnaire that dealt with their parents' conflicts. He did so in part because he felt that he could not ask the parents themselves whether they were physically aggressive with each other and get an honest answer (he has since discovered that under the right conditions people will admit to beating their wives or husbands [see Straus, 1979]). Straus found that verbal aggression and physical aggression are positively related. In other words, arguing and yelling, rather than having a cathartic, or tension-releasing, effect, may increase the chance that violence will occur. I say *may increase* because we have no way of knowing from Straus's data whether or not the two kinds of aggression are causally related. Still, the findings are interesting, especially in light of what seems to be happening in the Breel home: according to Mordecai, his father and mother's boxing matches almost invariably begin with one of the two (usually his father) verbally abusing the other.

The important question is, What makes Mordecai's parents so violent in the first place? One possible explanation is that Adelaide and Manfred are medically or mentally ill. Another is that they are victims of stress. Still a third is that they are involved in a struggle for power and are eager to win at any cost.

As far as the first explanation goes, without additional information, we cannot determine whether Adelaide and Manfred are suffering from a disease of either the body or the mind. As for the second explanation, it is also difficult to know (given the information we have) whether they are under stress, although there is some chance that the birth of their daughter has created financial pressure. Mordecai does, however, mention several things that would lend support to the third explanation—that Adelaide and Manfred are fighting to gain and/or maintain control in their marriage. He says, for instance, that his father would often verbally abuse his mother for not cleaning the house or for spending too much money on food but that the physical abuse did not start until his mother began to stand up for herself. This suggests that Manfred may be using force to discipline his wife because his preferred tactic—verbal abuse—does not work any more (cf. Allen and Straus, 1980; Goode, 1971). How does Adelaide respond to being beaten? More often than not, she is no match for her husband ("Dad shoved her under the table one night. . . . He wouldn't let her get out. He kept running around and kicking her when she tried to get up"). However, every now and then, she apparently gets in a few blows of her own ("Another night she must have hit him pretty hard, because when I got in there his nose was bleeding").

The critical issue in this situation is where Manfred got the idea that violence is an effective and legitimate way to deal with a "disobedient" wife. The answer is that violence against women is embedded in our culture and social structure; since early times, men have had the *legal* right (though certainly not the *moral* right) to beat and in some circumstances kill their wives to keep them "in their place" or punish them for "stepping out of line" (Dobash and Dobash, 1979). Ironically, in fact, the family has throughout history been a source of love, as well as an arena for violent combat (Gelles, 1974; Straus and Hotaling, 1980). Thus, Adelaide and Manfred would seem to be but a single link in a very long and very strong chain. In and through them, history repeats itself.

The Breel Family

Thomas J. Cottle

TWELVE-YEAR-OLD MORDECAI BREEL has a rather peculiar habit, peculiar, that is, until one discovers what it means. Periodically he walks calmly out of the back door of his apartment house into the small back yard and pushes his heel into his mother's herb garden. He only pushes down once. Then he goes out the back gate into the alley where his father parks his car and kicks one of the fenders. His kick does little if any damage; the crushed herbs come back after a rainstorm and some gentle handling by his mother.

When I first began visiting the Breel home several years ago, Mrs. Adelaide Breel always insisted that we sit outside in the yard. There we talked about her life as a mother of three children, her relationship with her husband Manfred, an automotive executive, and her plans to resume working as a secretary or bookkeeper when their youngest child was old enough to manage without constant attention. Spring afternoons were especially pleasant in the Breel yard. Adelaide seemed eager to talk, and while her husband was naturally suspicious at first about the sort of research I was conducting, he gradually came to like the idea that someone would be interested in his family.

"We're sort of an ideal family, I guess you could say," Adelaide told me one June day as Andrea, then a baby, slept in a white crib near where her mother was weeding the garden. "I never thought anyone would come to visit us and talk about our lives, but I can't say I'm not pleased. I think it's kind of exciting. I mean, I'm not trying to keep the problems from you, believe me. Actually, I think fate brought us all together, don't you?"

"Could well be," I answered, sipping orangeade she had made for her son Mordecai, who would soon be returning home from school.

My friendship with the Breels began through a chance meeting. I had been speaking with several men employed at a large Boston automobile sales and service plant. In time I came to know sev-

Excerpt from pages 3–17 of *A Family Album: Portraits of Intimacy and Kinship* by Thomas J. Cottle. Copyright © 1974 by Thomas J. Cottle. By permission of Harper & Row, Publishers, Inc.

eral of the executives, Manfred Breel being one of them. Soon after our discussions started, he suggested that I visit his home and
meet his wife and children. As Adelaide was then pregnant with
Andrea, I proposed that we "let the baby come first and the inter-
viewing later." Manfred smiled and agreed that plan would be
best.

In the beginning, just as Adelaide Breel suggested, the family
was what I always imagined a fine family to be. The two older children were growing nicely; they were creative and yet obedient in a
kindly way. Schoolwork came easily for them, especially for Mordecai, whose intelligence and grace were evident at our first meeting. Manfred's job payed a more than adequate salary; he would
have liked more money, naturally, but his wife never complained.
And the three-bedroom apartment on the ground floor with access to the yard and free alley parking constituted a lovely
environment.

"A man can work hard all his life and never achieve that,"
Manfred said after my first visit to the house. "There's no guarantee. Not until a person accumulates great wealth is there ever really
a protection against everything you have falling part. I watch the
papers quite regularly for indications of job loss at the middle levels. It happens more and more now. You see lots of engineers losing their jobs when the government cuts back their projects. Take
a business like mine. No one on the outside knows how we're
doing. Fact is, the accountants sitting right over there," he
motioned to a row of glass-partitioned offices, "I'm not even sure
they know half the time. You got to go to Detroit to find out what's
really going on. For a person like myself, right now everything's
working out well for us. It took a while, you've only known me the
last few months. I didn't have it so easy for ten years. I've done lots
of things in my time that netted me next to nothing. But I stayed at
it. I don't want anything else. The baby will come, with God's help
we'll get a nice healthy girl to go with two super boys, and we'll
hope the economy settles down so people will have lots of money,
and they'll buy their cars here." Manfred laughed freely. He is a
tall, handsome man with a big chest and strong arms. "Which re-
minds me," he joked, slapping my shoulder, "how's that little bug-
gy of yours holding up? 'Bout time for you to trade it in on something a little more in keeping with your life style, isn't it?"

I must have looked embarrassed.

"I'm only teasing you," he said. "That's what we call the soft sell. It's like planting the idea. Good way to sell a car is to convince the buyer he should feel ashamed driving an old car. Don't do it," he advised seriously. "If it starts in the cold weather and keeps running, hold on to it. None of these cars is ever run as many miles as it could."

My visits with the Breels were always pleasant. They were open with me about their interests and concerns and still discreet in their descriptions of personal matters. I rarely saw Manfred and Adelaide together, but based on everything I could see, they could count on the stability of their family.

Then I went away for a year. At the time I left, my visits with them had been no more frequent than twice a month. Shortly after my return to Boston, I stopped by their house one afternoon without phoning first, hoping to surprise them. Waiting at the front door fearing that the long delay in answering meant that no one was home, I imagined for the first time little Andrea walking. Time passes, I thought, peering through the front hall window to see whether the house was empty.

As I was about to leave, my idea of a surprise deflated, the door opened and there stood Mordecai. He wore blue jeans and a bright yellow shirt and looked as though he has just washed his face.

"Hey, Mordecai. My God, you've grown a foot!"

Mordecai was glad to see me, but a shyness I had not observed before was part of this "new" young man.

"Are you back for good?" he asked, as we walked into the living room.

"I am. Got back a little while ago and wanted to see you all. Where is everybody?"

"Ah, my brother Martin went to a friend's house. Andrea's asleep. Mom and Dad are out."

"Mom and Dad? Together?"

"Yeah. You want to stay in here?"

"Sure. Want to sit out in the garden?" I asked.

"No. It's too hot. Let's stay here so I can let them in if they come home."

Mordecai's way, it was easy to see, had been changed by something far more significant than a year of growing.

"Is everybody all right?" I asked gently. "Andrea okay?"

"Everybody's fine," he said, although not without some bitterness. "Everbody's just as strong as they always were."

"Strong?" It was not the adjective I would have expected him to use. "What do you mean strong? Was somebody sick? Your dad okay?"

"Yes."

"Mom?"

"She's fine too. Well, not really."

"You want to talk, Mordy?"

"Sure, I'll talk, except you can't tell them I told you, though they'll probably tell you when you see them."

"I'll see them. I've been planning on it. Where are they?" I asked suddenly.

"They're out seeing some psychiatrist, a marriage counselor, maybe. Someone like that."

"Marriage counselor? They in trouble?"

"What do you mean 'trouble'?" he asked calmly.

"I mean, you know. Are they thinking of getting a divorce?"

"That shake you up, Tom?"

"As a matter of fact it does. Why, doesn't it you?"

"You kidding me? Shake me up? You know what I've been doing for six months? I've been a referee for all their fights." We had walked into the dining area. I sat down at the table. Mordecai stood at one end behind the chair in which his father always sat.

"They fighting?" I asked quietly.

"Just about every night."

"Bad words?"

"You can say that again. The worst."

"Hitting?"

"Blood."

"Your dad?"

"Mother too. Both of them. Screaming, hitting. Wrestling each other all over the place. Breaking furniture. The whole thing. Then they're all right for two or three nights, then they're back at it."

"What's been going on? I mean, was this happening when I used to visit?"

" No. Of course not. You saw us then. You knew everything was normal, real stable." I was surprised to hear him use these words. "But the last six months, they've been fighting almost every night."

"But what started it?"

"I don't know. It was just one night, I heard them yelling. They used to do that so I was kind of used to it. But like, this one night, I think maybe it was New Year's Eve, I was in bed and they were fighting, and Mom kept telling Dad they were going to wake us up, but he kept yelling at her. Then he pushed her or hit her, and she fell. I waited for a while and then went in there," Mordecai pointed behind him in the direction of the living room," and she was lying on the floor. She had this big cut over her eye. I had to push Dad away, which isn't easy with Dad."

"I know, he's a big man."

"But I did it. Another night I carried Mom into my bedroom. She was barely conscious. I locked the door and told Dad he couldn't come in. He pounded on the door. I thought he was going to break it down. He could if he wanted to. Then another night she must have hit him pretty hard, because when I got in there his nose was bleeding. It wasn't broken, but he was crying and she was crying. I heard them fighting that night, too. They didn't wait like they usually do until we're asleep. They just started."

"You want to sit down, Mordy?" I asked when it seemed he had nothing else to say.

He shook his head and remained standing behind his father's chair, his hands holding its back. It had been fifteen months since I had seen this boy. He had not spoken to anyone about his new role in a family all of us had thought was as secure as a family could be.

"Dad gets awful angry, you know."

"I didn't know."

"Well, he can. I never saw him hurt anyone, but he's always picked on Mom. For little things, like not getting the house cleaned up or spending too much money on food, stuff like that. My brother and me, we're pretty used to it. We took it in stride." He looked at me. The phrase "took it in stride" made me think of him as being twenty-five instead of twelve. "But pretty soon she began to fight back, and when she did, his anger, like, never was worse. I couldn't do my homework with the two of them yelling and fighting all the time. I'd come in and tell them to be quiet. Or I'd pull him away from her, like I told you."

"What would your dad say?"

"Oh, he would tell Mom she's a failure and that she's letting herself go to hell, and he's going to find someone else. And she said 'go ahead' and he said 'I already have.' Then she would cry a lot, and he'd say she was a little girl because she couldn't argue or stand up for her rights like a grown-up. Then she'd say he was acting like a baby, and that would make him angry again."

"Did they swear at one another?" I don't know why I asked him this.

"Swear?" Mordecai blew out a long breath and shook his head sadly. "A football team could have taken a lesson from them."

"Your mother too?"

"Mom's just as bad. I didn't even know she knew all those words. I thought just boys learned them."

I smiled at him, hoping to lighten his mood, but there was more he had to tell. It seemed, too, that he wanted to get it all out for fear that I might leave again or that his parents would come home and, seeing us together, would realize that he had divulged too much.

"Dad's always been hard on Mom," Mordecai was saying. "Like, she might be talking about something political, and she'll say the wrong thing. Nothing serious, but it will be wrong, and Dad will really lay into her for being dumb. Mom never went to college, you know."

"Yes, I know that."

"So she hasn't really got a good defense. If Dad says she's wrong and stupid, she always feels she has to take it. Except for recently. Wow, she's been tough. She was breast feeding Andrea, you know, and then she had to stop. Something happened, and no more milk came. That really made her upset. Then one night I heard her tell Dad that it was because of him that it happened. He was drinking that night," Mordecai's head dropped down, and his voice became so quiet I could barely hear him. "He threw the drink in her face and laughed at her. Then she threw her glass at him. It broke all over the place."

"You hear this?" I asked,

"Saw it. I was standing right over there." He pointed to the entrance to the living room, his manner not unlike a trial witness pointing at a defendant.

"Are they drinking, Mordecai?"

"Hmm."

"A lot?"

"Every night. A real lot. They both get plastered. Mom puts the baby to sleep, and then she drinks too."

"And then they fight?"

"Not really. They fight even without drinking. I think Dad made Mom drink more. But they hit each other when they drink. So I have to be like a referee deciding whether to keep them from hurting each other or just let them do it."

"You must get pretty angry yourself, don't you?"

"Yeah. I do." He answered this question with the same uneasy calmness with which he had related everything else. "Sometimes I think I'll go into the living room and hit both of them. I'd rather hit my father, usually. But sometimes my mother. Not a lot, but she's pretty dirty too sometimes. I've seen Dad crying after their fights."

I nodded. I couldn't imagine, actually, how at her size Adelaide could stand up to someone as strong as her husband. Nor could I imagine them slugging one another as Mordecai had described.

"Dad shoved her under the table one night. Right under here." He bent down slightly and pointed underneath the small, rectangular dining room table. "He wouldn't let her get out. He kept running around and kicking her when she tried to get up. Mom didn't have a lot of clothes on but she was yelling."

"Could you help?"

"I made him let her up. She just stood there. She wasn't even embarrassed that she was naked. Dad kept telling her to put some clothes on, but she just stood there swearing and yelling at him until I calmed her down and got her to lie down on her bed. That was one of those nights I told you about, when I had to lock the door to keep Dad out."

"Did your mom talk to you?" Again and again I had to tell myself that this was a twelve-year-old boy recounting these episodes. I found myself thinking that when I was twelve, I went to camp for the first time and cried when my parents put me on the train.

"I don't know. A little. She always says that I'm a good boy, the only bright spot in her life. On the really bad nights she always want me to sleep near her, on the bed or on the floor. She's afraid Dad will come in and beat her, maybe even try to kill her." Mordecai's tone was unchanged. There wasn't a quake in his voice or a missed syllable, nothing to suggest he would give in to the pain or tears.

"What do you do?"

"Nothing. I never stay with her. When I was little I always wanted to sleep in the same bed with Mom and Dad. Between them, you know. I couldn't see why they wouldn't let me, but Mom said that every person has his own bed and that's where I belong. Besides, Martin would get lonely if I slept with them. That's what I tell her now when she wants me to stay with her. 'Everyone has his own bed, Mom,' I say. Dad ends up sleeping on the couch in there. The first time he slept there I thought it would be better if he slept in a bed, with covers and a pillow. I could sleep with Martin and Dad could sleep in my bed."

"That was a very generous thought, Mordy."

"Well, maybe." He seemed embarrassed by my remark. "But it wasn't a good idea," he added quickly, "because I didn't want to let Martin know what was going on. He'd figure out things were pretty strange if all of a sudden he woke up and found me sleeping with him and Dad sleeping in my bed. And Dad really gets looking pretty bad on those nights. He usually falls asleep with all his clothes on. With a drink in his hand too." Mordecai's voice always dropped when he mentioned the drinking. "So when he doesn't make it to bed or when she won't let him come in, he falls asleep on the couch and I go in and put some covers on him. Then I make up stories to tell Martin the next morning. It's a good thing Andrea's too small to understand what's going on. Martin's only nine, so this shouldn't bother him too much, but she's just a baby. It could really affect her, couldn't it?"

"I guess it could," I agreed.

"Yeah, that's what I've been thinking. People's personalities can be affected by these things."

"Yours as well, Mordy?"

"Sure." He said the word as if responding to an invitation to play baseball. "That's what really has me troubled. I don't mind being the referee for them, but I can tell that it's starting to bother me. In the beginning I sort of was frightened when I heard them fighting. I tried to block out the noise. Once I sneaked out the kitchen window and took a walk. It was real late and that made me even more scared." Mordecai smiled shyly. "But now I'm scared and angry. I don't know how much longer I'm going to be able to keep going, do my homework and all my chores around here and help Mom and Dad too. I sometimes wish I were fifteen or sixteen. I wish they could have waited a little." He looked at me, shifting his weight onto one foot. "But then it would be Martin and Andrea, so either way somebody gets hurt, especially Mom and Dad. But sometimes I think I may end up going crazy from all this."

"It's hard to stay so angry and so hurt, isn't it?" I said softly.

"You know what I've been doing? Every time they have a fight I push my foot down in Mom's garden, and then I kick Dad's car. It's silly, but while I'm doing it I feel better. That's because I feel better knowing the next morning I'll be able to do it. They know. I get pretty angry, but I can't do anything just lying in bed. That's another thing. I've been losing a lot of sleep, which isn't so good. And it gets hard to eat breakfast the mornings after the fights, too. You have to sit there looking at them pretending nothing's wrong. It's hard to believe they really love each other. I'll bet sometimes Mom and Dad go to bed at night and cry just like I do."

"Have you been crying, Mordecai?"

"Lots of nights. Some nights are good, I mean, they don't fight. So I try to do a lot of homework, get ahead on my work just in case they have a fight the next night. They've been starting earlier and earlier too, so I have to get ready."

"You must be at a point where you're ready to tear up the whole garden by now, huh?"

Mordecai grinned as if pleased to have someone condone his anger.

"I think I'd like to leave the garden and pull the house down. I try not to hurt the garden. I can stamp my foot so the plants are just bent a little. I don't want to hurt innocent little things like Mom's herbs, but I want to get back at her."

Throughout our conversation, Mordecai's eyes rarely met mine. Each time I looked at him he looked away. In response, I purposely stared at nothing just to allow him to see my expressions. These were moments when it seemed he might have liked to cry.

"I don't think I have anything else to tell you," he was saying. "I just hope I make it through. Things have really changed. I know I'm going to have to change a lot too, since I'm so young. My voice hasn't even changed yet. But I didn't think this was the way it had to be. They're going to have to stop pretty soon or my head is going to bust."

"What do you imagine they'll do?"

"Well, they're seeing this psychiatrist, which I guess is good. I don't know him. Dad didn't want to go at first, but now he is. I don't think they should get a divorce. They're not ready for it. Dad says he could, but he's worried about Mom."

"He tells you this, I take it?"

"Yes. And Mom tells me the same thing about him. She thinks Dad couldn't manage on his own. They've been married almost fifteen years. They aren't old, but they aren't *that* young either."

"And the children?" My questions sounded as if they were addressed to an attorney.

"We'll go where they want us to go. Probably with Mom, although Dad would like to see us, even if he gets remarried. Andrea, though, she'd probably have to stay with Mom, don't you think so?"

"Yes, I guess she would." I was beginning to sound like a probate attorney myself, settling the remains of an estate.

"That's what I thought, too," Mordecai said knowingly. "Little children need their mothers more than their fathers. Martin and I are old enough. We'll go with whoever wants us."

"You're twelve now, aren't you, Mordy?"

"Right. Why?"

"Just trying to catch up on you after all these months," I smiled.

"Do I sound older?"

"Yes."

"I know. Twelve is just a number of years. I feel older."

For several minutes he said nothing. The more I studied his face, the more he continued to concentrate on invisible objects. Both of us watched the patterns of afternoon light that moved about the blond hardwood floor. A modern lacy curtain caught the light the leaves had already played with and made it dance on the floor and on the dining room table. I thought about Mordecai's need to fulfill this new role exactly as he was fulfilling it and, by doing so, to hold his family intact long enough for someone, hopefully, to come and help them. His presentation was not characterized by that dull and incongruous emotion one hears in troubled people, depressed people, people heading for a serious fall, perhaps at their own hands. He knew he was inadequately schooled for this type of emergency aid, working over his head and holding strong until real experts could come. And his only outlet for this overwhelming burden was to push his foot into a tiny herb garden, carefully, too, so that no permanent damage would be caused and to smack the fender of his father's car in just the right way so as not to cause dents.

Still we said nothing. I moved uncomfortably in my chair; Mordecai continued to hold the back of his father's chair. There was a noise at the front door as Manfred and Adelaide Breel returned home. I rose quickly and followed Mordy to the entrance hall.

"How are you, Mordecai?" Adelaide asked perfunctorily, laying a heavy bag of groceries on a wooden chest. Then simultaneously the two of them saw me.

"Well, I'll be," Adelaide exploded with surprise. "When did *you* get back?"

"Stranger!" Manfred echoed her loudly. "I thought you were gone for good." He reached to shake my hand.

"Didn't you get my card?" I asked, shaking hands and watching Mordy as I did.

"Sure, we got it," Manfred answered, "but we haven't had a word since then. We thought you stayed out there in the middle-America scene. Thought you gave up on us New Englanders once and for all."

"You've gained a little weight, Tom Cottle," Adelaide teased me. "Cook better there do they? Mordy, love," she turned to her son, "have you asked this too-long-unseen visitor whether he wants something to drink?"

"A beer? I got some imported stuff," Manfred offered graciously.

"No thanks," I answered.

"Mordy, be a good boy and see what we have in the refrigerator," Adelaide ordered kindly, pushing the boy gently toward the kitchen.

"No thanks really, Adelaide," I said. Mordy stopped, waiting to see what would be decided.

"A small beer." Manfred persisted, pulling me into the living room.

"Okay. I'll split one with you."

"We'll split one, and then we'll see whether we go for two. My God, it's so early in the day. What's to fear?"

"Let me put some things away in the kitchen, and I'll join you two beer hounds," Adelaide said gaily.

Mordy seemed unsure where he was wanted. "You come with me, son." Adelaide smiled at her son, took him by the hand, and directed him to the groceries with a gesture that said, into the kitchen.

Then Manfred and I were sitting opposite one another in the living room. Beyond him I could see the spot in the dining area where Mordy had stood.

"So my friend the traveling reporter, what news do you bring from Iowa? Indiana?"

"Illinois," I corrected him gently.

"Illinois. Illinois. Why do I say Indiana?"

"All the I's probably."

"I suppose that's it."

"The word is," I began, "that they're still out there in the Middle West. And it was good. It was a terrific year."

"That's great, Tom. It was worth being away, then, eh?"

"It really was. It couldn't have been a better year."

"That's beautiful," he replied in his big voice.

"And you? How goes it here?" I stared directly at him, but he was reaching down to pull off his shoes.

"Everything's the same, Tom. A little change here, a little change there, a little more money one month, a little less the next, but anyway you count it, it nets out the same. You know what I mean?"

"You win some, you lose some," I said.

"Exactly. Spoken just like a businessman." He looked up at me from his crouched over position and smiled broadly. "Adelaide," he yelled good naturedly, "you've got two thirsty boys here waiting on you. Let's have something already."

"Be patient, thirsty boys," she yelled back from the kitchen. "We're just about ready. Mordy, take a Coke in there for yourself," I heard her say. "Don't say anything, Tom, without me. I don't want to miss a word of this. It's over a year since you've gone. You realize that?"

"I really don't have that much to tell," I said to Manfred who was now sitting with his feet up on the coffee table. He continued smiling at me, nodding his head up and down, waiting for me to begin my report. I hunched up my shoulders. "I really don't have anything exciting to tell you." I made a gesture to say, it's really true.

"Just getting along, eh?" he tried to encourage me. "Kind of surviving?"

"Yeah, like that."

He nodded his head. "I guess that's everybody's business. Just surviving . . ."

Adelaide interrupted him and rescued me for the moment when she entered with a tray of beer and glasses.

"Right here on the table, wife," Manfred laughed, clearing space for her. "Now, we're going to relax, be with our friend again, and hear his story start to finish. Isn't that right, Mordy? Come on over here, son," he motioned to the boy, who stood quietly in the entranceway holding his Coca Cola. "Pull up a chair and join us. There's nothing Tom has to say that isn't fit for a young man's ears." He winked at me. "Careful now what you say in front of my boy here," he grinned.

Study Questions

1. What would you do if you were Cottle? Would you mention to Adelaide and Manfred that you knew about the violence in their marriage? Would you contact a family or community service agency and recommend that the children be taken from their parents? Would you call the police and have Adelaide and Manfred arrested for assault or for child abuse and neglect? Would you do nothing? Why?

2. Mordecai plays several informal roles in the Breel family. What are they and what are their functions for keeping the family going?

3. Mordecai says that his parents fight even when they are not drinking but that they hit each other when they drink. It is common for family members to drink before, while, and after they hit each other, but it is not clear whether alcohol causes people to be violent or whether it facilitates the use of violence by providing a socially acceptable *account* (Scott and Lyman, 1968) for committing a crime (e.g., "It wasn't my fault, I was drunk"). Most sociologists would probably say that the second explanation is the correct one: drinking, rather than a cause, is a convenient rationalization offered by aggressors and accepted by victims to prevent a serious examination of the situation (Gelles, 1974). Sociologists would also point out that drinking is not the only account used to excuse and justify violence between family members. For example, some husbands say that wives ask to be hit, implying that abused wives have only themselves to blame. And some parents tell their children that they hit them because they love them. What other excuses and justifications can be used to rationalize family violence? Why are some accounts more legitimate (i.e., more socially acceptable) than others? What do you suppose are the consequences in a family if, every time violence is used, it is excused and justified; in other words, what do you think will happen to the family in the long run?

4. If you were to put together a theory of husband–wife violence, what would it look like? What variables would be the most important? What variables the least? How would family culture, interaction, structure, and identity fit into your theory? Finally, what solutions to the problem would you propose, based on your theory?

6

Therapeutic Change

CAST OF CHARACTERS

Mr. S., electrical engineer
Mrs. S., electrical engineer, part-time
Billy, Mr. and Mrs. S.'s twelve-year-old son
Larry, Mr. and Mrs. S.'s eight-year-old son
Psychiatrist, Richard Fisch

MOST THERAPISTS—whether they are psychiatrists, psychologists, counselors, or social workers—take an individualistic approach to therapy. In other words, they assume that the causes of poor mental health (e.g., schizophrenia, phobia, chronic unhappiness) are located within people's personalities, much the same as medical doctors assume that the causes of poor physical health are located within people's bodies. However, a small but growing cohort of therapists, known as *family therapists,* see poor mental health as a family problem. And when they receive a call for help—a call that typically involves one family member (the *complainant*) seeking a cure for another family member (the *identified patient*)—they insist on treating the family and not just the person who is presumed by the family to be sick.

An interesting thing about family therapy is that it is based on principles that have a distinct sociological bent. A lot of attention, for example, is given to family norms and family interaction. Also, the idea that the family is a system—a collection of elements related to each other in a complex way—is central to both diagnosis and treatment. Considering the link between family therapy and sociology, I thought it might be informative to include a case study showing how a family therapist goes about his work.

90

Richard Fisch, a psychiatrist with the Mental Research Institute in Palo Alto, California, outlines how he attempted to help a twelve-year-old boy by treating the boy's family or, more specifically, the boy's relationship to his father and mother. Unlike the other cases, this case includes a considerable amount of interpretation by the author (inserted in parentheses) because Fisch's diagnosis and treatment is what makes the case noteworthy and, I might add, controversial.

Here is what happens. Mr. and Mrs. S. meet with Fisch to ask for his help in dealing with their son Billy. It seems that Billy has been getting into fights at school. He also watches television a lot, something that bothers his parents a great deal because they feel he could make better use of his time by going out and finding new friends. Finally, they reveal that Billy is "neurologically and physically handicapped"—he suffers from psychomotor epilepsy, has a spastic left hand because of a lesion on the brain, and is dyslexic.

To help Billy with his problems, Mr. and Mrs. S. have created a "supportive" social environment. They have, for instance, encouraged Billy to do things that would make him feel good about himself, and they have tried to reward his accomplishments, however small. But they are now extremely discouraged because, no matter how much they try to help Billy, his behavior seems to be getting worse.

While Mr. and Mrs. S. tell him their story, Fisch listens intently. He makes no suggestions during the first session but says he would like to meet with Billy alone.

Four days later, Billy is in Fisch's office explaining his problem as he sees it. To Billy, his lack of friends is not nearly as troublesome as the fact that other children constantly "bug" him about his spastic hand. Fisch asks to see the hand and then tries to imitate Billy's hand movements, but without success. In the process, however, he presumably communicates to Billy that his spasticity can be seen as an ability rather than a disability—an idea that intrigues and delights the boy. Next, Fisch asks Billy whether there are any children who do *not* bug him about his hand. When Billy says yes, Fisch instructs Billy to attempt to get one of these children to bother him about his hand. The purpose of this prescription is ostensibily to show Billy that he has some control over the reactions of his peers. Billy leaves the session excited about the game he has been asked to play.

Six days later, Mr. and Mrs. S. come in for their second session, and they report that something strange has been happening around the house. Billy is showing off his hand rather than keeping it hidden, as he had done before. For reasons that will become clear as you read the case, Fisch congratulates Mr. and Mrs. S. and attributes the change to their positive influence on their son.

By now, Fisch thinks he knows what the family's problem is, and he is ready to start treatment. Essentially, he believes that Billy is a normal boy despite his spastic left hand but that he has been made self-conscious by his parents' well-intentioned attempts to help him. However, Fisch does not share this diagnosis with Mr. and Mrs. S. Why? Because this interpretation is contrary to what Mr. and Mrs. S. have assumed all along, namely that Billy is the problem. If Fisch were to share his interpretation with them, they would probably reject it. He thus comes up with a diagnosis that, on the one hand, will make sense to Billy's parents and, on the other, will provide a rationale (or "leverage") for the behavioral changes he wants them to make. In family therapy terms, Fisch is *reframing* (i.e., reconceptualizing or redefining) the family's situation in a way that will facilitate corrective action (Watzlawick, Weakland, and Fisch, 1974).

The interpretation that Fisch offers to the couple is that, with everyone paying so much attention to him, Billy has developed a fear of being too powerful, of being able to make his parents jump whenever he wants them to do so. This, Fisch explains, is why Billy does not want to make friends with other children: he is afraid that he would end up controlling his friends as well.

Fisch prescribes two things. First, he says that from now on what Billy does at school is the school's concern. Billy's misbehavior in the classroom is not to be allowed to affect the activities and routines of his parents. Second, instead of urging Billy to go out and make friends, Mr. and Mrs. S. are to encourage him to stay home and watch television—in other words, to encourage him to do just the opposite of what they really want him to do.

Fisch contends that his diagnosis "made a lot of sense" to Mr. and Mrs. S. because it "confirmed their own suspicions that they were not handling Billy right." After a few more sessions, during which Fisch continues to reframe and to prescribe corrective (and often paradoxical) action, Billy is apparently cured of his inability to socialize. The truth, however, is that in a matter of months (not uncommon, in fact typical in some schools of family therapy), Fisch has restructured the family itself—that is, the norms for dealing with Billy and the family's pattern of interaction.

The S. Family

Richard Fisch

MRS. S. CALLED ME. She said her son needed help. He was 12 years old and was having trouble with other children at school and at home. She wasn't sure how to set up the appointment but would leave it to my decision. I asked her if her son would be resistant to coming in and she replied that she wasn't sure but that he had no trouble relating to adults. When she began to elaborate on that I told her it would be best to leave any further description of the problem till we met in my office. I further suggested that it might "be better in the long run" for me to meet only with her and her husband, at least for that first session. She was agreeable to that.

(I discourage patients from giving me much information on the phone. I do this because I want to convey that treatment is a "getting down to business," not a casual affair to be discussed over a phone. I also want to convey a separation between my office and their lives outside of it. This helps set the stage when, later in treatment, I can further convey that, while discussion may be needed, it is action in their lives that is more important. As for whom I see in an initial session, this will often be determined by my assessment as to who, in the family, is the complainant and not, necessarily, by who is the identified patient. In a child-centered problem, it is almost always the parents who are the complainants, not the child, and since they are also the power in the family, I usually anticipate I will be doing the greater bulk of the work with them. Thus, having the parents come in initially conveys that *they* are initiating treatment and are asking my help in *their* dealings with *their* child. On occasion, I may see the child with his or her parents in the first interview, but I will never see a child alone the first time.)

Session 1

Mr. and Mrs. S. arrived on time. She is thirty-seven years old and he thirty-eight. They are an attractive couple; both are slim, youthful and athletic looking. Both are engineers working in the

From "Sometimes It's Better for the Right Hand Not to Know What the Left Hand is Doing" by Richard Fisch, M.D., in *Family Therapy: Full Length Case Studies* edited by Peggy Papp, M.S.W. Copyright © 1977 by Gardner Press. Reprinted by permission of the publisher, Gardner Press.

electronics field, although Mrs. S.'s job is part-time. In addition to their 12-year-old son, Billy, they have an 8-year-old boy, Larry. Mrs. S. reiterated her concern about Billy.

The principal problem had to do with his difficulty in socializing with children, especially with those his own age. In school, he often got into fights and seemed to be generally hostile to the other children. The problem had reached its peak about two years ago when he got into a "rage reaction" at school and had to be sent home. While the problem had subsided some in the last two years, it was still considerable and treatment was precipitated by a recent call from his teacher; that he had had another "outburst" in class and was sent home for misbehavior at school, although not all of it for "outbursts" or "rage reactions." They added that Billy's difficulties were not limited to school. He had no friends in their neighborhood either and he would spend "75 percent" of his time watching television. They would scold him for spending so much of his time in front of the TV set; would try to limit the hours of watching and urge him to go outside and meet with other children, but this was to no avail. When I asked how he got along with Larry, they said they frequently squabbled with each other but did not identify this as any particular problem; it was not excessive in their minds, did not reach uncontrollable levels, and it appeared to be a mutual bickering rather than any harassment by Billy, per se.

Then they launched into a rather pessimistic picture. Billy was "neurologically and physically handicapped." At about 4 or 5 years of age he was diagnosed as having psychomotor epilepsy and through the years had been maintained on anti-convulsive medications. This had markedly limited his seizures so that in the last year or two he had had only four episodes. These, they described, came on only at night and while he was asleep. However, he had also been diagnosed as having a "porencephalic cyst" and that this lesion had left him with spasticity of the left hand. For this he had also been receiving physical therapy and while function had improved he still had noticeable spasticity and difficulty with fine touch movement. But this was not the end of his "neurological" problems. Later, during his schooling, he had been diagnosed by school personnel as having "dyslexia" and because of this diagnosis had been placed in special education classes for the last two years. It seemed that such placement was also determined by his hostile behavior in class and the decision to transfer him was precipitated by his "rage reaction" and the teacher fearing she could no longer control him. Finally, Mrs. S. said that because of all the problems Billy presented she had been able to look back and realize that from birth he was "hyperactive" and difficult to handle.

In asking for Mr. S.'s views, he echoed much of what his wife had said. However, he added that Billy also suffered from some kind of frustration he was unable to put into words. They would often question him—"Why are you upset? What really bothers you?" And they would be dismayed when he responded in a self-denigrating way: "I always botch things up. Why is everything I do a boo-boo?" They attempted to help him by giving him "environ-mental support"—trying to find things for him to do he could feel good about himself in accomplishing, taking him on special trips skiing, golfing, bicycle riding, picnics. When the parents went out they made a special effort to find sitters who would be "supportive" such as male college students. They acknowledged this tended to limit their social life since such sitters were hard to come by. Finally, they would make "contracts" with Billy and give him special rewards for being a "nice kid."

(I made no comments throughout this narrative. My sole activi-ty was to raise questions to clarify the points they were making: what they regarded as the problem, what had precipitated their decision to seek treatment, how they had attempted to deal with or help Billy overcome his problem and what kind of outcome of therapy they wanted. I had gotten a rather clear picture of the problem and how they had been attempting to "solve" it. My prin-cipal uncertainty was how to evaluate the neurological picture and how to find the leverage to deal with the parents' implicit pessi-mism about their son. As for the former, I was more concerned about the epilepsy and the spasticity than I was the "dyslexia." I do not regard "dyslexia," "minimal brain damage" or "learning disa-bility" as valid or constructive ways of explaining a child's school difficulties. In addition, I know that these diagnoses can be very loosely used and are resorted to by some schools to protect their own educational philosophies of hidden coercion—much as "schizophrenia" is used to obscure parental or social agency mis-management. But I also knew that these parents had firmly accept-ed this definition of Billy's trouble and that this enlarged their pes-simistic expectations of him. These expectations were then mani-fested in the numerous "helping" efforts they had described which had turned the school and the home into treatment centers for him and could, at the very least, only add to his one-down self-consciousness. I anticipated that, whatever else I would do, I would want to get the parents to move away from that position. I, therefore, anticipated with them that I might have to work with Billy through them, explaining that since he had been subjected to such a profusion of special services it could be counter-productive for me to work with him directly while he struggled with the additional stigma of having to see a "shrink.")

Before ending the session, I said that as a next step I felt it important to see Billy but that after that I might ask to see them again. They were agreeable to that and we stopped.

(In seeing Billy, I had in mind to check out the report of his gross neurological problem as well as get my own appraisal of his general demeanor and his accounting for his difficulty with other children. Seeing him alone could have another use. Should I need some rationale for supporting any advice to the parents they might question, I could refer to "material" that presumably came up in the session with Billy, material that could not be challenged because of the privacy of the session and my own "expert" interpretation of that material.)

Session 2 (Four Days Later)

Billy was a pleasant looking boy and more outgoing than I had anticipated. He was slightly small for his age but in the course of discussion it never came up as a consideration on his part and did not seem to be any problem to him. I told him that his parents had seen me because they were concerned about his not having friends at school or at home. I asked him if this was a problem for him or were his parents being overly concerned? He appeared slightly uncomfortable in answering that question and said that he did have some friends at home. He acknowledged that he had no friends at school and did little with the friends he had at home, but on further elaboration about what he did do with his friends he implied that he had no dealings with them and that he did spend most of his free time watching television.

(I did not make any point of this "confession" nor confront him with it, but merely accepted his statements as helping me to be clearer on things. With children, as with adults, initial sessions are devoted to data seeking and are conducted matter-of-factly but with specific questions designed to elicit special information. My principal goal at that stage is to get a clear, concise picture of the

significant transactions in the patients' lives, especially those re-
volving around the problem. Also, I am always looking for
"leverages"—what is important and meaningful to [patients] which
I can use to get them to accept suggestions from me; suggestions
which redefine a situation or ones which influence them to take
some necessary action in their lives and regarding their problem.
Since my highest priority is on action and little or none on "insight," "confrontation" plays a minimal role in my therapy.)

I shifted in my questioning. I said that while his parents might
be concerned about his not having friends, it might not be of any
concern to him; was there something different *he* was concerned
about. He readily answered that his biggest complaint was that he
has been "bugged all my life." He explained that he has been made
fun of and harassed about his left hand. I told him that his parents
had mentioned his left hand to me but that I would appreciate it if
he would show me what kind of trouble he had with it. He then
demonstrated by slowly and jerkily picking up a nearby ashtray,
holding it between his thumb and forefinger and explaining while
he did so how much trouble he was having and that I should notice
how his "fingers didn't work right." I moved my chair closer to his
and watched with apparent curiosity as he performed this spastic
task. When he put the ashtray down, I told him that I found that a
very intriguing way to pick up the ashtray and would he please
show me again just how he did that. He seemed pleased to oblige
me and as he repeated the task I made my own comments on the
complexity of movements required by his hand and fingers to be
able to pick it up in just that fashion. I asked him to perform other
tasks with his hand and marvelled, each time, at the way his hand
performed it. Then I began trying to imitate his hand's movements but I always failed and expressed frustration that I couldn't
do with my hand what he so easily could do with his left hand. He
was surprised at my failure and this allowed me to tell him that I
would bet his father couldn't do it either. When he challenged this
I said, "I'll tell you what. I bet that even your right hand can't imitate your left." He tried, but as I anticipated, he was unable to do it.
For some moments, then, he looked at his left hand wonderingly
and admiringly.

(Since for him, perhaps not his parents, the most meaningful
problem was focused on his left hand, I decided to see what I could
do with that. I had not anticipated this before seeing him nor even
in the earlier part of the session. But since I am always looking to

use whatever is thrown my way I began to formulate a way of working with his hand to redefine his one-down position to a one-up. I began this redefinition by expressing interested curiosity in his hand, then by referring to its spastic movements as worthy of further, greater attention, then by referring to the movements as an *ability*, and finally as an ability that was unique and implicitly superior to those of mine, his father and even his stronger hand. His response to that indicated his acceptance of the redefinition and rather than labor the point, I shifted to a slightly different area.)

I asked him, as if it were a new and sudden thought, "Are there any kids at school who *don't* bug you about your hand?" He said there were. I said, "You know, you don't have to just wait for some kid to bug you, you can be in charge of some of the bugging." Since he appeared intrigued by that thought, I challenged him to see if he could pick out one kid who had never bugged him and, *without saying a word,* see if he could get that kid to bug him about his hand. He was quite agreeable, almost gleeful about the idea and we ended the session on that note.

(I was assuming that Billy's apprehension about being "bugged" would, through his defensive and withdrawn posture, invite harassment and recreate a self-fulfilling prophecy. I was, therefore, attempting to interdict that cycle by getting him to be *curious* about the "bugging" and, at the same time, even less defensive by defining it as something he could control—not simply be victimized by.)

Session 3 (Six Days Later)

Mr. and Mrs. S. came at my request. I said that I had had a most instructive and enlightening session with Billy. They commented that something of some significance must have happened since he had gone around for several days after showing them what he could do with his left hand. Before he had tended to keep it hidden. I told them I had shown great curiosity in his hand but I expressed surprise that it had made such an impact on him. In passing, I attributed this welcome change in Billy to their innate curiosity and patience.

(When I have had any beneficial impact on a child, I attempt to minimize my own influence and, instead, attribute progress to some quality or effort of the parents. I always want to strengthen the idea that it is *their* ability to positively influence their child and, thereby, enhance their optimism and willingness to take further steps.)

I told them that in that session I was able to get a handle on what might be underlying Billy's poor self-esteem, his unhappiness and, therefore, his asocialization. I explained that with his disability and all the years of doctors' appointments, treatments, special programs and the attention that has surrounded his difficulties he had become fearful of being in the omnipotent position of reordering his parents' lives; that while he had some concern about his own possible fragility, he was more concerned that his parents were too fragile and intimidated by him and his disability and that he was in control. This fear, I continued, held him back from risking approaching other children. As could be seen, all their well meant urgings, encouragements, special outings, and the like, were seen by Billy as evidences of their intimidation and he was unable to profit from them.

(The above explanation to the parents regarding Billy's "fear of omnipotence" is an example of a type of framing I often find necessary. In this case I had already formed some general idea of what I wanted the parents to do, principally to stop the well meant campaign of intrusiveness in his life through their questioning, exhortations, "special programs" and the like. I believed that all that could only add to his self-consciousness and therefore his difficulty in socializing.

However, it is one thing to know what the parents should do, it is another to get them to do it. I could have simply told them what I believed, that he is essentially a normal boy despite his left-handed motor problem but a boy made self-conscious by their well intended help. But this would have run counter to all their beliefs about him; they saw the problem as starting almost from birth, over the years their lives revolved more and more around his problem and they viewed him as having deficits—neurologically and psychologically—that set him apart from other "normal" children. To have ignored their views would have run the risk of their discounting any further input I could provide and, worse, set them to seek a more pathology-oriented therapist for their son. Thus, I felt it necessary to frame any further advice by an explanation which incorporated their own belief system but with some elaboration of my own that would make any ensuing suggestions "logical" in their minds.

In its essence, they were seeing Billy as having some significant psychological problem which led him to have a poor image of himself and in turn contributed to his difficulty making friends. Since I was the "expert" I was then free to describe what, in my "expertise," had come to light regarding the exact nature of that psychological problem. It was not too difficult to refer to "a fear of omnipotence." I had reason to use that framing before for parents who needed to treat their child matter-of-factly, at times punitively, but who were intimidated by the notion the child was "mentally ill" or "sick." To tell parents, then, that their child's "sickness" requires a departure from "egg-shell" handling allows them to shift more easily to a matter-of-fact management. In this case, as in many cases, the parents are overly conscientious and this reframing also allows them something to *do* for their child. In any case, it is more certain that people will back off from some traditional position if they are given something to do that requires a 180 degree shift.)

They said this made a lot of sense but confirmed their own suspicions that they were not handling Billy right. Since their implied sense of ineptness might interfere with their getting on with what they needed to do I said that most of what they had done for Billy was necessary and should not have been different and that I was commenting on those *few* things that might not, *at this point,* be useful to continue. In any case, what they did was born from their sincere desire to help him and for most children would be logical. Since they seemed to relax on hearing that I proceeded to detail what they now could do.

I reminded them that what I was about to suggest might still seem strange, but they were to keep in mind that it stemmed from my awareness of Billy's need to overcome his feared omnipotence. To begin with there needed to be a separation between Billy's world at school and his world at home; that whatever difficulties he had at school should not intrude [themselves] into the activities and routines of his parents. Therefore, the school should be notified that whatever problems they encountered with Billy were to be handled by them and under no circumstances should he be sent home for any misbehaviors. I said that it would help the school authorities relax if they were also told they could use their own judgement in handling Billy in any way they deemed appropriate. In keeping with this, I further suggested that they not punish him for any delinquencies that occurred at school; this would not only avoid reduplicated penalties but, more importantly, convey to him that he is not in a position any longer to "force" them to go out of their way to impose disciplinary measures simply by acting up at school. Finally, I asked them that they not only discontinue urging him to get out of the house and make friends but that they actively discourage it. I suggested this might best be done by telling him that they prefer he stay home as much as possible since it's easier to keep track of him and avoids the possibility of his bringing home some noisy children. Instead, he could "watch those nice shows on TV." Mrs. S. agreed quite readily and seemed to sense some humor in it. She smiled and said, "Well, at least that will be some switch." However, Mr. S., while agreeing to the plan, expressed concern that Billy might simply follow their instructions. I said that was possible, but since they had already made a concerted effort to get him out of the house with no success, there was nothing to lose by shifting tack. I added that what I was suggesting might not initially aid Billy's socialization, but that it was directed to a first or more basic step, their conveying to him that his friendlessness was not a burden to them. This seemed to reassure Mr. S. and we ended the session with the plan to meet in two weeks.

(As the reader can tell, all these suggestions and comments were designed to aid the parents in backing away from a management of their son which I felt could only be confirming and adding to his self-consciousness and difficulty in socializing. In effect, I was attempting to get them to stop *creating* a problem. For further elaboration of this rationale, the reader is referred to *Change—Principles of Problem Formation and Problem Resolution* by Watzlawick, Weakland, and Fisch, W. W. Norton, 1974.)

Session 4 (Twelve Days Later)

When they came in, Mrs. S. began right away saying that they had done what I asked and a few days later Billy had brought home two friends. She laughed as she said that he had even made lunch for them and she didn't mind the mess he had made in the kitchen. He hadn't repeated that since but she expressed amazement that their new tack would have such rapid and definite results. I expressed amazement also; that while I had hoped for some sign of less tension on Billy's part, I was surprised that it went further and I indicated that I was disconcerted that improvement had gone so fast.

(When patients or parents come in and announce a definite improvement, an improvement they are clearly acknowledging, I am most likely going to take the position that "things have moved too fast" and that, therefore, no further improvement should take place "for the time being." I may offer various rationales for this position but most often will simply say that in my experience, there is more danger changing things too fast than too slow. There is little, if any, error in this strategy since it is my general view that problems are more likely to arise when people are working too hard at things rather than at a leisurely pace. While patients are encouraged by initial success, it is too easy for them to become apprehensive lest the improvement isn't sustained. Their intensified and urgent efforts can often be counter-productive and produce a demoralizing retrogression. If, on the other hand, their therapist looks a bit worried about the unexpected efficiency of their efforts, it underscores the potential for change and, at the same time, puts them in the more relaxed position of not having to keep up the effort. Often, I may not only suggest that things should not improve further, but I will suggest that they make an effort to have things slide back a "peg or two." Thus, should any retrogression occur, this is not demoralizing since it is "according to plan." In actuality, it is rare for things to retrogress, and more often than not patients come in and smilingly tell me they had "failed" in their efforts to hold things back.)

They also reported that the school was quite willing to cooperate with their request, in fact almost seemed relieved. They said they couldn't add much more since "things have been quiet" on the school front since then. As we were about to end Mr. S. said that they had been planning to send Billy to a special school for dyslexic children sometime in the fall and what did I think about that. I attempted to discourage it by saying that while it might be necessary this school semester had just begun and there wasn't enough time to evaluate Billy's potential for progress; that it might be better to wait further. I added that while such a special school could have its advantages in meeting some of Billy's needs, it would have the disadvantage of gearing his educational experience even further away from the more regular context than the special classes he was in. This could have a bearing on the very problem they were coming in about, his difficulty in socialization and the marginal position he has been in vis-à-vis other children. I then asked that we meet again in about three weeks.

Session 5 (Three Weeks Later)

Mrs. S. came in by herself. She said that her husband had wanted to come in but since he was starting a new job they both felt it best he not take too much advantage of working hours. She said that Billy was "still holding his own." He had had friends over again, was spending more of his time out of the house and consequently less time watching television. She also reported that one morning when he had missed the school bus he simply took his bicycle and got himself to school. She regarded that as significant since characteristically he would ask her to drive him to school. She said he is still reluctant to attend school and she feels it necessary to get him up in the morning, urge him to speed up in getting ready so he won't miss the bus and the like. I suggested that his slowness in preparing for school was another facet of the overall problem—his fear that his own difficulties could push the parents around, and that it could be dealt with as they had done the school and his getting out of the house after school. I therefore suggested that at least on one morning she make an effort to get him to be late and we discussed some ways of implementing that—not setting the alarm, being slow in serving breakfast, etc. However, I told her that while I thought this might be helpful to him, on second thought, it might be taking things a little too fast again. I wasn't sure so she should think it over but not feel she should rush into it, beneficial as it might be. I ended the session and, again, suggested we meet in three weeks.

(As mentioned previously, I feel there is more danger in attempting to move patients on after there has been a report of improvement than in taking the position of "go slow." At the very worst, should I underestimate the confidence of the patient in moving ahead, he will make it clear to me that he is quite impatient and the impetus for change will all the more come from him. Therefore, while Mrs. S. was describing another facet of Billy's problem, she was defining it as a lesser one and the previous improvement he had shown was still holding up. I felt it important not to press it further but to appear to withdraw my suggestion. In implying that it would, nevertheless, be a beneficial move, I could allow her to go ahead with it but in a relaxed way since I was attaching no importance or urgency to it.)

Session 6 (Three Weeks Later)

Mr. and Mrs. S. came in together. Mrs. S. said that Billy was coming along fine, especially with friends. His contacts with children in the neighborhood were now more and more frequent and there had evolved some visiting at each other's houses. She seemed quite pleased but Mr. S., while acknowledging those gains, looked uncomfortable and tense. He expressed concern that, while things seemed to be going well, they might not be *fully* attending to Billy's needs, for example, his need to be more responsible. On further exploration, it turned out that Billy's "irresponsibilities" were minimal and Mr. S. acknowledged that they weren't any problem. He explained that the *real* problem for him was his anxiety that they weren't doing their best; that he was not carrying out my suggestions *correctly* and that they were making mistakes that would show up sooner or later. Since Mrs. S. didn't seem bothered by this, I directed my comments to her husband. I told him that since Billy's trouble had as one element a lack of confidence, it would be greatly beneficial if his father could convey that by making mistakes himself even in his handling of Billy. This might now be his most beneficial effort with Billy, while his wife could continue the previous tack we had discussed. Therefore, I urged him to make sure he made some mistakes with Billy, at least from "time to time." He relaxed on hearing that and I concluded the session by saying that I felt we should meet in two weeks.

(On hearing the mother's report, that gains in Billy's socialization had been maintained, even elaborated on, I anticipated that this might be a terminating session. While the reader may feel this is rather precipitous, I believe there are fewer risks in terminating treatment after a small, but strategic, change has occurred. Billy's asocialization had been a rather long-standing business and in a matter of a short space of time he had done quite well. The leap from no friends to one friend is a much greater one than from one friend to two friends. Much of the business of doing therapy briefly is knowing what *not* to meddle with. However, the father's reaction discouraged me from bringing up the offer of termination. I therefore decided to redefine his "incorrectness" as a therapeutically beneficial and necessary feature of the overall treatment. Although he showed some visible relaxation following that, I thought it would help to plan the next session sooner than we had been accustomed to.)

Session 7 (Two Weeks Later)

Mr. and Mrs. S. came in and said that things were going quite well with Billy. Both were visibly pleased. Neither could think of any complaints about his deportment and as far as they could tell analogous improvement had taken place in the school setting. They said that they had some unexpected trouble, not from Billy, but from his brother, Larry. He had taken some money from a younger child. On learning of it they had taken him over to that child's home, had him apologize to the boy and his parents, return the money and, after some brief discussion with the boy's parents, took Larry back home.

Again, Mr. S.'s main concern was not that Larry was becoming a problem, but wondering whether they had handled the incident thoroughly and correctly enough. Since I felt they had handled it quite well, I limited my comments to predicting that the only error I could be sure they would make at any time in the future would be to underestimate their beneficial handling of situations that arose with the kids. I would never fear they hadn't done enough, only that they would never feel they had. They acknowledged that this had been an old Achilles' heel of theirs, especially his. Mrs. S. then said she felt confident enough about the kids and their handling of them that she was planning to quit her part-time job and divert her time to endeavors of a more leisurely sort; things she had been looking forward to for many years.

I then took the opportunity of suggesting that we either stop treatment or, at least, take a long vacation from it. They said they were really quite pleased, even amazed, at the progress Billy had made and they preferred to stop treatment at this point; perhaps leave things ad hoc should anything come up.

Follow-Up (Two Months Later)

Mrs. S. called and said that things had been going quite well. Billy was doing fine in school, not getting into fights, making friends there as well as in the neighborhood. They were having no further trouble with Larry. She added that she and her husband were quite pleased with the outcome of treatment and thanked me for "what almost seems a miracle." I said that I appreciated their thanks and that while I needed all the credit I could get, I knew they deserved a major portion of it for the efforts they had made, the willingness to try out some "crazy stuff" and the way they went about it. I promised her, though, that since I did need the credit, I wouldn't divulge to anyone that they had had any part in Billy's improvement. Mrs. S. recognized my facetiousness and we ended the telephone conversation.

(As I mentioned in the opening of this case, I always want to convey that it's the parents' child and their effort that will count. I do not back away from this position because a case has gone well or has terminated. In my final rejoinder on the phone, I simply used humor to convey that message.)

Study Questions

1. How does Fisch perceive the pattern of interaction in the S. family: (a) before the family came to him for therapy, (b) during therapy, and (c) after therapy? In other words, what, in Fisch's opinion, is the pattern of verbal and nonverbal behavior in the family at these three points in time?

2. Family sociologists and family therapists are both interested in the nature and causes of social change, or in knowing how people change and why. An important distinction when studying change is the distinction between first-order change and second-order change. *First-order change* is change that occurs within a given social system that itself remains unchanged. *Second-order change,* on the other hand, is change on a higher level: the system itself changes. For example, when you sleep you can have a number of dreams. The change from one dream to the next is a first-order change. But when you wake up, you move from being asleep to being awake. This change is on a different level altogether and is essentially a second-order change (Watzlawick, Weakland, and Fisch, 1974). Fisch changes the S. family. Of this, there is no doubt. But does he accomplish a first-order change or a second-order change? And what difference does it make to know the level at which change takes place?

3. There is an approach in sociology called *labeling theory* that is very much like the framework that Fisch uses when he diagnoses the S. family's problem. According to this approach, deviance is a function of how people label behavior (Becker, 1963; Schur, 1971). If I do something that a significant number of people or a number of significant people label wrong, evil, weird, etc., then I am a deviate. What is more, if I know that I have been labeled a deviate, my actions are likely to reflect this negative label. Thus, for example, Billy's hand is labeled unusual by both his family and his friends; Billy, knowing how others view his hand, begins supposedly to act self-consciously and to

have difficulty socializing. The remedy? Change not the hand (which cannot be changed) but the way people *react to* the hand. How does the labeling process work? Why, for instance, are some acts singled out and labeled deviant, while other acts are ignored? And why can some people get away with doing things that others cannot? Focusing on the family, can you think of any reason that family members would deliberately try to thrust a deviant label (e.g., troublemaker, failure, do-nothing, or rebel) on another member? If so, what would be the advantages for the labelers?

7

Child Socialization

CAST OF CHARACTERS

Mr. Hines, mailman
Mrs. Hines, high school teacher
Jane, college student; Mrs. and Mrs. Hines's daughter
Peter, high school student; Mr. and Mrs. Hines's son
Beverly, elementary school student; Mr. and Mrs. Hines's daughter

AMERICA IS OFTEN TOUTED as the land of opportunity, one of the few countries in the world in which a child born of humble origins can realistically hope to increase her or his social rank and perhaps someday be "somebody." What this means, in sociological terms, is that Americans claim to value a society in which differences in income, power, and prestige are a result of individual achievements (e.g., education and hard work) as opposed to immutable characteristics (e.g., family heritage and place of birth).

Needless to say, the ideal does not coincide with the reality. While America does offer many opportunities to move up the social ladder, by no means is it a perfectly open or fluid society. For one thing, not every American believes in equality of opportunity. A lot of people feel that certain ascribed characteristics, like race and sex, should dictate an individual's social rank (e.g., lower-class whites believing that blacks should not be allowed to compete for their jobs). Second, getting ahead takes more than know-how and motivation. Even if everyone did believe in equality, an individual's advancement could still be thwarted by the absence of jobs or by a series of misfortunes. Thus, upward mobility in the United States depends on a mixture of factors—personality, opportunity, and chance (Schiller, 1970).

This case study offers a portrait of a father and mother's efforts to give their children whatever is necessary to help them succeed, and it is a good illustration of how personality, opportunity, and chance can become overarching concerns in achievement-oriented homes. The fact that it is also a story of a black family makes this case especially relevant. No other racial or ethnic group has had to struggle to succeed as much as black Americans have had to do because no other racial or ethnic group was subjected to slavery upon arrival in this land.

The principals in the case are Mr. and Mrs. Hines and their three children, two of whom are adopted. It is worth noting that the Hineses are both employed in the public sector: Mr. Hines works for the post office; Mrs. Hines is a city school teacher. Black people have traditionally had to rely on government jobs to make a living because they have been systematically denied access to the generally higher paying jobs in private industry (Willie, 1981). Hence, the social mobility of black Americans has been hindered by an opportunity structure that was (and is) designed to keep them in a subordinate position. The Hineses' willingness to expand their family through adoption in order to give two children a home is also significant. Recent studies have indicated that upwardly mobile, middle-class blacks are involved in strong kin–help networks just as their lower-class counterparts are; in other words, extended family ties seem to be an important source of strength at all economic levels in the black community (e.g., McAdoo, 1978).

What factors are the most important in determining who moves up in our society? This is a controversial question (e.g., Bielby, 1980; Jencks, 1980; McClendon, 1980). Nonetheless, most sociologists would agree that a child's chances for upward mobility are greatly improved if that child is (1) raised in a family that encourages curiosity and a desire to learn; (2) given a secure home and neighborhood environment; and (3) provided with a sound formal education. Mr. and Mrs. Hines, along with millions of other parents, undoubtedly feel the same way since they have worked very hard to give their children these things and more. For instance, reading is an activity that is very much valued, as is mastery of a musical instrument and an appreciation for different dance forms. When it was felt that the neighborhood in which they were living no longer offered a proper atmosphere for the children, the Hineses resettled in the suburbs. And, finally, all three children have been taught to believe that a college degree is indispensable, perhaps because Mr. and Mrs. Hines attribute much of their own success to their university training.

There is another element that permeates the Hines family and that may actually be more important, at least in the family's mind, than all the other factors combined. That element is the belief that they can do anything they set out to do. Thus, the Hineses evince a quality that is characteristic of Americans in general—an almost intractable faith in the power of individuals to change the world.

You might be interested to know that the Hines case study was written by a black woman enrolled in Charles V. Willie's undergraduate family course while he was teaching at Syracuse University. Willie, who is one of our foremost black scholars and who is currently on the faculty at Harvard, requires all of his family students to conduct interviews and write case studies because he firmly believes that direct contact with families is an invaluable educational experience.

The Hines Family

Beryl M. Dakers

MR. AND MRS. HINES have been married twenty-four years. Both parents are employed full-time. Mr. Hines is a letter carrier for the U.S. Post Office and Mrs. Hines is a high school science teacher, employed by the City School System. The family's income is slightly above the national median. To supplement his stable income, Mr. Hines often seeks extra employment as a yard man. The children are also employed in various part-time jobs to cover their minor personal expenses.

Mr. Hines was born in Atlanta, Georgia. Orphaned at age eight, he was raised by an uncle and aunt who had twelve children of their own and little extra money or love to spare on an additional child. He vividly recalls the trials of this early childhood, particularly the pangs of poverty and hunger. At age seventeen, Mr. Hines came to Raleigh, North Carolina to work his way through college. He did this by securing a number of indiscriminate and often low-paying jobs. Majoring in history, he graduated from college *cum laude* and taught school for two years before being drafted for World War II.

Mrs. Hines was the oldest of five children born to a rather prosperous farmer in rural North Carolina. Her family was extremely close-knit, and education and religion were stressed as the foundations for a good life. Mrs. Hines attended State College, where she met Mr. Hines at a football game. They dated rather infrequently, both as students and later, as young teachers. With the outbreak of the war, Mrs. Hines went to Washington, D.C., where she worked. She continued to correspond with Mr. Hines and accepted the engagement ring he sent her from overseas. Upon his return, they were married, and returned to Raleigh to make their home.

Unable to find steady employment in a well-paying field, Mr. Hines accepted various odd jobs at the Veterans Hospital. To supplement the income, Mrs. Hines became a secretary. Eventually, Mr. Hines became a postal employee and Mrs. Hines stopped working to await the arrival of their first child. They began making payments on an old, two-story house in a quiet, residential black section of town.

Daughter Jane was born at mid-century; then Mrs. Hines returned to work. The baby was cared for during the day by an elderly couple who lived across the street. At age two, Jane got her first taste of school, when she entered the neighborhood nursery.

During the next eight years, the young couple worked very hard. Meanwhile, Mrs. Hines had secured a Master's degree and was again working as a teacher. The couple had paid off the mortgage on the house and owned all of their dilapidated furniture and second-hand appliances.

At just about this time, one of Mr. Hines' foster brothers died and a seven-year-old son was left homeless. The Hineses decided to adopt the child as their own—and Peter became a full-fledged member of the family. Parents and children seemingly enjoyed the enlarged family set-up and soon began clamoring for another sibling. Through a process of "familial consensus," they decided to adopt a little girl who really needed a family. The result was the addition of Beverly, who was then four years old. Both child and family evidently made the transition quite easily, as there is no outward evidence of discrimination on the family's part, or insecurity on the child's part. Beverly is treated as any other "baby of the family."

All of the Hines children were brought up in an upwardly mobile family group. Each child was given music lessons for the instrument of his or her choice, and each was sent to dance school for at least four years. Explains Mrs. Hines, "We wanted to give them as much culture and refinement as we could. Besides, any musical endeavor is worth encouraging."

There is a strong emphasis on education in the Hines family. The bookshelves overflow with five sets of encyclopedias, assorted textbooks, and remnants of numerous Book Club memberships. Interestingly enough, all three children are avid readers. Jane has proved herself to be a very intelligent young lady and is remembered to have "practically read herself blind as a child." The most enthusiastic reader is Peter, often referred to as the family egghead. An aspiring young scientist, he reads just about anything he can get his hands on. Like Jane, he has been an Honor Roll student all through high school. Beverly, on the other hand, has trouble in school. Math is her personal cross—whether old or new. "She just can't seem to buckle down in school," says her father.

Nevertheless, Beverly is faithful to her books and brings home at least two books a week from the school library. Last summer she begged for membership in the Children's Book Club and most of her present allowance is spent on books.

Another major influence in this family's life is the church. Mr. Hines is a Baptist deacon and staunch church-goer. His wife was born and bred a Methodist and has remained true to her native denomination. Characteristically, each of the children expressed a preference for "Daddy's Church" while they were young. Now, Jane goes to church with her mother, Peter attends a Baptist Church (different from his father's) where he plays the organ, and Beverly attends the Lutheran Church on the corner. "We don't care where they go to church," remarked Mr. Hines, "just as long as they go."

The character of the Hineses' neighborhood underwent a rapid transition as the older residents died. Their single-family homes were converted into low-rent apartments, and those neighbors who could afford it began to migrate to the suburbs. The Hineses talked it over and decided they, too, should move, for Beverly was picking up traits that Mrs. Hines did not particularly appreciate. Thus they built a home in a previously undeveloped suburb. This section has now developed into one of the more prosperous black sections of the metropolitan area. The Hineses are quite content with this neighborhood and feel that it provides the "proper atmosphere" for rearing children. They do not anticipate moving again. When asked what he liked most about the neighborhood, Mr. Hines replied, "The neighborhood is nice, clean, and secure. It is easily accessible to churches, schools, and shopping centers. It is spread out enough to give you some sense of freedom, and yet, compact enough to ensure a sense of community."

The Hineses are quite active in civic affairs. Mr. Hines is president of the Community Club and works hard to establish solidarity among the neighbors. He takes an active interest in the welfare of the children and, despite his age, coaches a Little League baseball team. He is president of the Parent–Teacher Association at Beverly's school and works actively in several civic and civil rights groups. Mrs. Hines works basically with professional organizations—especially those dedicated to bettering educational opportunities for blacks. She is the voting ward representative for her area and spends much time encouraging others to vote and to participate in citizenship activities. Though their interests are diverse, the Hineses express a mutual respect for each other's independence. They do believe that their activities stem from like concerns and that they are working for the same types of goals.

The Hineses are a rather close-knit family, although individuality is important to them. The family rarely eats together during the week, but seldom does a member eat entirely alone. The varied schedules usually allow for at least two people to sit down at the table together. However, weekends are different. For Saturday breakfasts, Mrs. Hines eats with the children, and everyone waits for Mr. Hines to join them at Saturday's impromptu dinner. Sunday breakfast is the meal the family considers most important, as they all gather around for prayers before eating. Sunday dinner is a major production and everyone is involved, either in its preparation or in cleaning up afterwards.

The parents do not indulge their children's whims. However, they see to it that the children have everything they need—and more. Thrift and industry are necessary components of each child's upbringing. Each child was encouraged at a very young age (six to nine) to get a weekend or part-time job, and to use his or her earnings to buy some of the things he or she wanted. Each of the Hines children receives an allowance, with a starting weekly rate doled out at age five that increases regularly until age eighteen. Commenting on this somewhat meager allowance, Mr. Hines said, "It lets them know that Mom and Dad are willing to help financially, but it gives them the incentive to get out and do for themselves." Apparently this logic has been pretty effective, as all of the children earn their own spending change, as well as contribute substantial amounts to their savings accounts.

The Hines children are fiercely critical, and yet extremely tolerant and extremely protective of each other. They class themselves as a tough lot to beat, saying, "We are stubborn like Daddy and independent like Mom—and that's quite a combination!" Though they all evaluate themselves as being somewhat shy and reserved, they come across as being very self-confident and quite capable of any task they may undertake. They are competitive among themselves and their peers, but not jealously or covetously so. "Competition," says Jane, "keeps you from stagnation. It lets you know that no matter how good you are, you can always be better."

The Hines children have an enormous respect for their parents and a deep appreciation for the way in which they have been brought up. Commented Jane, "Mom and Dad instilled us with certain basic values and then allowed us to apply these values to our individual personalities. We may express ourselves differently, but I don't think any of us will ever really depart from our upbringing. We know and respect the difference between right and wrong."

When asked if there was a generation gap within the family, Peter replied, "Only when it comes to money. Pops still doesn't realize that things cost more now than they did in the twelfth century when he was growing up. Other than that, he is much more liberal and eager to understand than are the parents of most of my friends." Mrs. Hines' response to inquiries about a generation gap was this: "I want to understand my kids, so I ask and listen to find out what they are thinking and why." She feels that she is able to communicate well with her children as a result of this effort. "If there is a gap in this family, it is more likely to be between me and my husband," she laughs. The children agreed. Beverly summed up the whole question by saying "They are pretty hep for old folks!"

Father—Mr. Hines, over fifty—is a rather easygoing man. He is a big man (200 pounds), with a rather stern countenance, but a quick smile. He is devoted to his family and to fulfilling what he considers to be the "fatherly" role. He respects and admires his wife's independence, commenting that he could not have married a "tie-me-down" type woman.

Recalling his boyhood poverty and deprivation, Mr. Hines is determined that his family have the basics for a good start in life. These basics include: a good home (food, shelter, clothing), and education, good principles and love. He is a concerned father who disciplines his children with a heavy hand and admits that he often listens after he strikes. He takes an active interest in whatever the children are doing, always joining or organizing a corresponding parent group. He shows his affection for both his wife and children mostly in play, admitting that it is hard for him to be affectionate in the conventional ways.

Mr. Hines is indisputedly the man of the house, and the final authority—but not, he insists, the authoritarian. "We are a family," he says, "not a military company."

Mother—Mrs. Hines, middle-aged—is a typical, atypical mother. She is bouncy, yet often fatigued; fussy, but understanding; older in age, but young in actions; quiet spoken, but quick to make her opinions known. She is rather short and about fifteen pounds overweight (a nervous eater she says.) She suffers with every conceivable ache and pain (a typical hypochondriac her husband says), yet lets nothing slow her down.

During the course of the interview, her face changed back and forth from school teacher and disciplinarian to loving, compassionate mother. While acknowledging obstacles and personal limitations, Mrs. Hines firmly believes "you can do anything you put your mind to doing" and hopes she has instilled this feeling in her children.

"My husband and I worked long and hard to give these kids the opportunities we never had. We are not going to force them to take advantage of their chances but if they choose to do so, they will have enough stamina and love behind them to make the best of any opportunity." So said, and apparently, so believes, Mrs. Hines.

Daughter Number One—Jane—is a coed at the University of North Carolina, where she is enrolled in the pre-medical program. She hopes to be a hematologist. An honor student throughout high school, Jane excelled in many things and participated in practically everything. She is a good musician, being an accomplished pianist and a "half-cocked" flutist. She is a member of the Modern Dance Troupe at school and has been (to her parents' dismay) excessively active in the Black Student Movement. She does not consider herself a militant, but she does believe in asserting the rights of the individual.

Jane is easygoing and appears, at first glance, quite reserved. She can, however, get very excited over some idea she is interested in and often finds herself thrust into leadership roles. She says of herself, "I am an incurably romantic, realistic idealist. I know what the world is really like and I accept it. At the same time, I want it to be better, and deep down inside, I believe someday it will be." "I am," she says reflectively, "the product of my parents' love, wisdom, and being."

Son—Peter, a teenager—is a big man on his high school campus. President of his senior class, he is both an athlete and a scholar. Particularly interested in physics ("I get it from Mom," he grins), he hopes to major in bio-physics at Cornell, MIT, or Harvard. He is a very outgoing young man with both an easy smile and a quick temper. He is incredibly honest, hates phonies, and will go to any end for a friend. Very industrious, he works at a gas station on weekend days, plays with a jazz band on weekend nights, and is church organist on Sunday morning. When asked which of his parents influenced him most, he replied, "I guess Dad had the most influence on my manliness, while Mom influenced my being the kind of man I am."

Daughter Number Two—Beverly—is a perky, button-nosed miss. Often called "The Brat" by her brother and sister, she is the most precocious of the Hines children. Although she is active in many groups, she confesses that she often gets very lonely. Unlike her siblings, Beverly has an acute dislike for being alone and often feels compelled to seek out friends for company.

She idolizes her older sister and brother and adores her parents. When asked what her family was like, Beverly said, "They are like my family—you know, like you wouldn't want to belong to any other family but them." An engaging little girl, Beverly has the amazing ability of switching instantly from "Little Imp" to "Little Angel." Extremely outgoing around adults, she is somewhat timid of new friends her own age. An avid member of the "Now Generation," Beverly thinks that all in all, her family is a real "groove." . . .

Study Questions

1. Every family develops, over time, a theory about how the world works. This theory, which is part of the family's culture (or, more specifically, its belief system), determines in part how well the family copes with both everyday stressors and periodic crises. For instance, the family that assumes that life is a game of chance would behave differently from a family that assumes that life is a game of skill. So, too, a family that assumes that the world is incredibly complex would behave differently from a family that assumes that the world is basically simple (Reiss, 1981). How would you describe the Hines family's theory? What would you say are the major factors contributing to this view?

2. The Hineses seem to be trying to combine a solid group identity with a strong intrafamilial competitive spirit. Is this a realistic goal? How can a family group—or any group, for that matter—simultaneously emphasize we-ness and I-ness?

8

When Children Leave the Nest

Art, foreman at diecutting company; Betty's husband
Betty, homemaker; Art's wife
Martha, college student; Art and Betty's twenty-year-old daughter
Richard, semiskilled laborer; Art and Betty's eighteen-year-old son
Joan, elementary school student; Art and Betty's ten-year-old daughter
George, Betty's brother
Bridget, George's wife
Grandmother Santangelo, Betty and George's mother
Randy, Richard's friend
Eric, Richard's friend
Black Beauty, the Neumeyers' dog
Road Runner, George and Bridget's dog

THIS CASE STUDY describes the activities of the Neumeyer family as they celebrate Christmas 1972. The date is important because world and national events during the early 1970s provide a historical backdrop to the family's mode of interaction.

The Neumeyers were observed and interviewed by Paul Wilkes, a journalist, who thought it might be educational to follow "an average American family" for a year and report on what he saw. The Christmas segment you will read covers events that took place near the end of his year-long visit with the Neumeyers, which may partially explain the case study's vividness and poignancy. By the time the holidays rolled around, Wilkes apparently had gotten to know his subjects fairly well.

Whether any one family can be characterized as average is, of course, open to debate. Nevertheless, the way Wilkes went about finding the Neumeyers is interesting and worth reviewing. Relying on the 1970 census, Wilkes figured that the average American family would consist of a father, aged forty-five, a mother, aged forty-two, and two children, aged nineteen and seventeen. They would live in a mortgaged house in a suburb of a metropolitan area and have one air conditioner and 1.25 cars. The parents would have twelve years of schooling, and the father would be a craftsman, foreman, or operative earning about $10,000 a year. Wilkes distributed his profile to various people around the country—friends, friends of friends, teachers, personnel managers, "busybodies" (his term), writers, and editors. He at first thought that he would have little trouble finding the so-called average family and that his principal problem would be convincing people to participate in his study. But he was mistaken on both counts. Families fitting his criteria were extremely difficult to locate; however, once identified, they were almost all eager to be subjects for his book. After wittling the list of candidates down to fifteen and visiting each family in its home, Wilkes chose the Neumeyers (and the Neumeyers chose Wilkes). Though the Neumeyers were not perfect in a demographic sense, in Wilkes's mind they more or less fit the bill.

Several people figure prominently in the case, but Betty Neumeyer, who is the wife and mother of the clan, is probably the central character. She is the one who seems to be running things (if only behind the scenes), and she is the one whom others in the family seem to be trying to please. Part of this impression derives from the fact that Christmas 1972 is a very important holiday for Mrs. Neumeyer. With her twenty-year-old daughter about to graduate from college and her eighteen-year-old son constantly at odds with his father, Betty genuinely believes that this particular Christmas is the last that her family will spend together. In an effort to make the holiday a memorable one, she tries to orchestrate one final family celebration, one final we-oriented gathering. But, unfortunately for her, not everyone in the family is willing to go along. Betty's husband and son, for instance, repeatedly slip into a pattern of provoking each other—a pattern that they have evidently nurtured for years—and Betty is thrust into the difficult position of having to cajole and beg the men in her life to stop fighting until Christmas is over.

Significantly, the event that motivates Betty to put together a special Christmas is the very event that nearly prevents her from succeeding. It is the perceived loss of her two older children that both precipitates her maneuvering and makes her task a formidable one. When a child grows up and leaves home or is on the brink of leaving home, it is not uncommon for the family to go through a period of *boundary ambiguity,* as the members of the family try to clarify who is in the family and who is out (Boss, 1980, 1982). Boundary ambiguity is but one aspect of the tension that typically exists between personal identity and group identity (or between identity in one group and in another), and it is a phenomenon that often accompanies changes in families, especially changes that involve the subtraction or addition of family members (e.g., birth, death, divorce, or remarriage).

When you read the case, you will see that a lot of the conflicts in the Neumeyer household are actually efforts to make the family's boundaries either less ambiguous or more ambiguous. Art and Betty attempt to make the boundaries *less* ambiguous by reinforcing the boundaries that have existed for some time now—the boundaries that define their older daughter and son as in the family. By comparison, Martha and Richard (but especially Richard) want to branch out on their own and therefore strive to make the family boundaries *more* ambiguous by challenging the status quo.

This conflict of interests is indicative of the *developmental stake* each family member has in minimizing or maximizing intergenerational differences. Art and Betty have a stake in minimizing the differences between them and their children because focusing on *intergenerational continuity* (seeing their children as their heirs, for instance) gives meaning to their own lives. In contrast, Martha and Richard have a stake in maximizing the differences between them and their parents because focusing on *intergenerational discontinuity* (seeing their parents as different and seeing themselves as unique) validates their own lives (Bengston and Kuypers, 1971).

The boundary ambiguities and developmental stake issues that the Neumeyers are confronting cannot be fully understood without placing the family in a historical context. For example, Martha's and Richard's decision to leave the family when they are in their late teens or early twenties is not a function of some inborn biological need that has been mysteriously triggered by chronological age. Rather, Martha and Richard have reached a time in their lives that is socially imbued with significance. We know that the importance that people place on being eighteen or twenty-one is a *socially constructed* (versus biologically constructed) reality because anthropologists and historians have conducted studies that indicate that the timing of the transition to adulthood is variable (e.g., Aries, 1962). During the Middle Ages, for example, a child of seven or eight was assumed to have the mental abilities of an adult and hence was treated as an adult. Thus, what is critical from a sociological point of view is how the Neumeyers' pattern of interaction—especially their boundary maintenance and restructuring activities—is a product of large-scale social forces. Like the other families in this book, they mirror the society in which they live.

The Neumeyer Family

Paul Wilkes

ON FRIDAY, DECEMBER 23, Betty lingers at home until she has just enough time to walk to her one-o'clock appointment at the hairdresser. Once there she has been shampooed and rinsed when she hears Miriam, one of the beauticians, telling a caller that Betty can't come to the phone. But before the caller has a chance to leave a number, Betty, her hair dripping from beneath a towel, grabs the receiver.

It is, as she has hoped, Richard.

Miriam hurries Betty through a set and drying and less than half an hour later Richard is outside to pick up his mother.

"I hugged him and he hugged me back," she excitedly tells Art that evening when he comes home from work.

Art looks down at the smudge on the rug at the top of the stairs and proceeds to hang up his coat. "You can tell he's home," he says flatly.

Joan and Martha screamed with delight when they first saw their brother that afternoon. Their mother cried. But tonight as Art walks about the living room and kitchen and his son remains a floor away, lying passively on his bed, reading a health food magazine, each knows the other is in the house; neither is willing to make the first move.

Finally, it is time for dinner. Betty motions to Art with her head and a smile. He knows what she is trying to tell him, so he lights a cigarette and goes into the basement. The sound of rubber heels on linoleum is audible in Richard's bedroom, but he does not look up as his father approaches the room and stands in the doorway. Art inhales deeply. "Supper's on, Richie. Hungry?" he says in a monotone.

"Yeah, wow, starving," Richard says, leaping out of bed and coming toward the door. Art reaches for his son's hand. They shake hands in silence. Richard moves past his father, ready to bound up the stairs.

"Same rules," his father says dryly. "Put a shirt on for supper."

As the family digs into the steaming mounds of spaghetti spread with Betty's mildly flavored sauce and topped with meatballs, the talk dances about the week's events as if Richard had never been gone.

"Thought we were going to see a walkout on Sunday during the pastor's prayer about the war," Betty says.

"Should stay out of politics," Art responds.

"I read we dropped more bombs in a month on Vietnam than we did in the whole Second World War," Martha says. "Geez, we're just making bigger holes over there. Nothing left to bomb."

"Creep Nixon," Richard says with a sly smile on his face.

"You should talk about creeps, Richie," Art says. "You didn't even bother to come back to vote for your wonderful McGovern."

Betty quickly switches to Christmas shopping and relates how Francine Duprey noticed that "nobody spoke English" at Sav-Mor, a discount department store. "She said they were Puerto Ricans and every different kind of race. Where are they all coming from?"

"Wipe that smirk off your face, Richard." Art almost shouts at his son. "Now that you're home, show a little respect for people."

"Merry Christmas," Richard says softly.

After the meal, with Richard downstairs, the three women of the family spontaneously converge on Art. Joan's plea is first. "Daddy, if you're mean to Richie, he's going to go away and we won't have Christmas together."

"I didn't come home for all these hassles, Daddy, and if it's like this I'm . . . I'm taking the next plane back."

"See, Daddy, see?" Joan says plaintively.

Betty has tried to speak, but after her daughters are finished she does nothing more than look at her husband and then turn away, a hurt look on her face.

"I think you're being very obnoxious to him," Martha adds. She takes Joan by the shoulder, and they go downstairs to talk to their brother.

Art lights his after-dinner cigarette, thinks for a moment, then looks at his wife. "I'm not saying anything about his long, filthy hair. I'm not saying anything that he blew hundreds of dollars and then had to cry for help from home. But if he's going to live here— even for a while—he's going to live by our rules and he's going to talk with respect."

"OK, Artie, OK, but can't we just take it easy until Christmas is over at least? Please, honey." Betty drags out the words. "This is our last Christmas together. Let's make it one that everybody remembers with a warm spot in their hearts."

"Do you see the clothes—the rags—he's wearing? Just tell me what he's going to wear tomorrow night. He's not going out with us like that."

Do you want him to go to church or not?" Betty says, looking out the kitchen window into the darkness outside.

"Of course."

On the day before Christmas, Art, Betty and Martha take Joan to the Dupreys for a piñata party and return home by midafternoon. Art takes the television set to the recreation room to watch a football game while the female members of the family make final preparations for that night and the next day. One of Grandmother's presents is still to be wrapped. A huge baking dish of lasagna and an apple pie are taken out of the freezer to thaw. Joan will sing in the choir tonight, so Martha helps her wash her brown hair, which almost reaches to her waist.

Betty, on her way upstairs from the freezer, smiles at Richard as he comes out of his room. "Look at those ribs. I'll bet you don't weigh a pound over a hundred."

"You want to bet? I'm not that skinny." He smiles boyishly back at her.

"Get out the scale. I'll give you a dollar for every pound over a hundred."

Richard pulls the scale out from under his bed and steps on. The needle flickers, then settles at 140.

"Wait a minute," Betty says, playfully pushing him off. She gets on the scale herself but as Richard looks down to check her weight she jumps off as if the scale were electrically charged. "Oh, no, you don't. I'm porky but I don't weigh that much. This shag rug is throwing it off. Put it out on the linoleum."

Richard is laughing loudly as he puts the scale on the floor outside the recreation room. He gets on and the needle stops at 120. "That will be twenty dollars, please."

"Is my credit good?" Betty says.

"Not for long."

Richard bounds up the stairs and Betty is left standing by the scale with a huge smile on her face. She glances at Art to find him looking at her over the television set. He shakes his head slowly. "How could you get rooked into a deal like that?"

Betty's smile is her answer.

Since they moved to the suburbs, the Neumeyers have made it a practice to have their Christmas Eve meal in a restaurant. This year, because Joan must be at church before the seven-o'clock service, Art has told his wife and family they must leave at five. With the early hour he has not felt it necessary to make reservations at Billie's, a more expensive restaurant they only go to on special occasions.

It is four thirty and Joan and Martha are dressed, Betty is almost ready and Art, who has already picked up Grandmother Santangelo, stands at the Christmas tree, trying to find the burned-out bulb on a darkened strand. Richard trudges slowly up the stairs, his jeans hanging loosely off his bony hips, a towel over his shoulder.

Art wheels around. "Are you going to take a shower now?" The tone of his question stops the chatter between Joan and Martha and their grandmother.

"Yes, sir," Richard says cavalierly. He walks slowly toward the bathroom and locks the door behind him.

Betty, who came out of the bedroom when she heard the tone of Art's voice, immediately heads for her husband. "Art, this is Christmas. Let's all relax and enjoy."

"So we can sit around and wait for him to take a shower," Art says, the words spilling out of his mouth. "He sits around all day; why does he have to take a shower now? Why? And what is he going to wear, Betty? Those crummy jeans?"

A few minutes before five Richard saunters across the living room running a towel through his hair. Art glares at his son but says nothing.

"We're going to Billie's, Rich; come over as soon as you're ready, OK?" Betty says. "And get a move on so we can eat together."

Richard nods and goes down the stairs.

Art, Betty, Martha, Joan and Grandmother Santangelo silently get into the red Chevrolet and head for the restaurant, about a five-minute drive away. As they approach it Art can see there are just three cars in the parking lot and the restaurant seems dark. He leaves the car engine running as he parks in front of the restaurant and starts to get out of the car.

"Don't bother, Daddy," Martha says from the back seat. " 'Closed Christmas Eve,' the sign reads."

"And now we have to wait for your son before we find another place to eat," Art says, slamming the door behind him.

"He won't be long," Betty says brightly. "He was almost ready when we left. Joanie, how many songs will you be singing tonight?"

Five minutes later Art sees the Mustang, which has only one headlight plus a bashed-in fender from the accident, and he pulls out. Martha rolls down her window and shouts, "See you at the Mariposa." Because of the shortness of time, the family has agreed to eat at their old standby, the Mariposa Diner.

Art and the family are settled at a table when Richard comes into the dining room, which has but a half dozen of its fifty tables occupied. Art takes one look at his son and returns to studying the menu. Richard is wearing dark red velvet trousers, a flowered shirt, a blue sweater vest and a short blue suede jacket. Also he is wearing purple-tinted granny glasses.

Art continues to study the menu, holding his hand to the side of his face as if he were shielding himself from something. Richard leans back precariously in his chair and gazes around the nearly empty room. The four females talk among themselves paying little attention to either Art of Richard. They talk about the Christmas Eve service last year; they wonder if Bridget and George will arrive while they are at church; they tease Joan about not getting any presents because she has been a bad girl this year.

When the waitress comes to the table for the third time, Art says, "Would everybody please order so we can eat and get there on time."

"I'm not very hungry," Martha says.

"It's so early, Daddy, and I had so much stuff at the party," Joan adds.

"Lovely things here, Artie, but I'm not too hungry either, I'm afraid," Grandmother Santangelo says, widening her ever-present smile.

"If nobody is hungry, I am," Art says. "And I plan to eat." His voice grows calmer. "Now everybody pick out whatever they like so this lady can get to her other customers."

"Well, I'll have a cheeseburger," Grandmother says.

Art winces slightly.

"Give me a pastrami sandwich," Richard says.

"Roast beef for me," Martha says.

"I'll have a cheeseburger too," says Joan, smiling at her grandmother.

"The shrimp salad, please," Betty says.

Art points to the large featured item on the menu, a prime rib dinner. "I'll start off with cherrystone clams," Art begins his order.

After the meal, Martha gets into the car with Richard for the ride to church. When the faded blue Mustang and the red Chevrolet arrive in the parking lot at six thirty, the two older Neumeyer children tell their parents they will go inside later. Martha offers her brother a Salem. "Fucking cigarettes taste like shit," Richard says blowing out the smoke loudly. "Been smoking nothing but grass down South, Martha—Panama Red—really the best stuff. Much healthier for you. Dynamite."

"Daddy is really pissed at you, if you haven't noticed."

"That's his problem. They'd do anything to have me home, so I'm not going to change just for them."

"Just try to be a little bit civilized. I know it's not always easy."

"Fuck it, Martha. I'm my own man now. I'll be the way I want to. I was living off bitches down in Florida. Old broads too."

"For how long?" she asks with no inflection in her voice.

"Well, for a time," he stammers. "Anyway, I'm not taking their shit."

"You had to call home for money, and they sent it. I'm going inside; it's cold out here."

"I'll be right there. Randy Short said he was coming. The place'll probably crumble when he walks in."

Martha walks through upper fellowship hall, which is bustling with people, on her way to the sanctuary. It is reminiscent of Easter, with effusive hellos from old acquaintances followed by strained smiling silences. Betty and her mother have already been seated in a row on the right side of the church, and Art, who is ushering, hands his daughter a program and leads her to them. Just before the processional hymn, Richard and Randy slip into the row from the other side. To the triumphant organ strains of "Hark! the Herald Angels Sing," Parkside's senior and junior choirs start up the center aisle, followed by Pastor Firth MacIntosh, his deep baritone voice resounding as he moves slowly toward the front of the church. Pots of poinsettias take up much of the room behind the communion railing so the choir members and pastor carefully work their way through the holiday obstacle course, going to their assigned positions.

Parkside United Methodist Church is almost filled this evening, recalling the days when the church was troubled over where to put people rather than how to keep and attract them. The dim overhead lighting and the soft radiance from the candles lining the aisles lend a homey yet religious atmosphere and also mask the need for the paint job that still remains in committee. Throughout the church, the family portrait is repeated: neatly dressed father, mother and children stepping down in size from the oldest to the youngest. Some college students are home; some newly married couples are worshiping with their parents. In the middle of the church are the Neumeyers, who will be joined by Art after the collection is taken and his duties are completed.

Betty smiles broadly at no one in general as the congregation sits down. The pastor dispenses with the conventional Bible reading of the birth of Christ and reads a fourteenth-century monk's poetic version. Betty looks over her shoulder and winks at Art. Art, who has been looking her way, winks back.

ART: It's a typical Christmas, I guess. It's different in that when the kids were younger we didn't trim the tree until they were in bed. Christmas is a big holiday for us, but it looks now that Martha probably won't be able to spend too much time with us at Christmas, and who knows about Rich? I guess I can accept the fact easier than Betty that children grow up and go away from home. Women are more emotional than men.

We've always made a big thing of holidays, and Richie has that in him, so I knew he'd be home. Anybody can see he's trying to be extra nice to his mother because if a person is raised that way it always comes out. But I'm pretty damn tense about some things about him. Just don't want to leave for work in the morning and still have him laying around in bed. He's got to find a job. I want Betty to have a nice Christmas, so I'm trying to keep my mouth shut. But wait. The holiday spirit will wear off and her nerves will get frazzled. It will change.

One of the older boys in the Carson family, all of whose members have musical talent, steps out from the choir and stands in front of the lectern, a guitar in his hand. In a low voice that seems incongruous with his seventeen-year-old face, he begins to sing a folk song about a cherry tree that bent down to present its fruit to Mother Mary on the first Christmas night. Betty settles into her seat, the warm smile beginning to fade from her face.

BETTY: The way Richie lives, I don't know if his body can stand another year of the abuse he's giving it, living so transient without anybody taking care of him. God was very good to give us this nice Christmas, with Richard wanting to do what he did. He didn't have to come to church but he did it to please me; I know that. For Martha, it's easier; for Richard it was an extreme sacrifice and a gesture of love. So if something does happen, it's so much easier to end on a pleasant note, happy memories. It's important to Joan, too, because we tell her God is love, and if anything happened, we'd be able to tell her: Remember Christmas and everything was good?

The frustrating thing is we weren't able to get Richie things he needs. We never put the accent on giving a lot of unnecessary things, but good articles they can use. But I wouldn't want to give Richie anything he had to carry around. He left his radio in one place and he broke his watch so we're finished with that kind of stuff now.

I can see him twitching over there, tapping his feet on the floor and beating his fingers on his knees. But it seems as the service goes on, he's more relaxed. It makes me proud he brought Randy too. Rich is like a missionary. It's not a lecture; he's just showing Randy by his example that you do some things because they make other people happy and that's what makes the world go around.

The events leading up to Christmas were so nice. To have everybody in the house doing things. Martha doing, Joan doing. Regardless of what Martha says, she loves all the commotion around a holiday. And underneath it all she's glad to be here in church. When she looks back on it, the church was her whole thing at one time because she wasn't so active at school, except for being in athletics. She belittles church now, but how many kids had earthshaking things happen to them at fourteen or fifteen? She learned how to teach in Sunday school; she forgets that. She just forgets the enthusiasm she had for church.

The candles that line the aisles flicker as a draft from an open door wafts through the church. The younger children in the congregation especially are drawn to the dancing flames that had been so still they could have been electric imitations. But soon their attention, as well as that of the older members, is drawn to a story of a rabbit and a field mouse on a cold winter's night. Told by a boy of about fifteen, whose shoulder-length brown hair bobs in the soft light at the lectern, it takes the worshipers to a touching ending where the rabbit wraps himself around the mouse for body warmth, saving that life but losing his own.

Sitting next to her mother, Martha starts to slowly chew on her calloused thumb, hiding it from view by swirling the ends of her hair forward with a slight movement of her head.

MARTHA: I guess it's been coming for a long time, but this is the first time going to church for Christmas was totally nothing. Almost a painful thing to have to go through. And that bothers me.

I always assumed I was a religious person, always read all those little doctrines of the church and thought I believed them. I went to church, stood up for prayers, stood up for hymns, but I never internalized any of it. It was funny when I went to make my confirmation. I expected the skies to open up when I first took communion that day. A whole new me. Rebirth. Something really fantastic. That was such a disappointment because I sat down and, other than the taste in my mouth, I didn't have anything to remember.

I don't even know if I believe in God now, and that's the scariest part of it all. And just yesterday the pastor asked me to speak on Youth Recognition Sunday. Should I really say what I think? I found out I wasn't really a church person when I went away to college and realized they were saying the same old crap I had heard here. Right out of the Bible. Be a Christian but never think that Vietnam or racism or politics have anything to do with religion. I probably think more about religion now than I ever did before—then it was just a case of buying whatever my mother and father said.

It wasn't till I went away to college and stopped going to church that I formed any religious beliefs at all. Right now I don't know about a God, but I believe there's some sort of force, some power in the world that is basically good, and there's real good in each man to some extent. I'm living in a scientific age, and if it can't be explained somehow, it's hard for me to believe it. But I want something to hold onto.

Art and three other ushers march with military precision up the aisle to the front of the church. They fan out in front of the pastor, who hands them shining collection plates lined with felt. Richard leans over to Randy to say something, and smiles come over both their faces. Richard digs into his tight-fitting trousers for some change. The plate is passed, and soon Art is handing it to the first person in Richard's row.

RICHARD: This is kind of cool. Not the idea of church or anything, but it's a pretty service with the flowers and candles and everything. I like churches. I've seen a lot of them traveling around. I haven't gone inside any, but I dig the architecture and stuff so I really can get into it like I never did before.

It makes my mother happy that I'm here and it doesn't hurt me, so it's OK. I guess my father likes it too. They don't know it, but I'm not going to be around long. Probably about a month. Then I'll split. I might not be back till next Christmas. My old man is pretty uptight about me—do this, don't do this, take your feet off the furniture—so I'll just split sooner if he leans on me. Now that I've been around and know I can go any time, his shit doesn't penetrate any more. It's a good place to visit, but I wouldn't want to live at home.

I get the feeling that my folks think I just came home from around the block. They don't want to hear about it. They don't pursue anything about where I've been or what I've seen or what I've done. Same way when I came home from California. It's just that I'm home, that's important, not all the experiences I had. I'd dig it if they said they wanted to sit down for a couple hours and listen to what I did. They just walk away; Joanie's the only one who listens. They just think I was out there for kicks. You do what you please, but it just ain't all kicks, that's for sure. Why aren't they interested enough to listen to me?

I don't want anything for Christmas especially, just for them to be friendly to me. But I'm glad my mother lent me the money for Christmas presents. It feels pretty good to give shit to people. The only trouble I'm having right now is that I have this boil on my ass and it hurts like hell on these pews.

At the end of the service, all the church lights are turned off as the pastor lights a small white candle and then offers the flame to the first person in the first row. Slowly, Parkside United Methodist Church takes on a mellow glow as the small candles everyone was given at the beginning of the service are lit. In the choir, Joan giggles as she drips some wax, waiting for the candle of the girl next to her to catch.

JOAN: All Christmases are the same because everybody is here. But next year Martha and Richie aren't coming home; I'm sure of that. Martha will probably be teaching and they don't get any money for that, and I don't know if my mother and father will treat her. Richie will probably be someplace else.

I like Christmas because we play games and tell jokes and talk and my aunt and uncle come. It's a couple of days that we celebrate that Christ was born. Presents really don't matter that much. Seeing the new ornaments we get every year, that's fun, and they're all going to be mine when I get married. Yeah, and when I get married everybody's going to come to my house, just like Grandma does now.

After the service, holiday greetings are exchanged by various members of the Neumeyer family with people they hadn't seen beforehand—all except Martha, who excuses herself and almost runs to the church basement. She catches up with her family before they get into the cars and join the stream of vehicles leaving the church parking lot.

As Art approaches his house, he sees an unfamiliar station wagon parked in front. The car's radio is blaring through the open windows on this mild winter night. Someone laughs inside the car and an empty beer can is tossed out, first landing softly on the grass close to the street, then giving off a tinny rattle as it skitters onto the sidewalk.

Inside the red Chevrolet there is silence as the family watches. They get out of the car in the driveway and walk into the house, averting their eyes from the station wagon. Richard parks on the street, slams his car door shut and walks jauntily toward the house.

"Richie, what's happening, man?" A voice comes from the station wagon.

"Not much, man," he replies, recognizing the voice. "Just got back from Florida. All the tourists go there for Christmas, but I come north." He smiles, obviously proud of his quip. Randy, who has just pulled up, follows Richard into the house.

As Richard comes in he sees his father looking out the front window from behind the curtain. The grass next to the station wagon is littered with beer cans, cigarette butts and waxed paper and cups from a McDonald's drive-in.

Betty puts her hand on her husband's shoulder. "Artie, let them be. They're troublemakers."

"Bums," he says, his eyes narrowing.

"Artie, I've seen Eric carry dead squirrels and rabbits up the block that he shot on the golf course. Sick, he had a sick look on his face when he was doing it. All the kids in that family have been arrested for drugs."

"Who is it, Betty?" Grandmother Santangelo asks.

"One of the Murdock kids; they live four houses up."

"I'd like to call the police," Art says.

"The only one who can get hurt out of this is Joanie," Betty says. "They might do something to her. Come away from the window. Artie, it's Christmas," she pleads.

As Richard and Randy go downstairs to play pool, Joan is told to get into her nightgown. The house is momentarily quiet when Martha walks slowly into the living room, her head down.

"What's wrong, baby?" her father asks, only half seriously.

"Nothing."

"Come on, baby."

"Daddy, quit it." She walks into the kitchen and says softly. "It just so happens I threw up after church. That's all."

"Are you all right?" Betty says. "Do you want an Alka-Seltzer? Something wrong?"

"Just forget it, Mother. You know I throw up all the time; I have for years."

Art shakes his head and goes into the kitchen to fix daiquiris for himself and his wife. Betty calls downstairs, "You boys want a beer? We have some wine too."

"Yeah, just bring the bottle of wine down," Richard hollers back.

"No," Art says in a loud voice. "You have a glass like other civilized people."

"Artie, the boy's been out for three months and could have had anything he wanted," she says quietly. "Now you're worried about a little wine. Come up and help yourself, Richie," she calls out.

About nine thirty the doorbell rings and Joan runs to the door, shrieking a high-pitched "Whee-e-e!" She leaps into her uncle's arms and reaches over to give her aunt a hug and then a kiss.

Black Beauty yelps as exuberant greetings are exchanged between Betty and Bridget, George and Martha, George and his mother. Art waits at the top of the stairs to shake hands with George and then to give Bridget a kiss. "Where's Richie?" Art asks.

"We saw him outside," Bridget says. "He's out there with his friend in the car."

Art glares at the already closed front door. "Did they come for him?" he asks Joan.

"No, he and Randy went out a little while ago," Joan says. "And they're drinking beer and everything out there." In the silence that follows, the rattle of a beer can hitting the sidewalk is heard.

Betty gets Art aside and whispers, "They look so tired, don't they?"

Art looks at George, whose eyes have faint red circles around them. That color is accented by the pallor of his face, which Art has branded "grocery-store yellow." Bridget has dark half-circles under her eyes. Her blond hairpiece hangs askew at the back of her head. Because she parts her hair in the middle and hasn't had it peroxided recently, a brown line at the roots is all the more noticeable.

George loosens his tie and falls onto the sofa, coming down with such force that the legs move from the indented spots on the carpet. "What a day! Started out slow; then it was dynamite. They were buying cold cuts like they were starving. Bologna, salami, liverwurst! Cleaned off the bread rack. We should have had roller skates, right, Brij? Got a new display for pet stuff: bird seed, doggie bones, all that stuff. Nice display, doesn't take any floor space. They were in today buying gifts for their pets. Brij, what would you say? Didn't we do fifteen bucks in pets' presents?"

"I don't know, George," she says in an exhausted tone. "All I know is that holidays for everybody else are madness for us."

"Madness, Brij? What're you talking about? I'll bet we did . . . well, we did plenty today."

"You got to take more time off, Georgie, you look so tired," Grandmother Santangelo says. "Even your father didn't work Sundays."

"I will, Ma, I will. We're going to take Wednesdays off as soon as things settle down."

"Been saying that for the last three years," Art says blandly.

It is after ten o'clock and Richard is back in the house—having been greeted by a father's glare and a mother's smile—when Betty tells Joan it is time for bed. The youngest member of the Neumeyer family puts some of the Christmas cookies she and Martha made on a plate, pours a glass of milk and leaves them on the kitchen table as a snack for Santa Claus. Then she thumbtacks the red felt Christmas stocking with her name on it to the newel post at the top of the stairs and calls to her brother and sister for them to do the same. As Martha pins hers up, there is a strained look on her face. Richard, who has had several cans of beer and glasses of wine, lets a cigarette dangle out of his mouth as he puts his stocking up. He laughs. "Santa, Santa, fill it full of the stuff I need."

"Stuff we need." Randy laughs too.

Soon after, Randy leaves and the family makes final preparations for the morning. Christmas presents emerge from all corners of the house, from George and Bridget's car, from the garage. A pile of presents builds for every member of the family. When all the presents are set out, Joan's is by far the biggest mound. The two smallest piles contain the few gifts for Road Runner and Black Beauty. Even the gifts for the dogs are handsomely wrapped and tied with ribbon.

After this chore is done, the family members sit down to talk in the living room. Richard, who is shirtless, lies with his body half under the dining room table, lazily sipping on a can of beer, but his father says nothing to him. It is not long after the conversation begins that George's eyes begin to droop and Betty demands that everyone go to bed. By one o'clock all the beds and sofas in the house at 97 Birchwood Drive are occupied. Everyone sleeps except Martha, who has been assigned Richard's room. She lies awake into the night.

Christmas, 1972, dawns bright and crisp. A light breeze plays with the branches of the pines and nudges the waxed papers in front of the Neumeyer house. Inside, Joan is the first to get up. After she puts on her robe, she runs through the house, knocking on doors and shaking sleeping bodies on the sofas. "Get up, get up, it's Christmas!" She dances about, jumping up and down, clapping her hands. "Oh, oh, oh!" she exclaims as she sees her stack of presents.

One by one, family members find their way to the living room. Richard is the last to make his appearance, coming up from the recreation room only after repeated calls. Betty scans the living room, the people, the tree, the presents and the decorations and cuddles up to her husband. She leans her head on his chest and then wraps her arms around him and closes her eyes.

"Artie, I'm so happy."

"OK, everybody dig in," Art says.

Ribbons are eased off, paper crinkles and the range of voices and emotions go from Joan's "Oh, just what I wanted" to Richard's "I don't wear socks any more." Joan jumps with glee over Barbie doll dresses and a digital clock radio. Betty hugs Art and puts on the beige woolen cape that bears a note, "To the best wife, from Santa Claus." Art kisses her on the cheek as he looks at the certificate that says he's the owner of a new bowling ball. Martha tries to look appreciative of a tastefully made nightie. The only problem is its color: lavender again, like the one she got at Easter. It is a color that went out with Mark Hard. Bridget tries on slippers and finds them too small. Art and George open boxes to find sweaters or shirts. Richard tries on the snorkel coat from his parents and pronounces the sleeves too wide and bulky. Betty puts Joan's handmade wall hanging "Sing Praise to the Lord" on a doorknob and smothers her with a hug.

The weeks of preparation, the hours of shopping and wrapping have culminated in this morning. And, an hour after the present opening begins, that phase of Christmas is over. A gigantic heap of wrapping paper sits in the middle of the living room rug.

"You keep gabbing," Art says to the suddenly quiet, almost pensive group, "and I'll fix breakfast." In forty-five minutes a huge plate mounded with sausages and steaming ham is brought to the table, followed by a continuous stream of pancakes fresh off the griddle. It is the "big breakfast" Betty has settled on as the Christmas meal for this year. In the conversation that ensues over cups of coffee, Christmas itself is left behind except to negotiate which presents have to be taken back because they won't be used or are the wrong size.

Two people are silent. For one of them, Art, it is a natural way of reacting at a family gathering. For the other, Joan, it is not typical. She looks often at the kitchen clock, knowing that at noon her aunt and uncle will leave. She sits by her mountain of presents and listlessly handles two necklaces she's received. Betty notices this. As Grandmother and Art set up for bingo, she goes to her daughter and, without saying a word, gives her a hug. The tremendous buildup for this "last Christmas together" has peaked, and Joan already is anticipating that the coming down will be sudden and not as enjoyable.

As family members gather around the dining room table, bingo cards are purchased for three cents apiece and Grandmother Santangelo begins to call the numbers. After four games, George is winning, having amassed twenty-four cents. But also after four games, it is noon. George and Bridget begin to gather up their presents and to offer profuse thank-yous. Fifteen minutes later they are gone.

Richard goes downstairs to call a newly found girl friend in Delaware and spends the next twenty minutes reminiscing about their time in Florida and coming back in the car. ("How about that chick who was a diabetic? Sold her works to that junkie and we had money for pot, gas and food.") Once the phone is free, Art makes the perfunctory holiday call to his mother and sister. One by one, Betty, Martha, Richard and Joan take the phone to thank Art's side of the family for the presents Betty swore would not be reciprocated this year. But after Betty's blowup at the wedding, she said nothing about her vow not to send presents and went forward with the shopping as if nothing had happened.*

Throughout the afternoon the older members of the family doze on chairs and the living room sofa, Joan plays quietly in her room, Martha reads and Richard goes back to bed. At four o'clock the women gather in the kitchen to begin to prepare the evening meal, which mostly involves the heating of frozen dishes.

The evening Christmas meal is a feast, and where Thanksgiving saw plentiful food and no appetites, there are a group of eager eaters today. Antipasto with salami, peppers, artichoke hearts, anchovies, olives and Italian bread that George brought is first, and the platter is nearly cleaned off. Lasagna, followed by chestnuts, mints and coffee, completes a meal Art calls "the best you've ever made, Betty. I think it's about time we got married. I don't want to lose a good cook like you."

After supper, Betty suggests a game of Yahtzee and Joan perks up. Martha is less than enthusiastic about the idea, but she puts down *The Other,* a paperback book she's been reading, and goes to the kitchen table where the game is played. Joan scores three Yahtzees by rolling five of a kind three times and demolishes the competition by a margin of one hundred points.

It is nine o'clock when Joan says she is tired and wants to go to bed. Martha is reading her book once more. Randy and Richard are downstairs, talking. A few minutes after nine, after a lull in their conversation, Richard goes to the plastic Army tank he made in grade school that sits on a shelf over his stereo. He lifts off the turret and takes out a small foil-wrapped object, no bigger than a piece of sugarcoated chewing gum. He places it carefully in the

---

*Editor's Note: When one of Art's nieces got married, Betty sensed at the wedding that she was being snubbed by Art's side of the family, and she consequently told Art that "Starting this year, we are not exchanging Christmas presents." But, as indicated here, she did not carry out her threat.

pocket of his flannel shirt as if it were either very valuable or explosive. The boys leave the house. Soon they are sitting in a car alongside the golf course. Using the pipe Randy has under his seat, Richard lights a chunk of the hashish. They sit in silence for the better part of an hour, passing the pipe back and forth, staring out through steamed windows as Christmas day comes to a close. It is only when the bright lights of an oncoming car suddenly shine into his heavy-lidded eyes that Randy finally speaks up. "I'm tired. I'm going home."

At 97 Birchwood Betty has her shoes off and her feet on the coffee table. She exhales loudly and her husband turns away from last night's paper to look into her eyes, also tired and droopy.

"Everybody was here, Artie. I'm so happy," she says.

"Was it everything you expected?"

"Everybody was so happy. They all had such a great time."

"I asked, 'Was it what you wanted?' "

"Of course not." She hesitates. "It only lasted a couple of hours. I want Christmas every day. To last forever."

Study Questions

1. When Martha confronts Richard about how much their father is angry at him, Richard says, "That's his problem. They'd do anything to have me home, so I'm not going to change just for them." What does this indicate about Richard's power–dependence relationship with his parents?

2. Examine the interview segments in which Art, Betty, Martha, Richard, and Joan talk about what Christmas means to them. What do these segments tell you about the Neumeyer family culture?

3. On a long-term basis, boundary ambiguity can create a lot of stress in a family, but on a short-term basis boundary ambiguity may help a family cope with separation or loss. This is because "a period of boundary ambiguity may give the family time to cognitively accept the information that the status quo has been broken and that change is imminent" (Boss and Greenberg, 1982, p. 6). Is there evidence to suggest that the boundary ambiguity being experienced by the Neumeyer family is helping the family cope with the loss of Martha and Richard?

4. If there is any season of the year during which families feel compelled to perform, certainly it is the holiday season. This is the time that family members can *show* their appreciation and the time that family members try to *look* surprised and excited when they receive gifts from each other. Examine the Neumeyer case study as you would a play or film. Who is the producer, the director, the stars, and the supporting cast? What props are essential, and what happens when actors flub their lines? What is the theme of the whole performance?

9

Extended Families

Oscar, truck driver; Gloria's husband
Gloria, homemaker; Oscar's wife
Bea, Gloria's sister
Brenda, Oscar and Gloria's first child
Raymond, Oscar and Gloria's second child
Ann, Oscar and Gloria's third child
Edward, Oscar and Gloria's fourth child
Gertrude (Gert), Oscar and Gloria's fifth child
Naomi, Oscar and Gloria's sixth child
Susan, Raymond's girlfriend
Richard, Brenda's husband
Roberta (Bobby), Brenda's first child
Brenda and Richard's twin daughters
Little Ann, Edward's mate
Donald, Edward and Little Ann's son
Clara, family friend temporarily living with the Wards
Bettylou Valentine, family friend; author of case; Val's wife
Charles Valentine (Val), co-investigator; Bettylou's husband
Jonathan, Bettylou and Charles's son
Dee Dee, family friend
Roland, Bea's son
Eileen, Roland's wife
Justin, Roland and Eileen's son
Mr. Jay, family friend
Hank, family friend; Bernice's husband
Bernice, family friend; Hank's wife
Jack, family friend
Randy, family friend
Thaddeus, family friend

Bishop Wells, community leader
Reverend Tomes, minister who briefly led prayer meetings at the Wards'
Mrs. Tomes, Reverend Tomes's wife

THE WARDS are a black family who live on Paul Street in the community of Blackston, a fictitious name for one of the poorest sections of a big northern city. They, along with several other families, were studied by two anthropologists who wanted to document the everyday lives of people caught in a struggle for survival in a world of racism and poverty.

Using classic ethnographic techniques, Bettylou Valentine and Charles Valentine moved into Blackston with their one-year-old son for a period of five years and "inhabited the same decrepit, rat- and roach-infested buildings as everyone else, lived on the same poor-quality food at inflated prices, trusted [their] health and [their] son's schooling to the same inferior institutions, suffered the same brutality and intimidation from the police, and like others made the best of it by some combination of endurance, escapism, and fighting back" (C. Valentine, 1978, p. 5). Generally accepted by the residents of Blackston, the Valentines eventually became part of the community and, in a real sense, also members of the Ward family, which is remarkable given that they are an interracial couple (Charles Valentine is white).

No doubt one reason the Valentines were absorbed into the Ward family has to do with the fact that social norms in Blackston emphasize assistance between households. In other words, the Ward family is an *extended family*, a network of relationships that extends beyond any single household (to include not only people connected by blood or marriage but also friends, neighbors, and mates) and that is a carrier of values and a base for economic, parental, and emotional support (Martin and Martin, 1978; Shimkin, Shimkin, and Frate, 1978).

The case (written by Bettylou Valentine as part of her Ph.D. dissertation) revolves around the Wards' activities for but a day, yet the study manages to capture the essential features of the family and, in the process, the essential features of extended family ties in the black community.

We are first introduced to Oscar, whose position in the Ward family is paradoxical. As the provider, he plays a very important role in the group. However, the daily operations of the family seem to go on almost in spite of him. One reason for this is that Oscar is an alcoholic, and alcoholics often are not held in the highest esteem by their families (Wiseman, 1970). Another reason that Oscar is not involved more in the everyday affairs of the family is that, as the breadwinner, principally he is responsible for maintaining steady work, which he does against all odds, as you will soon see. Thus, Oscar is the family's economic ballast in a sea of turbulence.

Oscar's wife, Gloria, on the other hand, is the family's "organizer, peacemaker, and focus." She is the one responsible for coordinating the caring for and raising of children (not only her own but others'), and she is the one who plans the meals, directs family activities (e.g., reunions and religious services), mediates family disputes, and, most important, strives to develop a collective identity among the members of the group (cf. Martin and Martin, 1978).

Although more often than not, she will be at the center of whatever happens to be going on in the family, it would be a mistake to assume that Gloria is a matriarch or that the Ward family is matriarchal in structure. A *matriarchal family* is dominated by women (Staples, 1971). Gloria does not dominate Oscar or anyone else in the family. The Ward family is, however, matrifocal. A *matrifocal family* is a family in which the mother–child bond takes precedence over the husband–wife bond and in which the day-to-day problems of family living (especially child care and socialization) are managed by women (Safa, 1971). A number of families—both black and white, extended and nuclear—could be classified as matrifocal. It is a popular family form throughout the world.

One way to analyze the structure of the Ward family is to imagine a series of concentric rings (cf. Holloman and Lewis, 1978). The inner ring includes Oscar and Gloria and their six children. The next ring encompasses Oscar and Gloria's grandchildren, their children's spouses and mates, and Gloria's sister, Bea. The third ring includes family friends and neighbors who interact more or less on a daily basis with those in the first two rings and who are tied to these people by a norm of reciprocity. This is the ring into which the Valentines are absorbed. The outer ring of the Ward family consists of blood kin who do not participate in the everyday life of those in the first three rings and who are defined by others (and/or who define themselves) as peripheral to the group. Bea's son, daughter-in-law, and grandchild belong in this ring, as do some of the fathers of the Ward grandchildren.

It may be difficult to decide where a person is located in the family's structure. Bea, for instance, may be trying to become a member of the first ring when, as you will see, she puts Oscar down in front of Gloria. In fact, some of the things she does would seem to indicate that she already is a member of the inner circle. Bea also bemoans the fact that her son, Roland, refuses to become more involved in the family, and she might understandably object to my assigning him to the outer ring.

Generally speaking, in a black extended family the people who are central to the group reside in the *base household*, the place in which many family activities are carried out and the place that many members of the family call home, even if they do not actually sleep there (Martin and Martin, 1978). The base household for the Ward family is Oscar and Gloria's second-floor apartment. This is where family meals are prepared and where holiday festivities and religious services occur.

Finally, one of the things that is especially interesting about the Wards is their flexibility. For example, no fewer than nine people—Oscar, Gloria, Ann, Edward, Gertrude, Naomi, Little Ann, Donald, and Clara—live in Oscar and Gloria's tiny four-room apartment and two more are on the way—Gertrude and Little Ann are pregnant. In order to live peaceably, if not comfortably, everyone in the family, male and female, does some of the cooking (under Gloria's supervision), and eating and sleeping are typically done in shifts. Also, all the women in the family—whether they are part of the base household or not—share responsibility for child care and socialization. This is not to say that children do not have a special attachment to their parents or that parents do not prize their children. It means simply that in the Ward family, as in most black extended families, children are not considered the property of their parents but are perceived to be the legacy of the group and of the black community as a whole (Aschenbrenner, 1978).

The Ward Family

Bettylou Valentine

OSCAR JUST DIDN'T understand these women. Here was his sister-in-law Bea throwing him out of her house again. Other people in the neighborhood might call her Aunt Bea, but he didn't even want to be related to her at times like this. He felt he hadn't done anything—at least nothing much—just cursed a little. Anyway, Bea cursed more than he did. She sure could be mean when she was drinking. And Oscar, Bea, and Mr. Jay had been drinking since this morning. Bea must have had some money. She had sent Mr. Jay over to the liquor store, and Oscar had decided to join the party when he saw Mr. Jay walking back with a bottle held up under his coat.

One reason Oscar felt specially bad about being thrown out was that he had no other place to go. It was still too cold to be sitting out on that stone stoop. And he knew his wife, Gloria, didn't want to have him upstairs. She had said so just before he came down to Bea's.

Gloria would rather be surrounded by all those daughters and their friends and grandchildren. They all listened more to her than they listened to Oscar. In fact, his two sons weren't living in the house now partly because they didn't get along with him too well either. His older son, Raymond, preferred to rent one of Bea's three rooms, where he had privacy and didn't have to argue all the time, as he told his mother. And Edward, the younger one, who even contributed something to his mother each week since he started working at the same place as his father, claimed to live at home but spent more time staying with friends. Right now Oscar didn't give a damn where any of them slept. Nobody showed him any respect.

Hell, he was their father. So he was a bit of a drinker. In fact he drank a lot. Still, he had managed to keep the same job for twenty-four years. During all that time he had provided for six children, relatives that Gloria had taken in from time to time, and now grandchildren. Oscar had mixed feelings about his work. It was his life in many ways. Twenty-four years with the same company had meant factory work, loading-platform work, and finally his present job as a delivery-truck driver. But he also knew that after twenty-four years at the same job he made only three-fourths as much money as any garbage man in this city who had just begun working this year. Oscar knew that he wasn't the right color to get a job as a garbage man. They hadn't had any Black people in that job when he started work in this city, and they had few even now. He had read about their salaries in the paper last year when the garbage men were going on strike. And he knew it partly because Gloria kept reminding him about it. He sure felt tired.

He wasn't going to let them push him around. He'd go upstairs anyways and go to sleep on that bed that filled most of his and Gloria's room. They couldn't keep him out of there. Often he wished he could get Gloria to do something else with him there too. But instead she built up a living wall of babies between them whenever they were both in the same bed. He hadn't been able to make love to his wife in longer than he could remember.

Oscar stumbled up the steps and gripped the wobbly handrail. At the second floor he pushed against his apartment door, brushed past the people crowded into the communal kitchen of the apartment, and went into the back bedroom. He climbed into bed with all his clothes on. And now he couldn't sleep. It wasn't the noise that bothered him. He was used to living with six or seven adults and a shifting number of children in the four-room apartment. He couldn't sleep because he wasn't drunk enough. Damn it, he wanted a bottle of his own. But he knew he'd never get Gloria to give him money for liquor. During all these years he would try to keep back $10 or $20 before giving Gloria his paycheck. Sometimes he wasn't able to do so before Gloria took the money for the house, or he spent it before the weekend ended or lent money to his friends and like today was without a drink when he wanted one.

Too bad he hadn't had more to drink before Bea threw him out of her three rooms on the floor below. He would have taken more but Bea was sneaky. She kept the bottle closed and down on the floor by her chair. She was always trying to keep him from drinking, even when she was drinking a lot more than he got. Damn if he was going to beg her for a drink.

He couldn't go to sleep. Instead his mind seemed to wander

back to those early days when he was just up from the South and had met Gloria. She was so pretty then—small and light-skinned with long "good" (unkinky) hair and a sweet smile. Everyone who looked at that picture of the two of them on the rooftop shortly before they got married agreed she was pretty. He enjoyed carrying the picture around in his wallet and showing it to everyone. Right now Oscar felt Gloria would be prettier if she would just have her missing front teeth replaced. But he knew better than to try to get his wife to do anything she didn't want to do.

That stubbornness ran in her family. You could see it in Bea. And it sure was passed on to their oldest daughter, Brenda. She was dark like him, pretty like her mother, quiet, and stubborn as a mule. She had been stubborn when she got pregnant after high school and decided not to marry the baby's father. He had wanted to marry Brenda. He had come around often and brought things for the baby. Brenda had called him when she needed anything, but she had stubbornly refused to marry him. What she had done instead was to get welfare support for the baby, move into a place of her own, and go to work in an insurance company office. Gloria took care of the baby during the day until Brenda returned from work. Then Brenda would take her little girl, Roberta, back to her own apartment about eight blocks away.

Brenda was stubborn about other things too. She wouldn't do any art work even though she was good at it. The things she had done in high school had won some prizes. Gloria's wealthy employer had asked to "borrow" some pieces such as the sculptured head to display in his apartment. But Brenda just didn't seem to care about art work now. Sometimes that streak of stubbornness helped. Brenda put money in the bank every payday and absolutely refused to let it be used except for what she had in mind. The stubbornness was in Roberta too. It was hard to believe that his first grandchild, who liked to be called Bobby, was now in school herself. Her mother had finally married the son of good friends. Now she, her husband, Bobby, and the new twins lived in this same building. Oscar supposed that the money Brenda had put in the bank had gone into furniture after the wedding. But he didn't know for sure. Nobody ever told him anything.

At one time Oscar had hoped that a son might be closer to him. He was pleased when their second child turned out to be a boy. He was a good-looking and healthy baby. Gloria had insisted on naming him Raymond after her own father. Somehow Oscar and his first son had never become very close. Then Ann was born. It wasn't until after they had a second son that Oscar got to name a boy after himself, Oscar Edward Ward. Still, Edward looked and acted more like his mother. After Edward II came Gertrude Gloria, named for her mother but better known as Gert. Finally, their "change" baby, Naomi, had been born when Gloria was forty.

Maybe the reason Oscar hadn't ever become very close to any of his children was that Gloria provided all the love and attention they seemed to need. And most of the time Oscar was at work or out drinking with his friends. Oscar felt good that he had kept his job throughout this time of babies and moves from one place to another. He had stayed at the same job even though the company he worked for had changed owners three times. Each time the union had also changed, and each time Oscar lost his union seniority and benefits. But he had supported his growing family as best he could. Only occasionally, between children and after the first-born daughter, Brenda, was big enough to help look after the younger ones, did Gloria do some domestic work in the White suburbs.

Oscar finally felt himself dropping off to sleep, still thinking about his family.

Meanwhile, out in the kitchen, most of the female members of Oscar's family were doing their own things. Naomi, a preteenager, the youngest but by no means the smallest of the Ward sisters, was still at that age where all the other males and females, family and friends, were constantly telling her to do something. Naomi, find my blue shoes! Answer the door! Give me my cigarettes, there they are on the sink! Feed the dogs! Bring me a Pamper! So although it was fine in some ways to be a part of the give and take of grownup interaction, Naomi clearly took more than she was allowed to give.

One of the people who bothered Naomi the most with her bossy, pushy orders was Little Ann, mother of her brother Edward's baby. Little Ann had moved into the Wards' four-room apartment when she became pregnant while she was still in her late teens. Edward, who had quit school without graduating, after several unsuccessful attempts to find an acceptable trade at a technical school of his choice, had met Little Ann through friends. After quitting school Edward volunteered for service in the navy. He came out of the navy with no more of a lead to a job than when he left the trade school. But in the meantime he did begin a family and brought Little Ann back to his parents' home.

Little Ann was called that to distinguish her from Ann, the second-oldest girl in the Ward family. Naomi didn't need any help in telling the two apart. Her own sister Ann used Naomi too, but for the most part Ann was quiet, even-tempered, and less bossy. Ann was really very different from Little Ann. Naomi felt that Little Ann pushed her around as if she owned her. And now that Little Ann was pregnant again she was more trouble than ever. Even the whine in her voice seemed uglier. Naomi was angry because Little Ann lived there, ate there, and didn't do any work.

Naomi wasn't alone in her view of Little Ann. All the other girls were bothered by her surly, bossy ways. Edward, who had brought this all about, didn't spend much time at home. He sometimes slept there only a few nights a week. So he missed most of Little Ann's troublemaking. And most of the time Little Ann was smart enough not to bother Mrs. Ward with her troubles.

Gert, Noami's next older sister, wasn't bossed around by Little Ann. Gert was also pregnant and not inclined to give one inch to Little Ann's demands. Gert and Little Ann shared the second bedroom with Ann, Naomi, and their friend Clara, who had moved out of her parents' home across the street after a family fight. Some of this sharing was made possible by informal sleeping shifts. Ann, who was a clerical trainee in a downtown investment company, left the house early in the morning, as did Naomi, who was still in elementary school. Little Ann and Gert and Clara often slept through the morning, sometimes into the early afternoon, and consequently went to bed much later than Naomi or Ann.

Gert was officially still in school although she didn't often get there. She went to a special program operated by the public school system for girls who became pregnant while still students. The emphasis of the program was on preparing for the coming baby through courses on hygiene, nutrition, and child care. Conventional school work in academic subjects was secondary. Gert was only slightly more interested in the child-care lessons than she had been in her regular school work. She knew the baby would come whether she went to school and learned about it or not. She knew the baby would be fed and raised in this household where any number of babies had been fed and raised before. Whether she went to nutrition and child-care classes didn't seem very important.

Gert knew these things the same way she had known she would get pregnant someday. She remembered talking to Noami's godmother about this over a year ago. Bettylou had asked her then whether she used or planned to use anything for birth control. Gert's answer then had been "no" to both questions, and they joked about how soon it would be till Gert became pregnant. Gert knew that whenever it happened she wouldn't be unhappy about it. But she sure as hell was a little tired of it now. Her breasts were hurting, and she knew she'd be even bigger and more uncomfortable when the weather got hot.

Gert was the most outspoken of the Ward girls. She remembered that when she was about eleven years old and Bettylou and Val were moving onto the block, she had been one of the first people to talk to them. If she hadn't introduced them to her mother, Naomi might not have them as godparents now. Then she had called them Miz Val and Mr. Val. Now she only called them that to tease them. Gert enjoyed teasing people, insulting them, or otherwise being outspoken, even provocative in speech. Sometimes this got her into trouble, particularly at school. But shit, she couldn't help it if people couldn't take it.

Putting her thoughts into action, Gert started in on Naomi, who pouted and called to her mother to say that Gert was bothering her again. Ann's reaction to the fuss was to get up from the table and go into the living room to watch the TV set that played nonstop throughout the day. Gloria turned from the stove where she was cooking and gave a half-hearted order to Gert to stop bothering her sister. She then turned to Naomi and told her to stop making a fuss. Gloria could and did raise her voice and demand attention and action when she felt it was needed. But she reacted to this momentary hassling with only momentary attention and conviction. Then she went back to her conversation with Dee Dee, her next-door neighbor, who often spent hours here in the Wards' kitchen.

Dee Dee and Gloria continued to talk about their experiences with the nearby hospital. It was a Jewish hospital which now had many Black and Spanish patients, especially in the older section of wards and in the clinics. Gloria had had a great deal of experience in dealing with health institutions and seemed to get a certain delight in discussing illnesses, injuries, diagnoses, and treatments.

Dee Dee, somewhat older than Gloria's grown daughters but younger than Gloria, was often able to relate and interact with both generations. The night before, she had gone to the opening day of the large nearby amusement park with the younger generation.

Today she was functioning as the mother of a ten-year-old daughter and the head of a household that included her two children, her own younger brother, and her mother. Dee Dee's mother was an active Muslim who wore floor-length dresses and kept her head and arms and body covered with modest and loose-fitting clothing. She did not interact with any neighbors or other individuals on the block.

Dee Dee, on the other hand, was one of the most sociable people on the block. When the recently formed block association decided to put on a block party for the children this past summer, Dee Dee was active in planning, shopping, and the work of the event itself. One of Dee Dee's favorite spots was her second-floor front window, from which she would watch the activities on the street below. Unlike her modest and proper mother, Dee Dee was most likely during these hours of watching to wear a bathrobe.

It was from this window perch that Dee Dee saw the public part of the family fight that led Clara to take up residence with the Wards. Clara's mother, a preacher at a church located in a nearby community, did not become involved in the street part of the family squabble. But Clara's father, a hip man-about-town in his own estimation, and her drug-addicted older brother were both trying to suppress Clara's assertions of independence. Clara's feeling of independence had been growing since she spent time as part of a Job Corps group in a neighboring state.

Clara was now adding some of her experiences in the Job Corps to the discussion about health care that Gloria and Dee Dee were carrying on in the Ward kitchen. Even Gert became involved when the talk got around to her own stay in the Jewish hospital during an operation on her leg. Except for the early pain in her leg, Gert had had an enjoyable time visiting with her friends and listening to the stories of how they had lied about their ages in order to be able to go up and see her in the hospital. Gert also remembered enjoying the fried chicken, greens, and potato salad her friends had smuggled up to her to offset the skimpy kosher meals served by the hospital.

At that time Gert's hospital stay had been made possible by her father's job-connected insurance. Gloria had never used that coverage for herself, but she was glad it was available to take care of the children.

There were two other hospitals available to pregnant women, and neither Gert nor Ann had decided which to use. One was a

Protestant church-connected institution on the northern border of Blackston. Although it was much smaller than either the Jewish hospital or the County Hospital, some women from the block who had given birth there recommended it highly. They felt it had concerned doctors, many of whom were foreigners, a warmer atmosphere, which they associated with the small size of the institution, and more flexible rules, especially as concerned mother–infant interaction. The County Hospital was considered by many, not only the patients from this area but also some of the staff of other hospitals, to have a superior department of pediatrics and maternity. But the size of the hospital worked against any personal doctor–patient relationships and against flexibility in applying rules. In addition, the distance of the hospital from Blackston affected the ease with which family and friends could visit. Both Gert and Little Ann were more interested in this latter consideration, since they expected no medical complications.

Dee Dee was arguing in favor of the Jewish hospital, but Clara pointed out that the local community council had recently boycotted it. A Black baby and a Spanish baby had been allowed to die in the emergency room through medical neglect, the council said. All of the women became involved in the argument, and Ann returned from the living room to join in too.

During all this, Gloria continued cooking in the several pots on the stove top. The oven door remained open in an attempt to heat the house, since it was midway between the periods when heat was turned on. The thirteen-year-old family cat climbed up onto the washing machine that was fitted in tight against the kitchen sink. The dogs were tied to the bathroom door and dozing in front of the apartment door they were supposed to protect. Brenda's daughter, Bobby, was watching TV and keeping her eye on her half sisters, the infant twins, and on Donald, Little Ann's small son. When Brenda returned from work, Bobby and the twins would go back upstairs to their own apartment. During all of this, Oscar continued to sleep in the back room.

When Oscar woke up and came out into the kitchen, the group had changed somewhat. Dee Dee had gone back into her own apartment across the hall. Oscar wished she'd spend more time there and less in his kitchen. His youngest daughter had gone to the corner store for Aunt Bea. And Val, Naomi's godfather, had come to visit. Already Gloria had set a big plate full of food in front of Val. If anyone ever left the Ward home hungry, it wouldn't be Gloria's fault.

Oscar said he wasn't hungry. But his presleep thoughts had put him in the mood to reminisce. He did this by reminding Val of the occasion a couple of years earlier when Naomi had become their godchild. At that time Oscar and his family still lived on the first floor of the two-family house across the street. The six rooms had meant more space for the family, but even so, the apartment hadn't seemed large enough. There had been a bad spell of illnesses and other expenses in the family, so that Gloria fell more and more behind in the mortgage payments, and the upstairs tenant had failed to pay the money he promised. They had had to move when their overdue payments amounted to more than they could catch up with. At that time Val and his wife had been living in the first-floor rear apartment next door. They offered to hold the christening party in their apartment because the boiler had broken down in the Wards' house and no money was available to make the extensive repairs required.

Oscar remembered the christening party very well. Naomi seemed so tiny then. The presents she received from family and friends were piled almost as high as she stood. Oscar had contributed a two-pound jar of caviar from the specialty-foods company he worked for. Oscar didn't like caviar. And from what Bettylou told him after the party, no one else did either. She and Jack from across the street had spent several evenings doing various things with the leftover caviar. Sour cream hadn't helped, and when Hank and Jack decided to mix it into a biscuit batter, everyone insisted that the entire mixture be thrown out. Oscar knew from his job that caviar was an expensive item, and he had wanted to contribute something important to the party. So as far as he was concerned, the father had done his part.

Naomi's mother had arranged the church-related part of the christening. Although Gloria's own uncle was the minister in a church on Stanner Avenue, in another section of Blackston, she decided to call on "Bishop" Wells to do the christening. Bishop Wells was a community figure of long standing. At one time he had organized a "cadet corps" and band with help from the local War on Poverty agency. Gloria's son Edward had been a member of both. Whenever Bishop Wells was in the neighborhood, he would stop at the Wards' home. No one in the Ward family attended any church regularly or even irregularly. But they kept up church ties for ceremonial occasions such as christenings, weddings, and funerals.

Oscar remembered attending prayer meetings in his living room. It had come about this way. It was summer. The family was sitting on the front steps when they were approached by a man who explained that he was leader of a storefront mission in another district. He said he was walking through the Blackston area and felt that people needed help. He also wanted to increase his mission membership by working here on this block. Gloria agreed to hold a prayer meeting once a week on Wednesday night at the Ward house. Wednesday was chosen because many of the people who might attend would be busy on weekend nights with card games or parties, and the minister wanted the weekend to prepare his Sunday morning service at the mission.

The meetings had gone on for about two months. Oscar recalled only two things from those prayer meetings. One was that his drinking was frequently the most discussed item, and the second was that the most often repeated prayer was that he stop drinking the devil's brew. In the ecstasy and excitement of the meeting, Oscar sometimes promised to do so. But the next week always required new prayers that the Lord again forgive his continued drinking. Drinking or not, praying or not, Oscar was always able to keep up with his work schedule and bring home the weekly paycheck. He would remind himself of this when he felt especially bad about drinking.

Bettylou, who had recently moved to this area to do a study, came to each meeting at Gloria's invitation. The second thing that Oscar remembered from these prayer meetings was related to Bettylou. Oscar had seen but not heard the incident. It was only later, when Gloria and Bettylou told the story to others, that Oscar understood what everyone was smiling about. After one of the prayer meetings the Reverend Tomes had taken Bettylou's hand in both of his and gazed into her eyes while Mrs. Tomes continued playing "Nearer my God to Thee" on the Wards' out-of-tune piano. Still holding her hand the Reverend murmured, "My dear, I believe God has great things in store for you."

Oscar's tendency to ramble and reinspect earlier, happier times was brought to an end by Val's asking him to come across the street and help with a block-association project of repairing a fence. The fence was needed to keep garbage out of the vacant, block-long lot behind Oscar's old house. The vacant lot had resulted when all the homes and buildings on the next street across from the railroad tracks had been torn down as part of urban renewal. The various houses had been taken down by different contractors at different times, as they became city property through abandonment, years of nonpayment of taxes by the absentee landlords, or other neglect. The flimsy fences required by law around all razed property did not connect with each other. In addition, one fence had often fallen down before the next-door one was built. Some fences were even torn down by a later contractor who saved money by using the old fence on his present job. The fence only had to last until the city inspector came to approve the demolition job a few weeks later. What happened after that was of no interest to the contractor or to the city.

After all the houses that backed on this block had been torn down, the sanitation department had decided to use the street as a dumping place for all the garbage trucks servicing this section of Blackston. When the block association had complained to the health department and the city administration, the sanitation department had argued that all the garbage dumped in that area was removed by the end of each day. One city department convinced the other that dumping garbage on a city street, a half block from occupied dwellings, was necessary because it was too expensive and time-consuming for the sanitation trucks to go all the way to the official city dump far from Blackston. The residents on the street knew that the garbage remained for many nights and attracted rats as well as private dumpers, who added their loads to the city's garbage piles and thus avoided the fees charged to private commercial users of the city dump. The block association took photographs of the illegal dumping, called and reported violators to the city bureau that licensed [the private dumping companies], and tried to enlist the support of the newly formed Model Cities agency in Blackston. All of this brought no change.

Oscar was aware of the problem, and so were most of his age mates and drinking buddies on the block. But they were very cynical about fighting the city and didn't offer to help. Many of their wives were active in the block association, so they knew about all the efforts that didn't seem to bring any success. A few of the men on the block voiced their belief that it would be a waste of time to try to do anything. Although Oscar said he agreed with them, he couldn't refuse to help Val when asked directly.

Oscar got up to put on a warm jacket and made Val promise to bring back his copies of the christening-party pictures so they could continue talking about it. Although the Wards had a set of the same pictures, it was always a major job to find them among the clutter of such crowded living. After working a while on the fence, Oscar planned to try to get Val to buy a pint of whiskey too. But he didn't mention this aloud while his wife was with them in the kitchen. With mixed motives, Val and Oscar went out to fight city hall.

In the meantime, Gloria had finished most of the cooking for the day. She decided to go downstairs and talk with her sister Bea about their tentative plans to visit their father in a town several hours' drive away.

The food, which on this midweek day included roast pork, green beans, sweet potatoes, and biscuits, would be left on the stove to simmer or on the open oven door to keep warm. Each family member would eat when she or he got hungry. The older children would serve the younger ones. And sometimes three or four people might sit down together to eat.

Most of the time there was no formally agreed-upon or scheduled time to eat. On special occasions, such as Thanksgiving or some other holiday, a birthday, or a visit from special friends or family members from outside of Blackston, Gloria would put on a dinner party that sometimes sat as many as sixteen people in this combination kitchen/dining room. Such a dinner usually meant that the weekly paycheck went totally for food. There would be no payment of bills, no buying of clothes, no dry cleaning, no household items that week. After the leftover food was finished, it might even mean no food, or they would have to borrow to just get by. Everyone knew this and seemed to accept it as the price of a celebration, in the same way that no one seemed to mind being squeezed up close to the refrigerator, washing machine, dish cabinet, or stove at such a dinner. Attention was focused on being with one another and on cooking and eating.

One Thanksgiving dinner started with grapefruit halves and shrimp cocktail and featured turkey, chicken, ham, and roast beef. These were accompanied by the traditional Thanksgiving cranberries, corn, sweet potatoes, and mashed potatoes, as well as the usual collard greens, blackeye peas, and rice with gravy. For dessert there were cakes and pies prepared by Gloria the night before and during the early morning hours. Most of the dinner guests on this occasion were immediate family or aunts, uncles, cousins, and mates of these family members. The few nonfamily guests had arrived at the appointed time and entered a scene of ongoing cooking. They waited for nearly four hours for all the dinner items to be completed before eating.

Cooking was something that everyone in this household, male and female, learned to do, usually without very explicit direction or urging. Some family members specialized in certain items. For instance, Edward, who had spent some time in trade school learning to be a baker, preferred to work on baked goods. Often he and his sister Ann argued about who could, and how to, make the best lemon meringue pie. Oscar, the father, tended to cook one-pot mixtures that often included meat, vegetables, and rice or dumplings. Sometimes a particular youngster would be asked to fix something or keep an eye on a given pot. At other times several people in turn might stir, taste, comment on, or add to some cooking item.

Gloria was glad to leave her own stove and go down to sit and talk with Bea. They usually managed to get together at least once each day. Bea might be cooking too. Or, if she had decided to drink rather than cook, Gloria would send down a big plateful of food later. Bea's cooking tended to be more mainstream American or even ethnic Jewish than Gloria's, probably because of the differences in their past employment. Gloria had worked outside of her home on occasion when it became necessary to supplement Oscar's paycheck. But most of the time her family of seven had required that she spend time at home.

Bea, on the other hand, had only one grown son, had long been a widow, and was currently unmarried and living alone. She had spent large periods of time in the employ of suburban householders; often as a cook or as an all-round domestic worker. Bea had thus learned the food preferences, cooking styles, and customs of her employers and prided herself on being able to cook in a variety of styles. During this same time, the families for whom she worked, especially the children, learned about items common in Blackston and similar communities, such as grits and greens.

When Gloria walked into Bea's small apartment, she didn't see or smell anything cooking. Bea seemed very glad to see Gloria and opened up the conversation by telling her sister how she had thrown Oscar out of her house earlier that day. This was a scene often enacted and reenacted between the two sisters. Bea had been very critical of Oscar when her sister had first brought him around during the Second World War. And now, twenty-five years later, Bea still felt the same way. Gloria, in turn, seemed to agree with all

Bea's complaints, and an outsider might wonder why she remained married to Oscar. Oscar, for his part, wasn't there to hear today's complaints, but he had heard them many times in the past. He seemed able to live with the complaints, however unhappily, and to keep functioning as wage earner for his wife and children.

Part of the reason the two women agreed on this topic was probably related to their joint background. Their own upbringing had been in a solidly respectable northern town rather than a big-city ghetto area. Their father had come to the United States from the Caribbean, and although his grandchildren and great-grandchildren considered themselves just Black, Bea and Gloria still held to their Caribbean origins and background and expressed them to others. Each would make explicit if asked or challenged their belief that West Indians were smarter, harder-working, better-mannered, and otherwise superior to American colored people.

Oscar with his poor, southern country background, had always been treated like a country bumpkin by Bea. And although Gloria had gone ahead with her plans to marry Oscar and had lived with him for twenty-five years, she didn't often defend Oscar publicly or in private to Bea.

Bea began to tell Gloria her latest news of Roland, Bea's only son. Roland had been born when Bea was quite young, and much of his upbringing had not been in Bea's hands. Now Roland was a good-looking, fortyish Black man living in a middle-class Black suburb some miles from Blackston. He occasionally came to Blackston, sometimes in his sports car or on his elaborate motorcycle, to visit briefly with Bea and other family members who happened to be around, and quickly went off again. Bea didn't like Roland to find her drinking, but she wanted the visits, which were almost always unannounced and unpredictable. Even this problem was better than the many years during which Roland refused to have any contact with his mother. Bea knew that during that period he had been seeing a psychiatrist, but she never did learn from Roland whether this was related to his decision to get back in touch with her.

Today's news was about an invitation for Bea to spend Mother's Day with Roland and his wife and son at their suburban home. Bea was excited and proud. She had already begun to make plans about what to wear and was asking Gloria to fix her hair in a special style.

Gloria was the hairdresser in the Ward family. Most of her

teenage and young-adult daughters had recently begun to wear their hair in the Afro style that was becoming popular among their friends. Neither Gloria nor Bea was very happy about the Afro style and preferred to continue pressing and curling their own relatively "good" hair. Before the Afro became popular, Gloria had spent part of most days helping one or another of her daughters, their friends, and later her grandchildren to press (with a hot comb), braid, curl, or style their hair. Often this was done in the kitchen and served as a focus of activity for an afternoon. Just last weekend Gloria had done Bettylou's hair for a party while she sat and talked with Gert and Brenda about their school experiences.

Bea didn't want to talk or think about anyone else just now. She wanted only to plan for the upcoming Mother's Day trip. She began taking about possible presents she might take to her son's wife, Eileen. Eileen had been a high-school sweetheart of Roland's. She had called Bea "Mother" then and told her that the one thing in life she had determined would happen was that she would marry Roland. The two of them had been married now for almost eighteen years, and their only son, Justin, was a six-foot-tall teenage chess fan and high-school sports hero.

Bea had the money to spend on a gift now, since she had been working steadily for the past ten weeks for the dentist's wife who had been her employer in spells for the past five or six years. When Bea wasn't working for the dentist's wife, she was often working for the same woman's sister-in-law, who was married to a doctor. Sometimes Bea worked two or three days for each of them at the same time. At times like this she provided a common background for the small cousins in her charge and helped the sisters exchange gossip. In addition Bea did the cleaning, shopping, cooking, and babysitting. Both the doctor and the dentist had been promising to provide professional services to Bea at no cost or only at the cost of materials. So far neither had done anything, so Bea, like her sister Gloria, remained overweight and lacking a front tooth or two.

Before Bea had gone back to work for the dentist's wife, she had a half year of subsisting on a welfare check of $17 per week and about $25 more per week that she earned illegally by caring for the two small children of a working mother who lived in the city-owned apartment building across the street and for the small child of the anthropologists. She charged them $3 or $4 per day to provide three meals, constant attention, game playing, reading stories, or just watching the children while they sat or stood on the stoop during the warm weather. In addition, Bea would some-times agree to watch the infants or toddlers of her kin, even though this usually did not involve any cash payment. Bea often said that she loved children and wished she had had more. But she always added, "God didn't bless me with any more children, and that's why with everybody else's child I try to do nice things."

During this period Bea had been able to fulfill her food needs and provide some household necessities, but she never had much to spend for other things. She was able to pay her rent because the West Indian landlord in her building and the Jewish couple who owned the tenement next door paid her a small amount each month to keep the halls clean in both buildings, to see that the front stoop was swept and that the garbage cans lined up on the sidewalk in front of the buildings were kept neat.

Bea was able to keep up with these chores, plus the 7 A.M. to 6 or 7 P.M. babysitting, by hiring Randy, the addict from up the street, to mop the hallways. Bea herself swept off the stoops early each morning. There was very little anyone could do about the garbage cans, many of which were battered by the garbage men as they threw them around. Some of the cans were losing or had lost their bottoms or lids, and there were too few to hold all the garbage pro-duced by the large families in the six tenement apartments at both houses.

During the ten weeks of working for the dentist's wife, Bea hadn't been drinking at all. Today was the first day in several months of returning to alcohol. This was part of a pattern Bea had developed. For weeks or months at a time she would not drink at all. During these times she became very insistent upon "proper" behavior from her kin and friends—no swearing, respect for eld-ers, moderate or no drinking, set mealtimes, modest clothing, and other customs less honored during Bea's drinking periods.

But Bea's values weren't merely anchored to her drinking hab-its. Gloria reminded her today about the dinner party Bea had giv-en for Gloria and Oscar's wedding anniversary. The guests had in-cluded the Wards, Bernice and Hank, Val and Bettylou, and various of the Ward children and teenagers, who came and went. All the adults, including Bea, had been drinking for some time be-fore dinner was served. Everyone was seated at Bea's food-laden table when Randy and some other addicts knocked at the door. They had sacks of potatoes and onions and several cartons of canned foods taken from the freight cars on the siding nearby. Bea had immediately tried to send them away, saying that it was illegal and not right to be taking someone else's food and she wouldn't have them selling it in her apartment. But both Gloria and Bernice had gone out to the door, looked over the offering, and argued a little about price, and finally each had bought a sack of potatoes, a sack of onions, and various cans of food. The entire transaction had taken place in the hallway outside Bea's door with only the light from her kitchen to provide a little illumination.

Gloria called upstairs and had her son Edward come to carry her purchases up to their apartment. Bernice asked Hank to take hers across to their house. Bea allowed that, in order not to break up the dinner party further, Bernice could just leave the things inside the kitchen door and take them home later. Although Bea was willing to give in to expediency on that issue, she was very active in arguing that all this behavior was wrong. Bea pointed out, as everyone already knew, that Randy and his friends had stolen the items from the railroad. It was Hank who pointed out that stealing from the railroad wasn't like stealing from an individual in that the materials were probably already counted as an expected loss and/or completely covered by insurance. His wife, Bernice, agreed strongly. Gloria expressed the view that she couldn't possibly feed all her family each week and provide everything else that was needed on Oscar's paycheck, so she needed bargains like this to make ends meet. The Valentines took no active part in this conversation, so Bea was left arguing in a heartfelt and morally indignant way against the buying of stolen goods while her kin and friends defended it as fair in the circumstances and the only way to get a reasonable deal in the ghetto. Bea made the point, and Gloria agreed, that they had never taught the Ward children to steal; in fact they had been taught not to steal. But although Bea felt this point supported her argument, Gloria countered that it was only her own children for whom she was responsible and over whom she had any control. The morality, need for, and meaning of the transaction had been the main item of conversation during the entire dinner.

Bea didn't especially want to be reminded of the event. She still felt that she had been right but had not prevailed. But her main interest now was not in that question but in her plans for the upcoming Mother's Day dinner at her son's home. He was to come and pick Bea up in the late morning, and she was to spend the entire day with his family. Bea went on at some length about how wonderful her son, daughter-in-law, and grandchild were to do this for her.

During Bea's talk about Roland, she was interrupted several times by various of Gloria's children putting their heads in at Bea's unlocked door to ask their mother some question, or calling down from the steps between the two apartments. Gloria would answer or step momentarily out of the room to find something or settle a problem. Bea finally told Gloria that she didn't like trying to hold a serious conversation with her because Gloria couldn't sit still long enough. Bea, who could be very indulgent with children, often felt that Gloria was too indulgent with hers.

Gloria was used to this complaint. She never really tried to stop the interruptions, or at least her efforts weren't taken seriously by the chidren. It all made Gloria feel needed. For years she had been having chest pains, and when she finally went to see a doctor, who suggested that she go into the hospital for tests, Gloria refused. Her stated reason was that the house would fall apart without her presence as organizer, peacemaker, and focus. Only she knew the secrets and bargains necessary to make Oscar's check cover their expenses, and only she could keep after him to get free items like day-old bread from places where he made deliveries. Besides, as she pointed out in defending her refusal, Oscar's insurance coverage wouldn't pay for diagnostic work, as they had found when their daughter Gert had trouble with her leg. And they had no savings at all.

Gloria believed in preventive medicine, particularly for babies and children. She had fed her children vitamins, taken them to the well-baby clinic or a private doctor, and dealt immediately with any symptoms of illness. Yet all of this was for her children, nieces, nephews, and grandchildren. Gloria, who was following out her own line of thought, told Bea that for adults who had to be at home or at work each day there was neither the time nor the money for illness. Therefore many adults refused to think about their aches and pains and hoped that most physical problems would clear up without care. Bea didn't always agree, but she knew that Gloria would find many older people in Blackston who felt this way. Bea herself had gone to the doctor when she began to have pains in her hands, only to be told that there was nothing to be done about it except take aspirin when it hurt too much. Gloria had scoffed at this waste of money for a doctor's visit and told Bea that she could have prescribed aspirin. Besides, as they both knew, everyone hurt more as they grew older, and Bea and Gloria knew many such people in this community who made their own pains secondary to other immediate needs such as employment, child care, cooking, and similar duties. Oscar tended to agree with Gloria, but he worried about his wife's chest pains and dizziness. Yet on those few occasions when he insisted that he could run the household as well as work, Gloria dismissed the entire discussion.

Bea, on the other hand, who had no family obligations around which to focus her life, often warned her sister to take care of her health, stating that if Gloria didn't, she might soon be away from her family permanently. The two sisters obviously had a long-standing and ongoing relationship in which they criticized and supported each other. Today Bea continued drinking even though her sister Gloria wouldn't join her. Gloria drank only at parties or on special occasions.

This session was finally broken up totally by Naomi's return from the store, where she had gone for Aunt Bea. Gloria and Naomi returned upstairs to their own apartment to eat, and it was only on the way upstairs that Gloria remembered her earlier intention to talk with Bea about visiting their father. Oh well, she could see Bea later tonight or tomorrow. Bea, who had been drinking most of the day, began to feel lonely when she was left by herself in the apartment. She felt depressed and unhappy with her life. Bea recognized this feeling as a familiar one and knew that if she didn't do something about it she would be unable to sleep and would probably feel a need to begin the next day with a drink too.

Bea decided to go across the street to talk with Val and Bettylou. She had done so before. Both her father and her son had encouraged her to continue to do so if it made her feel better. Bea knew that she couldn't have an uninterrupted talk with Gloria. Gloria might just respond jokingly and not understand the emotional significance of Bea's feelings. Occasionally, as Bea now reminded herself, she had tried to talk with Roland. He had been mostly sympathetic, but he didn't like to be awakened by the phone in the late night or early morning, and this was often when Bea needed help most. In addition, there were some things Bea felt she couldn't discuss with her son.

When Bea knocked at the Valentines' door, both Val and Bettylou were at home. Their son, Jonathan, whom Bea often cared for, was asleep. Val had just recently parted company with Oscar after some post-fence-building drinks. Bettylou was gathering together the christening pictures she had promised to take over to the Wards' the next day. Bea asked the two of them to listen to her troubles, saying that she felt her drinking problems might get out of hand if she didn't deal with her problems first. The Valentines said they would and asked Bea if she would feel comfortable if a tape recorder was recording in the background. Bea agreed, telling the Valentines that she loved them, was sure they loved her and would not embarrass her or hurt her.

Bea was happy with the fact that she was able to talk uninterruptedly for as long as she wanted. She talked about her childhood, her father, her mother, and her grandmother, with whom she had lived for some time. Mostly she seemed to want to talk about her marriage, her husband's death, her fear and depression thereafter, and finally her present, deeply felt need for affection. She talked about all the children she enjoyed taking care of and repeated aloud for others what she had known for a long time—that her days were bearable if she had a lot of work, children to care for, and companions, but the nights, when she had to be by herself, were terrible. Bea talked about living in with the family she did housework for, as they had asked, but felt she would miss the neighborhood and her relatives. Besides, she did not see this as a solution to her problem, which she felt was in her head. It would also keep her from finding the social and sexual company of a man.

Val and Bettylou listened sympathetically and didn't comment until Bea said she felt talked out. Then they suggested that Bea's account indicated to them that she needed a "companion" and should regard even very strong desires for this as quite normal.

Bea didn't talk any more but she felt less depressed and left saying she thought she might sleep now. . . .

Gert was staring at a TV game show when she heard Aunt Bea call from the bottom of the stairs. She smacked the dog tied to the apartment door and told him to shut up as she stuck her head out to call back. Aunt Bea insisted that Gert come down, saying she didn't want to carry on her business in the hall. Gert and Aunt Bea were on neutral terms just now. Sometimes they were more friendly, sometimes less so. Some time ago, when the Wards lived across the street, Gloria and Bea had worked out an arrangement for Gert to move in with her aunt, so as to provide Bea with company and a little household help. Gert, for her part, was to get a quiet and more orderly place in which to do her school work. The arrangement had not lasted long. Gert had found Aunt Bea too bossy, and Aunt Bea refused to put up with what she considered unhelpful, ungrateful, and sassy behavior.

Gert slipped into her old shoes, which served as slippers since she had bent down the backs of the shoes, and flopped loudly on each step as she went down to Bea's. She had picked Donald up and carried him down with her despite his protests. Gert knocked on Bea's door and walked into the kitchen immediately without waiting for the "come in" shouted from the front room. The door to Raymond's room was shut, as it always was when he wasn't there. Earlier, when Gert had lived with Aunt Bea, she had shared what was now Raymond's room with Bea. Now Aunt Bea slept in the living room on a sofabed.

Aunt Bea was not sure when Raymond would be back, if at all, that night. She was often asleep when he came in. She would leave food for him on the stove. But she knew that Gert might see him, since the young people all seemed to keep late hours, or Raymond might call on the phone at the Ward apartment. Bea, like many Blackston residents, didn't have a telephone. The Wards had one now because Little Ann had worked briefly for the phone company and was not required to make a deposit before installation as were all other Blackstonians, in contrast with people from wealthier sections of the city. If Raymond called, Bea had a message that had to be acted on right away. The West Indian family in the third-floor front apartment in this building had decided to move into the area across from Blackston's southwest border. This area was a lower-middle-class community whose Jewish population was moving out and being replaced by West Indians, other Blacks, and some Hispanics—as had happened in Blackston a dozen years earlier.

The landlord had told Aunt Bea about the move and asked if she knew of anyone who would be interested in taking the apartment. He didn't want anyone on welfare. Bea immediately thought of Raymond and Susan.

If Raymond and Susan decided to take the place, Susan would be close to her in-laws and the rest of the Ward extended family. Brenda and Richard lived with Bobby and the twins in the third-floor rear apartment; Gloria, Oscar, and their remaining children in the second-floor rear; and Aunt Bea in the first-floor front. In addition, Susan would be able to remain close to her parents and among established friends and neighbors while Raymond was in Thailand.*

Gert liked the idea too because for her it would mean the company of someone near her age and a place to go when she got tired of her family's crowded and often noisy home. Gert knew she would receive some payment for her expected child from the welfare department. In fact she had already received a check to buy clothes and materials. But because she was under eighteen she would be discouraged from setting up an apartment or home separate from her parents. Gert wasn't sure she wanted to do that anyway. She expected almost without conscious thought that her mother would help care for her baby and leave Gert free to party and socialize away from home like other seventeen-year-olds. Her mother's doting treatment of Donald contradicted her occasional statements to Gert that she wasn't going to take care of any more babies.

Gert had neither planned for nor against a baby. She was very uncertain about whether she wanted to marry the baby's father. In fact, she had told her mother and others that she didn't want to be married to anyone just now. Her sister Brenda didn't get married until Bobby was nearly five years old, and she had done well. Brenda had kept up a job with the insurance company, bought nice clothes, and had an apartment of her own before she ever got married to Richard. From Gert's point of view marriage was no big thing.

Gert knew she couldn't say this sort of thing to Aunt Bea, so she didn't try. Instead she agreed to deliver the message to Raymond and urge him to do something definite the next day. The landlord had told Bea that the West Indian family expected to move out Wednesday and she could have the key to the apartment then. Aunt Bea often collected rents from the tenants as part of her work for the landlord.

Aunt Bea and the West Indian family had been quite friendly during the few months they had lived on the block. Bea had often taken care of their two school-age boys after school, before their father had returned from his daytime job as a security guard downtown and after their mother had left for her night shift of private-duty nursing. Aunt Bea expected that they would tell her about their new home in the next day or two, but like many people

---

*Editor's Note: Raymond was in the army and was about to be sent overseas.

in Blackston they probably would not let many others know. It always seemed safer to keep your business to yourself, especially if it involved property or changes related to income or residence. Yet Bea was aware, from having lived on Paul Street for over eight years, that many of the people who moved away in what seemed a day without word to friends were often back within a week or a month to keep up old social ties. Even people like Thaddeus across the way, who often spoke of hating this neighborhood, had admitted to Bea in early-morning conversations with her as she sat in her street-level window seat that this area was a community, a place of friends and ties that made for more than just neighbors in an impersonal, big-city setting. . . .

Study Questions

1. Describe the role structure of the Ward family. In other words, identify the various social positions in the family and specify the norms associated with those positions. Also, discuss the way in which the various positions and roles interlock. Try to diagram the role structure by using, say, squares to denote formal roles, circles to denote informal roles, and lines between the squares and circles to denote interlocking relationships. Don't forget that each individual in the family can play more than one role.

2. Some scholars contend that the black extended family was born out of poverty, that it is essentially a kinship system created by black people to deal with an alien environment (e.g., Frazier, 1939; Rainwater, 1966; Safa, 1971). Others argue that the black extended family is rooted in black culture, that it characterizes family life in many black societies—both in the United States and abroad (e.g., Mathis, 1978; McAdoo, 1978; Shimkin, Shimkin, and Frate, 1978; Staples, 1971). The obvious answer to this apparent dilemma is that the black extended family is a product of cultural as well as socioeconomic forces (which is, of course, true for all family forms). Focusing, for the moment, on the effect of socioeconomic forces on family life, describe how the Ward family's group identity—specifically, its emphasis on we-ness rather than I-ness—helps the family cope with racism and financial hardship.

3. Three distinct perspectives have been used by researchers studying black family groups: (a) the *cultural deviant* perspective, (b) the *cultural*

equivalent perspective, and (c) the *cultural variant (relative)* perspective (Allen, 1978). The cultural deviant perspective labels black families like the Wards as abnormal or pathological because they deviate from white, middle-class families, which are presumed to be the ideal (e.g., Moynihan, 1965). The cultural equivalent perspective deemphasizes cultural differences between black and white families while emphasizing what black and white families have in common (e.g., Scanzoni, 1971). Finally, the cultural variant perspective views black family life as a way of life that is both distinctive and well adapted to the social and cultural environment (e.g., Billingsley, 1968). Which of these perspectives do you think is the best one to understand the Ward family? Can you think of any reason that two of the three or even all three might be used, or do you think that only one perspective should be employed?

10

Alternative Lifestyles

CAST OF CHARACTERS

Michael, former journalist, now freelance writer; author of case; Ruth's husband

Ruth, mental health therapist; Michael's wife

Matt, Michael and Ruth's eight-year-old son

Anne, elementary school teacher; Gary's wife

Gary, physician working for the government; Anne's husband

Dan, former medical student, now unemployed

Leigh, organizer of the Health Information Project (HIP), a collective that advocates community health care; lived with Dan before joining the commune

Pete, a "doctor of science," whose occupation is not specified

Chris, high school teacher

Sharon, a friend of Anne and Gary's who visits the commune and is thinking about joining; she never does

THIS IS THE STORY of Cliveden House, an urban commune formed to provide a familylike atmosphere for its members. Dissatisfied with what they perceived to be the atomistic and individualistic character of modern life, the founders of the commune wanted to bring together under one roof a group of people who would be financially and emotionally dependent on each other, a group in which there would be few barriers to interpersonal contact and involvement. Like other communes, this commune was predicated on the belief that cooperation, sharing, and mutual responsibility are the best avenues through which to achieve happiness and fulfillment.

Contrary to what some people think, communes are not new; they have existed in one form or another throughout history. What is new, however, are the reasons currently being used to justify this lifestyle. In the past, communes generally were started for religious or politicoeconomic reasons; today, most communes revolve around efforts to create a romanticized version of a large family, the logic being that large families may be the only way to counteract the alienation and social isolation presumed to be inherent in postindustrial society (Kanter, 1972a).

We meet the commune when it is just starting out and we, thus, have the advantage of seeing in bold relief some of the most critical problems that confront virtually all communes. One of the first dilemmas that the commune must deal with is the membership of the group. This is an interesting issue because it demonstrates that communes are like conventional families and yet unlike conventional families; they fall somewhere in between a family and a friendship clique. The fact that communes, unlike conventional families, are voluntary has some decided advantages: people are less likely to get stuck in an uncongenial arrangement. On the other hand, the freedom to choose carries with it ambivalence, uncertainty, and discomfort. Experiencing something not unlike premarital dating and courtship, the members of the commune gradually move through a period of mutual testing and discovery until they reach a point at which they are willing to make their first commitment to each other—living together.

Formally adopting a common residence is not, however, sufficient to define a commune or, for that matter, a family. Besides being physically or spatially close, communal groups are also socially close. Indeed, as was mentioned earlier, social closeness or cohesiveness is typically the commune's reason for being. The commune strives to establish a social bond or group identity by employing several strategies for achieving and maintaining strong interpersonal commitments (Kanter, 1972b). The members of the Cliveden House commune decide, for example, to set up a modified form of economic communism, whereby a portion of their salaries and some of their personal property will be pooled and made available for general use. Interestingly enough, the commune opts not to buy clothing from joint funds because members feel that this is a matter of "personal preference"; yet many communes have argued that a collectively controlled wardrobe is indispensable for reinforcing solidarity and playing down individual differences.

The members of the commune also decide to meet as a group once a week to deal with the problems of living together and, more important, to "begin to build, in a conscious way, a network of engagement." In the case study we see how one meeting was conducted and how the members tried to deal with perhaps the greatest threat to the commune's stability, namely, the insistence on maintaining precommunal marital ties. Classifying the commune's preference for monogamy as a threat to stability may sound odd, given the strong feelings most people have today about traditional marriage. But it has been shown that one of the critical differences between successful and unsuccessful communes is the tendency of successful communes to discourage pair relationships (Kanter, 1972b).

In the group meeting depicted in the case, Anne and Gary disclose the problems that they have been having with their marriage and ask for help from their housemates. As the discussion gets increasingly heated, the boundary between Anne and Gary (as a couple) and the rest of the group becomes harder and harder to discern; the privacy of the couple's marriage is breached and, correspondingly, the family identity of the commune is reinforced.

Cliveden House

Michael Weiss

Origins

On July 18, 1971, I moved into a big old stone house in the Germantown section of Philadelphia which I shared with eight other people. The twin dogwoods that stood like gatekeepers in our patchy front yard were green and leafy in the summer heat. Now, fourteen months later, as I sit here looking out my bedroom window, the dogwood leaves are thinning and turning rust-red; bright orange-red berries have appeared on the trees, and the days are turning cool again. Seven of us remain in the house, beginning a second year.

Somehow our commune never got a name, although we toyed around with a lot of possibilities in the weeks before and after we moved into the house on Cliveden Street. We would sit in a big group on a lawn or in a living room and somebody would say, "How about 'Radish'? It's red and it grows." And two of us would be enthusiastic, three indifferent, and a couple more opposed. We went on like that until we tired of the game and our friends began to call us Cliveden House because it was convenient to call us something, and that name was obvious. I suppose being unable to agree on a name was one of our first lessons in the frustrations of living communally. Our bank, which was unaccustomed to communal accounts with eight co-signers, had the same problem: they finally decided that we were a club, the Cliveden House Club.

Our life together isn't some kind of counter-culture pablum: you do your thing and I'll do my thing and it'll be groovy. We proceed by arrangement. The people in the house didn't just flow into a commune on the tide of life, free and unencumbered. All of us decided to live together individually and in our own separate fashions; we each arrived on Cliveden Street with our own hopes, terrors, needs, fantasies, and ways of getting what we wanted. Gary, for instance, would never have moved in at all if he hadn't planned to leave Philadelphia in a year. He viewed communal living as an experiment, an adventure, and he still does, though as time goes on he finds himself more uncertain about how he will live in the future than he had anticipated. Leigh, on the other hand, was aiming to develop a community where she could bring up the kids she didn't yet have. She's still looking for a lifelong home, but is more hesitant now that she understands better what the cost will be.

Perhaps it was because we recognized from the beginning the many differences in our temperaments, ages, upbringings, beliefs, lifestyles, and desires that our group developed a studied, self-aware style. We work hard at living together, take pride in the happiness of our home, and cause some of our friends to suggest that we are more-communal-than-thou. . . .

Arrangements

One spring evening we sat down in our living room and began to talk, keeping a lot of what we were thinking to ourselves, but no doubt revealing more than we intended. We had to see if we liked one another, whether we could talk like friends. And it was just as important to know if we all had similar ideas of what it would be like to live together. We had strangeness to overcome, and genuine differences in how we had been living and what we valued, and fears of judging as well as of being judged. The possibility that one of us might not live up to another's standards, that somebody might have to say that he or she didn't want to live with somebody else there that night made for a hesitant, probing mood which prevailed every time we talked about our new house during the next few months.

I wanted to be accepting and understanding, and yet there was no way around looking at Pete or at Chris and wondering, can I live with that *stranger?* There were moments when I thought that it was crazy to be there altogether: swimming against the current of my culture required an unflagging resolve, lessons long ago learned broke over my consciousness like waves of doubt. To be sitting with people I hardly knew, speaking of sharing a home—a kitchen, a refrigerator, a bathroom. So much of what I am is symbolized by the details of my home, by the food I eat, the hair or lack of it in the bathroom sink—my home is an emblem of my aspirations. Just so. I accepted the doubt and indecision as among the less consequential costs of having decided to live in a group. But were these the right people? Except for Chris, who missed that first meeting, and Pete, with whom I had never really talked, I had begun to trust that everybody else would respect my sensitivities. And I was yearning for a home, the beginning of a future. I had decided that just like falling in love, picking your intentional family was largely a matter of luck, or instinctive trust in your own judgement: you played around and fenced around and waited to be excited, or comforted, or reassured, and in the end you guessed—yes or no—without ever knowing why.

Neither Gary nor Anne had ever lived in a commune before. For them, if they decided to chance it, it would be a leap into the unknown from four years of privacy, orderliness, and an increasingly involving marriage. They were, compared to Ruth and me, financially well-off—Gary was a doctor and Anne a teacher and they had a lot of furniture, books, records, paintings, artifacts, kitchenware, a car, a stereo system, a motorcycle. Anne had become interested in communal living before Gary, but by the time they arrived in Upper Darby that night in April, he was more enthusiastic. Anne thought that nobody would like her because she was too straight, too conventional. But she also knew precisely why she wanted to live with other people.

"I'm interested in living communally because I want more intimate relationships than just the one with Gary," she said in a voice that shook a little. "I want other people to help me grow, to help Gary grow, and to help us grow together. And politically I feel it's absurd for a person to have a car of their own, or their own couch."

She was blunt and spoke without embellishment. Eventually I learned that Anne sets out to get what she wants with a great force, a considerable will. What she was after was a happier life with Gary, and before long the rest of us would find ourselves enlisted in her campaign to get it.

Leigh was of two minds about Anne. She admired her outspokenness. But she was seven years younger than Anne, who was thirty-one, and she was worried about being excluded by the two older women. She could see how much Ruth and Anne liked each other, and she was afraid that they wouldn't respect the validity of her experience. So she kept testing, prodding them for reactions, especially Anne.

"I've always lived communally in a way," she said, thinking somewhat resentfully about how her father's house had been a harbor for his friends and patients. "I guess what I'm looking for is a situation where there's a lot of equality, where people don't get cast in one kind of role or another." This was directed toward Anne. It was both timid and a bit arch. "And a group that feels comfortable and supportive around what I'm doing in the women's movement and with anti-war stuff."

She thought she sounded defensive, and disliked herself for it.

Meanwhile, Dan was having his doubts about whether he could make a go of it with Gary and Anne, who seemed burdened by a lot of money and possessions, and who had a certain intangible security, as well. He turned the conversation toward possessiveness.

"The only thing I own that I guess I don't want ripped off is my sleeping bag," he said nonchalantly, as if that were an unquestionably sound and customary point of view.

Pete was keeping pretty quiet, sitting back on his haunches and watching the give and take. He was afraid of Dan. Although they had met at any number of political meetings, Dan seemed young and uncompromising to him, and he was sure that Dan would eventually scorn his more comfortable, accepting ways.

But Dan was also the most easygoing person in the group sprawled around the room that night. He could drawl the laziest loops around the staccato city talk which the rest of us kept in motion. In this, though neither of them knew it at the time, he and Pete were very much alike. Months later Pete would say that he and Dan "anchor the nonpsychological wing of the house."

"Well," Dan replied, when Gary asked him what he was looking for in a commune, "living with other people feels better. You have more fun with other people and you can always find people to do things with or get help. It felt good in a big family growing up."

Gary gave me the impression that night of being fidgety, eruptive. He kept running his long fingers through his thick, dark brown hair. For awhile he would say nothing, and then he'd let loose a torrent of words. He was intimidated by me, by my long black hair and beard, by my having lived in a commune before. I appeared mysterious and vaguely dangerous to him, and he couldn't imagine why I'd want to live with him. He suspected that I really wanted to live with Anne, and that she might be sexually attracted to me, too. Though he thought that I was sensitive and intelligent, he dwelled within himself on my strong, even dogmatic manner.

As the night wore on there was less tension. We talked the same language. And we looked and dressed alike, which gave us some superficial reassurance. The men all had long hair, and the men and women alike wore dungarees and work shirts or T-shirts, boots or sneakers. Before the others went home we decided to go to the beach the next weekend. Gary and Anne wanted to bring along a friend who was also interested in living with us, and there were no objections.

That first night, and in the next few weeks Ruth and I felt responsible for helping the others to reconcile their differences. We had brought Chris, Dan, and Leigh together with Gary, Anne, and Pete, and in that sense we were pivotal. Ruth and I were also the only people in the group who had lived in a commune which could serve as a rough model for what most of us had in mind for our new house. So there was a disposition, especially on the part of Gary and Anne, to view us as being especially knowledgeable and wise.

Saturday morning, after a half-dozen phone calls and a chaos of plans made and altered and made again—a style of group confusion about doing something which has characterized us ever since—we piled into three cars and headed for the Jersey coast. Anne and I sat together in a back seat, talking rapidly and easily about our marriages. It was a gray, damp day. When we got to the ocean, we walked and ran along the beach, huddled together on blankets, threw around a ball, and occupied the deserted dun and gray oceanside with our boisterous presence. I felt free and quick, loping along the sand, breathing deep gulps of the wet, salty air while the gulls glided and squawked overhead.

Having that fun together did more to loosen us up with one another than all the portentous talks in the world. I was really pleased. We bought a crateful of fresh New Jersey lobsters and a case of beer and headed back to Upper Darby where we tore into the food, blew off steam, shouted a lot and collided in tentative, friendly ways. Leigh, who was still wary of Gary, began to relax when the two of them made brownies in the middle of an incredible mess in the kitchen, and just acted loony together. They were both self-consciously restrained, but they were also enjoying each other.

Afterward, when we all sat down to talk again, Anne's friend Sharon included, our ease began to evaporate. Sharon's relationship to the rest of us was ambiguous because it appeared she was including herself in, and except for Gary and Anne nobody was at all certain that was okay.

After our day on the beach there seemed to be a subtle shift in our assumptions, as though the fun we had had together had made our intentions toward each other more explicit. It was like a courtship, yes, a group courtship. We had met and been attracted and so arranged a first date, which, though it had been awkward and unfamiliar, gave us enough promise of a possible future to warrant a day at the seashore. And there we had begun to laugh together. No passions were stirred yet, but we shared some sort of dawning recognition. At times, sudden personal discoveries broke past the bounds of propriety; at other times we bogged down in the sad, tense ambiguities of trying to make sure that we had the same future in mind.

Soon we began to talk about what Pete called arrangements, about conscious accommodations to what each of us wanted. And what a weighty load of subjects confronted us: money, possessions, sex, privacy, limits on our involvement, sex roles—in short, the politics of an intentional family. It was a marvelous opportunity, forming such an unconventional household. We were serious, we were truly disgusted with the way things were generally being done, and so we had all been swept into a restless seeking after more satisfying styles of existence; we were ready to begin deciding which cultural conditioning we could discard, which we wanted to shed but could not, and, finally, which values and behavior, like our own skins, wrapped us in forms which gave us coherence. . . .

We decided to try a plan under which each individual would put half of his or her earnings into a housefund and keep the other half for private use. We agreed that it would be a big step toward a feeling of collective existence, we would be pledging something more substantial than our benevolent intentions toward one another. It also safeguarded our autonomy by assuring each of us continued freedom to come and go within the limits of our incomes, by leaving us all some getaway money, and by guaranteeing each of us some measure of continued financial independence. And it seemed a cautious beginning, it didn't push us too rapidly past our actual limitations toward some ideal goal. Another consideration was that the six of us who were coupled off wouldn't be treated as appendages of each other; it would encourage us to treat one another as individuals and not in tandem, as married couples especially are usually treated.

Our plan was that the housefund would pay for rent, food, utilities, transportation and auto upkeep including insurance, all household expenses, and a ten-dollar-a-week allowance for each of the adults. The allowance was supposed to help us avoid situations where we might all want to do something together like go to a restaurant, but some people might not be able to afford it. We decided to pay for clothing out of our own pockets because we thought that how much clothing an individual had, and its quality, were too much matters of personal preference to be subject to collective control. We didn't want to find ourselves weighing a shirt somebody wanted against whether they truly needed it.

We agreed rather easily that we would support Matt collectively, and that if Gary and Anne had the kid they were planning we would also support their baby with group money.

Inherent in the entire agreement was an understanding that if one of the people with the higher incomes wanted to stop working after awhile, or wanted to change to a lower paying job, and if that created a need for more income, then one of us who had been indulged would be responsible for bringing in the extra that was needed.

What benefits did we envision? Well, we all felt virtuous doing something demanding and unusual just because we believed it was right. We were proud. And we thought that sharing half our incomes would enable us to live active, productive urban lives without always having primary responsibility either for making money or being a homemaker or both. We hoped to relieve the dependencies fostered by sex-role stereotyping in nuclear families, and to end the enforced loneliness of living in ones and twos: the pleasures and drudgeries of working, earning money, and caring for our own home were to be available to all of us equally.

We decided, too, that we would share the use and costs of the cars. And here Leigh enjoyed a certain ironic, private amusement. Nearly a year before, when she hardly knew him, she had just about bought Pete's Toyota, but then changed her mind at the last minute. Now, she smiled to herself, she would have the Toyota anyway, and without laying out a penny. It would be months before she was confident that Pete could enjoy the humor without resenting the truth of what had happened. In addition to the Toyota, our cars included a Volvo which Ruth and I owned, Leigh's Mercedes diesel, and Gary and Anne's Volkswagen.

We also acknowledged the existence of private property, of items each of us possessed that we didn't want to become common property. Gary and Anne were outspoken about this, and it made me wonder if they were really ready to go as far into communality as I thought I wanted to. They had more possessions than any of the rest of us, and seemed more emotionally attached to them. Still, all of us had some things we wanted to keep out of the way of harm and wear. For me, there was my typewriter, a fifteen-year-old Smith-Corona desk model. I've been talking to myself by pounding on it for a long, long time, and I want it to be with me for a long time more. When a key broke not so long ago I felt as though some vital vessel in a loved one had burst.

Our conversation about money and possessions lasted a long, exhausting night. At its end, we were all drained by the cautious, judgement-ridden negotiations, and by our private doubts. We still reserved the right to pull out, but turning back had become more difficult than going ahead: it appeared to me that we were half-willingly snaring ourselves into living together. Just before we broke up Gary said that he knew about a seven-bedroom house in Germantown which was up for rent.

Pete drove home that night very unsettled. The group was moving perilously close to an agreement, and he still wasn't sure whether or not he wanted to be part of it. He was uncertain about giving up his car and half his income to group use. It scared him just to think about it. His family had had very little, and he had worked hard for everything he had acquired. For years he had an almost Scottish stinginess, it had been hard for him to get accustomed to having and spending money on himself. Finally, though, he had disciplined himself to enjoy the life he could afford, and now he felt endangered by agreeing to give any of it away, especially to people whom he hardly knew and who were earning nothing or very close to it by their own choice. And yet he also knew that he was lonely, that for years he had talked and thought about living in a commune. He knew he would have to make a decision—and soon. And he knew too that he was thirty-five years old, and that this was probably the last opportunity he would have to live in a commune, that either he would join this group or very probably would never join any. Perhaps what eventually tipped the balance for him was knowing that Gary and Anne had many of the same doubts, that, if need be, they could huddle together and give each other succor in the new house. The new house! He really would just about start shaking when he said that, even to himself.

About a week later, in a more relaxed mood, we talked about

Matt. Anne, who had been teaching kids for nine years, was starting to like Matt. Sometimes she thought he was spoiled and bratty, but at other times she was amazed by how articulate he was, and how sensitive to other people. There was the time when she had been nearby when he leaned over and kissed a boy friend and said, "There! I did it! I've been wanting to do that for the longest time." Anne could see, too, that I had a lot of guilt about raising Matt in such crazy-quilt homes, and so sometimes withheld clearcut decisions when he needed them. She wondered what was the best relationship between Matt and the other adults, and what Ruth and I would want.

We told the other people that we intended to go on being Matt's only parents, but that we hoped they would become his friends and assume some responsibility for his well-being. That came very close to what most of the other adults wanted, too. Again, Pete was baffled, there seemed to be just one unknown prospect after another. He had very little idea of what living with an eight-year-old might really entail. Pete thought of Matt as just a cute little grown-up kid, not as a separate person.

I was reluctant to put Matt into a situation where he would be the only child among eight grownups, but I was even more reluctant to live just the three of us on his account, and then spend years thinking how grateful he should feel for all I had given up in his behalf. No, I wouldn't do that. But I went on doubting the decision Ruth and I had made, wondering if it was fair. I felt quite vulnerable in a way that nobody else in the group did, except for Ruth.

The question of Matt's being the only child in our group was incidental to Ruth's decision. She had looked for people with whom she wanted to live, and when she found them none of them had any kids. She wondered why not, why so few of the people she was closest to had children. It made her feel lonely.

We didn't talk about sex until after we had rented the house on Cliveden Street several weeks later and were already decided on living together.

"There's something I have to talk about," Gary said when we were all sitting around one night. "I haven't brought it up before because I was afraid of seeming too old-fashioned or something." There was a nervous pause. "It's that I'm very jealous about Anne's and my sexual relationship. It's not something I want to expand or share, and I'm worried that other people in the house might try to get us to break that down." His voice was a trifle reedy, and he sat cross-legged on the floor, looking agitated. At the back of his mind was his first college romance—he had broken it off when the girl had slept with another man, causing him agonies of rage and pain, like a fire in the pit of his stomach.

Ruth sighed audibly, but said nothing. "Well, monogamy is an issue that Dan and I are struggling around," Leigh said, trying to gather her thoughts. Gary so often emphasized his privacy and his fears that she thought he wouldn't ever push her to explore her own limits. "I can respect your decision about your own relationship," she said. "I don't want you to feel any pressure from me to change that if you don't want to."

I was drawn to Anne, and I immediately felt at a loss about how to sort out my feelings in this situation.

"You know Ruth and I have been talking about the possibility of sleeping with other people," I said cautiously. "But getting involved with somebody else in the house seems a little too frighteningly immediate and close to me."

"I think I'd feel best," said Ruth, who had fantasized about making love with Dan, "if we could reach an agreement that nobody would sleep with anybody else in the house outside of the couples who are already together."

"Why's that?" Dan asked sweetly and curiously.

"Because I don't think I could handle it," Ruth answered, not at all happily.

"I think I'd feel a lot safer like that, too," said Anne. She was thinking not only about Gary, but about the appeal that Pete, Dan and I had for her. But her investment was steep, and she intended to protect it. "I feel old-fashioned and everything," she said, "but that's just where I'm at."

Chris, meanwhile, was intensely uncomfortable. The level of sexual feeling and uncertainty in the room was high, but he knew that this was the time to broach what he was thinking about.

"I'm really worried about bringing this up," he said in a small, soft voice, "but I want to be sure that everybody knows I'm gay and is sure that's okay with them." And he waited for the axe to fall.

But it didn't. The men who had never lived with Chris or any other homosexual before—Pete, Gary and I—all had pretty similar responses. We each said that we found Chris' sexuality a threat, that we weren't interested in having sex with another man, and we thought that living with Chris would force us to confront ourselves more directly than we had.

Gary asked Chris why he was willing to live in a heterosexual group.

"Well, I didn't especially take that into consideration when I decided who I wanted to live with," Chris said. "I wanted to live with this group of people because of who they are, not because they're gay or straight." He anticipated that what problems he would have would show themselves subtly, in how people said things, in their attitudes and reactions.

I thought Chris' answer was incomplete, but was reluctant to say so. His decision raised questions about his own sexuality to which I would have liked some more answers, but I was sufficiently unsure of myself—and of him—to press him.

There was something else on Chris' mind which was even more difficult for him to bring up.

"I want to be sure that Mike and Ruth feel all right about my taking care of Matt, like if I'm ever alone with him, babysitting or something," he said in a choked voice.

I reached over and grabbed Chris' hand and said that I trusted him; Ruth came across the room and hugged him. I was angry, incensed at our culture for having taught us to so thoroughly fear homosexuality that a fine, gentle man like Chris couldn't trust himself or be sure he would be trusted around a boy child. But I was angry at myself, too, because I knew that his concern wasn't unfounded: I was worried that if Matt found out that Chris was gay, he would be upset. I trusted Chris to be alone with Matt, but there was nothing in anybody else's sex life I wanted to protect Matt from knowing about, I only wanted him to be taught with sensitivity. In Chris' case, I wasn't sure I wanted him to be taught at all.

Many, many months later Matt, who by that time was aware that other men sometimes shared Chris' bed, asked Pete and Ruth and me while all of us were in the kitchen on Cliveden Street: "What's a homosexual?"

"That's a man who makes love with other men," I answered after a pause and an exchange of glances among the adults.

A moment later Matt left the kitchen, his curiosity apparently satisfied. . . .

House Meeting

We had decided to meet once a week as a group, to hold house meetings. First of all, it seemed necessary in order to run a

cooperative household, the nuts and bolts of communal living—
schedules, chores, money and bank accounts, complaints, requests, cars, guests—all of these needed frequent attention. We
also wanted to stay in touch with one another's lives. Coming and
going as busily as a lot of us did offered scant guarantee that we
would ever spend an evening all together. But most importantly,
we wanted to have a setting for acting on our intention to talk
about our concerns and problems, to seek sympathy, understanding, and advice from one another, to begin to build, in a conscious
way, a network of engagement. After all, if living alone and in
pairs had been sufficiently satisfying, none of us would have chosen to live with a group. We sought the company of other people,
yes, but wanted something far more binding, too. Monday nights
were set aside for house meetings, and for an entire year we didn't
miss a week: our faithfulness to each other was unswerving. Very
soon we learned that the kind of life we hoped to build together
would probably be impossible without the meetings—they were
like a pressure release, the place where you could most safely let
off steam. Nothing was allowed to get in the way: we removed the
phones from their hooks, and told our friends not to come over.

We were so wound up for our first meeting, so tentative and
prickly, that nothing memorable happened. A week later, though,
we were ready to try again. After dinner Pete headed straight for
the kitchen to do the dishes, a much safer place, so far as he was
concerned, than the living room where the rest of us were supposed to be going. In fact, the nervous desire to avoid the house
meeting was at work in all of us. Gary picked just that time to get a
screwdriver and begin working on the stereo. Chris was
concentrating so intently on a book you might have needed dynamite to blast him loose from those protective pages. Ruth was cro-
cheting too rapidly to talk, smile, or acknowledge another human
presence. I kept running from room to room trying to hurry
everybody up. Leigh remembered a last-minute phone call. It was
close to an hour after dinner. Pete had finished the dishes and
boiled water for a pot of tea which he finally brought into the living
room on a tray, along with cups, sugar, honey, and spoons. Somehow, we all finally gathered together, sitting on chairs and cou-
ches, or stretched out on the floor around the low, circular table in
the center of the room.

We began to talk about routine housekeeping matters, our
nervousness abating so long as we talked about who was going to

fix the leaky bathroom faucet, and which car could be used at the co-op on Thursday. About ten o'clock we took a break and I put Matt to sleep. When I got back downstairs Gary was sitting cross-legged on the floor, his back to the fireplace, shifting nervously.

"I have something I want to talk about, but I don't know if it's appropriate to bring it up," he said, his voice just a bit higher and reedier than usual. My stomach tightened up.

"It's something I want to share about some of the problems Anne and I are dealing with," he continued. He wanted help, it was true; but it was just as true that he had decided to take the first plunge, had decided to take that on as his responsibility.

"Go ahead, Gary," Ruth said, as if the preliminaries were going to drive her up a wall.

"How do you feel about me talking about these things?" he asked Anne.

She was sitting on the rocker, across the circle from Gary, her blue eyes alert. One foot, in a furry house slipper, tapped lightly on the floor. Her small, square, compact hands gripped both arms of the rocker firmly.

"Sure, okay," she said.

There was a pause, while Gary seemed to take a mental deep breath.

"I feel like you're not accepting me the way I am," he finally said in a burst, looking directly at her. "You keep pushing me to change, and I don't understand what it is you want. But I feel like you want me to be something I'm not."

Anne answered rapidly, "The way you look at our relationship it's all about my problems. You make it sound like you don't have any problems of your own, so I wind up feeling like the fucked-up one." Her face was angry. "There's so much you aren't willing to look at. I feel like you're not really open to me and willing to share with me. I'd like us to be closer than we are."

I rolled my neck to loosen the taut muscles and unclenched my jaw. I was gripped by the enormous tension between them. My sympathy was more with Anne, yet that made me feel guilty, made me suspect that I was silently siding with her because she was a woman, rather than because of what she said. Way at the back of my mind there was a flicker of a thought that I wanted to see Gary punished for being so much like me. But more consciously I thought that they were serious, and by having it out at a house meeting they were indicating that they expected something from all of us, from me. I was excruciatingly self-conscious. I had to squelch an impulse to laugh, and another to say, "Oh, this is just a lot of crap." The division between sincerity and the ridiculous is flimsy at times, especially when I am called upon to give more than I am sure I have available. I felt as if I were set down upon a proving ground.

There were signs of similar recognitions among the other people. Dan stretched, and shook himself loose. Chris looked petrified, eyeballing around. Leigh was leaning forward, her fingers splayed across her thighs.

"What things do you want to share more of?" Gary asked indulgently.

"Like your family," Anne said, angry but not adamant, as if this ground had all been covered before. "Every time I say anything about how your family might have influenced the way you are, you react like I'm attacking you."

"Look, Anne, I've thought as much about my family as I know how," he said, his voice rising again. "I feel like you're pushing me to admit that I'm fucked up because you want me to feel the way you do about things."

"You see what I mean," Anne yelped, "you *always* make it that I'm fucked up. You're not listening to me. Every time I try to talk to you about any of this you get defensive and begin to intellectualize and verbalize and shut me off."

"Why don't you just let me alone then?" Gary shouted in exasperation.

"Because there's more I want from you," Anne shouted back. "I want you to start taking my perceptions seriously. I'm no dummy. I want you to understand that you've got problems, too, just like everybody else."

"For chrissake, Anne . . ." he said, his voice thick with frustration. He turned toward the couch where Pete, Ruth, and I were sitting. "What am I doing wrong?" he wailed. "I just don't understand." And though I was struck by the theatricality of his question, his bewilderment was so genuine that I softened at once.

"It doesn't sound like you're really hearing Anne," Pete said, encouraged by his ties to both of them. "Yeah . . . she's saying that you're treating her like a patient with a problem. And she's telling you that she feels boxed in by that. I think you're really trying to mold her into the image you have of a woman and a marriage."

"But you know, Anne," I said, "it really does sound as if you're pressing Gary to be what you want him to be, that you're not being patient about his way of working things out." I was aware of wanting to give Gary some support, worried that Anne would get so much sympathy that Gary would feel all alone.

"I know," Anne said. "But I feel so goddamn frustrated I don't know what else to do."

"Why are you taking your frustration out on me? That's what I don't understand," Gary said sullenly.

"It sounds like what you're saying to Anne," Ruth said slowly, concentrating on each thought, "is that you've got everything accounted for, that you understand what you need to. And that really frustrates her because it makes all the problems the two of you have her fault, it makes her feel guilty. It's like you're saying that she should straighten herself out, that it's not your problem. But she's got this enormous investment in you, in your relationship, and *that's* what's frustrating her. She doesn't want to walk away from your problems, and she doesn't want you to turn your back on them, she wants the two of you to work this out together."

"I don't know," Gary said sadly. "Everybody keeps telling me to look at myself, but I don't know what to look at." What an admission for him to make, staring into his own opaque depths.

"It sounds like you don't believe you've got an unconscious," Chris said, after a long hesitation during which he wondered if what he wanted to say was true, knew that he wanted to contribute something perceptive—the atmosphere of the house meeting seemed to demand nothing less—but feared that his shot in the dark would wound.

But in fact his thought fell like a pebble in the pool of Gary's musing, and set off ripples of meaning and understanding. An unconscious? Precisely what was meant by that? Gary wondered. He was learning that he saw himself differently from the ways the rest of us did. Just when he was being charitable, making an allowance for another one of Anne's damn irrational perversities, Leigh would tell him he was being sanctimonious; at just the moment when he was acknowledging that *everything* might not be the way he thought it was, Ruth told him he sounded defensive. He couldn't avoid knowing that he was missing the point. He was being told that there were more things he didn't understand than he had imagined, but being told by people whom he trusted—people who seemed to believe in him. He tried as hard as he could to be honest, because he expected that of himself. Now he had to confess that he didn't know as much about himself as he thought he did—a realization which presented itself anew every few years.

We talked on and on, until anxiety gave way to tiredness; tempers still flared but stamina was sapped. Early in the morning all the men were clustered around Gary, while Leigh and Ruth flanked Anne. When Gary and Anne finally went to bed, they were uncertain of where to proceed, of what to do next. But what had happened that night would inform the rest of our lives on Cliveden Street. . . .

By having the courage and trust to make the rest of us privy to the conflict at the heart of their relationship they had opened up a vast, flexible psychic space in which we could all begin to explore what we wanted to get from living in the house. It seemed during that house meeting, and in the weeks immediately afterward, that most of us were ready to accept some responsibility for being available to each other when asked, and when our own lives permitted. I felt more secure about making emotional demands because I anticipated that there would be a response. The next few weeks were animated by ceaseless conversation: all over the house, late at night and early on weekend mornings, over breakfast and dinner, we talked in twos and in groups, ever shifting, like cells involved in growth, seeking and giving, learning about one another. I began to think that if I slept at all I would miss something crucial, began to experience a deep, jealous possessiveness about the lives of the people with whom I was living. It was akin to the feeling when a man and a woman discover they have a passion for each other: most everything else is, for a while, crowded out of the forefront of their consciousness. Except that, because we weren't lovers, the mood was more one of unacted upon incest; the air was thick with longing. The house meetings were the points in time at which feeling coalesced.

A group identity was taking shape. . . .

Study Questions

1. According to studies of various communes (e.g., Kanter, 1972a), one of the most important cultural elements of a communal group is its *belief system* (i.e., what the members assume is true and what they assume is false). What are the essential features of the Cliveden House belief system? How do the members of the commune try to shape and maintain these features?

2. Typically, communes work out some arrangement of sharing finances. It is not unusual for the arrangement to be based on Karl Marx's well-known dictum "From each according to his ability, to each according to his needs" (1938, p. 10). Thus, for example, Dan, who is not working, is supported by others who are. How does this arrangement differ from the way in which money is allocated in traditional families? If you were going to start a commune, what kind of economic system would you create and why?

3. Cliveden House decides that no one will sleep with anyone else outside of the couples who are already together. In other words, the group decides to prohibit in-house, extramarital sex. Yet, often communes encourage sex outside of marriage, and some communes go so far as to ban monogamy in favor of group marriage, in which several men are married to several women. In terms of the advantages and disadvantages to the group, what are the pros and cons of (a) monogamy, (b) monogamy with extramarital sex condoned, and (c) group marriage?

4. Families like to erect boundaries around themselves; they want to identify who belongs and who does not (Kantor and Lehr, 1975). But when several families join together to form a larger unit, it is often assumed that these boundaries no longer exist. How many married couples, for instance, have an attentive audience when they argue, as Anne and Gary do? Again, what are the advantages and disadvantages to the group when pregroup privacy norms are no longer honored? Suppose that in order to build a strong group identity Cliveden House discouraged all pregroup bonds and in fact discouraged any pursuits and activities that did not have the complete support of the group. What would happen?

11

Divorce and Single Parenting

CAST OF CHARACTERS

Lynn, divorced mother; author of case
Jennifer, Lynn's older daughter
Joanna, Lynn's younger daughter

CHANCES ARE THAT YOU have had some contact with divorce. Either you know someone who has gone through a divorce, or you are the child of a broken home, or you have been part of a marriage that did not work out. Perhaps you fall into all three categories. But whatever your experience—and it is entirely possible that you do not belong in any of these categories, *at least not yet*—you have a stake in the divorce process simply because the institution of marriage is central in our society and anything that affects marriage as much as divorce does ultimately affects us all.

In this case study and the next, you will have the opportunity to learn how two people dealt with divorce. The cases are typical in many respects, although in different ways, and I suggest that you read them as a pair and try to pick out the similarities and differences.

Lynn's story is a first-person account of the five years immediately following her divorce. It is a vivid and fairly representative description of what it means today to be a divorced woman and single mother.

Lynn begins not by focusing on the legal aspects of divorce or the problems associated with dividing property but by declaring that when her marriage ended her "whole world" fell apart. Gone was the life she had dreamed of and planned for. Gone was the future she had assumed would naturally come to pass. Anyone who has been through a divorce can relate to what Lynn is saying. As difficult as the practical problems accompanying divorce are (how *do* you divide the stereo, the car, the children?), what often hurts most is that dismantling a marriage means dismantling a future. The simple fact is that a marriage is more than a commitment to share a home; it is a commitment to share a life, to intertwine your destiny with that of another (Davis, 1973). Thus, the most radical change that divorced people often have to learn to deal with is the change that takes place inside their heads.

Sensing a void in her life, Lynn does something that many single parents do: she turns to her children for emotional support. This eventually results in her developing a more flexible and egalitarian relationship with her daughters than she probably would have had if she had stayed married; interacting with one's children as both parent and friend tends to blur the boundaries that traditionally exist between one generation and the next. There are some authorities who see the absence of a clear-cut division of roles as problematic (e.g., Minuchin, 1974), but others see the ambiguity in positive terms (e.g., Greenberg, 1980). Lynn's story suggests that there is an element of truth to both points of view.

Lynn mentions several times the financial difficulties that she has had since her divorce. The economic burdens of single parenthood tend to fall more heavily upon women than upon men for a variety of reasons. First, faced with discrimination in the marketplace, women generally do not earn as much money as men do. Second, in part because of their lower earnings, women generally do not have as good a credit rating as men do, which means that women are more often denied credit cards and bank loans. Third, women are typically awarded custody of the children after a divorce and although it is common for the courts to instruct the father to pay alimony and child support, quite often these payments are late or withheld altogether.

The fact that divorce may mean economic hardship for both themselves and their children is one reason that many wives choose to remain in unsatisfying and even abusive marriages (Gelles, 1976; Kalmuss and Straus, 1982). Comparing married life with divorced life, they choose what they perceive is the lesser of two evils. Thus, only by reducing the financial dependence of women on men—which would mean attacking the sources of sexual discrimination in our society—can we begin to change what, for many wives and mothers, is a no-win situation.

Lynn

Lynn Gail

DURING JULY OF 1975, I found myself facing life with my four-year-old daughter, Jennifer, my one-month-old infant, Joanna, and no husband. After eight years of marriage, my husband and I had decided to separate. For me, the separation initiated a period of intense pain and anger. My whole world—one that I had so carefully dreamed of and planned for, and that I had existed in during the marriage—fell apart, completely.

Because her father had moved across the country and had very little communication with his daughters, Jennifer was afraid that I too might leave her. I had to assure her continually that I would never leave her and that the divorce was not her fault. I explained to my daughter that her father and I could no longer live together as husband and wife in a good, healthy way, but that we would always be her mamma and daddy.

Although a young child at that time, Jennifer knew me incredibly well. She had shared the rough periods during my married years and the pain of the actual break-up. She helped me to survive as a single mother just by caring for and loving me. She trusted me to keep the family together and to take good care of her and her sister. Jennifer and I became a team in a struggle for our lives. We kept our house a home. We served as supports, confidantes, and as outlets for our emotions—whether we were hugging, crying, or expressing anger. As mother and daughter, we were connected by feelings of loss, sadness, and anger. I needed her terribly.

Although my younger daughter was only a baby at the time of our separation, she also has been an important resource during the difficult five years of single motherhood. Her sweetness and tenderness have been a refreshing source of strength during these bittersweet years. Nursing and holding her, watching her grow and develop into herself, has been a wonderful experience. During tense times, the humorous and childlike interactions with Joanna helped Jennifer and me to laugh; we began to enjoy life as a family.

During the months immediately following the separation, I felt rage and chose to express it. I was furious with my ex-husband for deserting our family. I was also angry with myself for not creating a marriage that could "last forever," having believed that I could do so to such an extent that my whole world crumbled when the bubble burst.

Jennifer expressed her anger by refusing to really believe that our family of four—mother, father, big sister, and little sister—was gone and could never, ever be put back together. She continued to question me about whether or not I "hated" Daddy, or was still her friend, long after the divorce had been finalized. She was also hurt over her father's lack of communication with her.

We both released our anger physically by dancing, stretching, drawing, and punching pillows. We shared our expressions, thereby supporting each other's need to believe that it was all right to be sad and angry.

A nonverbal conversation and a closeness between mother and daughter, between friends, was developing. Later on, we were able to verbalize our feelings.

I felt terribly alone and frightened of facing my new singles world while taking care of my children. The evening hours at home were the most difficult for me. After the children were put to bed, too late for the phone to ring with a call from a friend, loneliness and sadness would haunt me. Tears would flow in rushes, finally expressing the fear and confusion of my life as a single mother, in financial debt, desperately trying to survive. When I became deeply depressed, and my frustration erupted into anger at my children, a pile of papers, a burned dinner, or anything, Jennifer would be there to support me. She would come over to me and stroke my hair slowly. She would hug and hold me, assuring me of her love. "Don't worry, Mama," she would say. "Everything will be all right. I'll help you."

Sometimes my life situation struck me as almost ludicrous: here I was feeling like a child and needing so much help, yet I was taking care of two children. Realistically, I had to be the strong responsible adult. Fortunately, I could also be a child with Jennifer and Joanna.

I wanted to share the truth about my life with my children: I was a mother first, but also a friend to my daughters. Sometimes it became confusing as to where the boundaries lay, and I recognized a need for a balance. For example, I had to keep my disciplinary rules firm, but I also had to be open to the emotional needs of my children. Beds had to be straightened before breakfast, toys and clothes picked up, and no running or yelling was permitted in the house. There is security in knowing that things have to be done in certain ways. By structuring our lives with consistent limits, I was definitely the mother of the house. But the doorway for intimacy was also open, enabling us to be friends and our individual selves, as well as family members.

One of the most difficult aspects of being a single parent was doing something for myself without feeling guilty that I was being selfish or a "bad" parent. I decided to attend graduate school in the expressive arts and then spent a great deal of time planning how my children would be taken care of while I was in school. I explained as honestly as possible my feelings that mothers have things they want and need to do. Because my daughters were already experiencing so many changes, I tried to be positive, sensitive, and strong when presenting any new developments in my life to them.

It was not easy to attend graduate school five days a week, drive close to an hour each way, be a mother to a five-year-old and a one-year-old, take care of the house, shop and cook, be a friend, and also be a single woman. Often I felt like a switchboard operator working with too many wires—plugging them in and out, hoping that all the connections would be made. Would Jennifer be left at kindergarten because my friend might forget to pick her up? Did I remember the car seat for the baby? Did I pay the baby sitter? Are all my notebooks for school in the orange bag? I needed to plan it out carefully so I could be comfortable each day and thus free enough to really get into the learning and processing at school.

I had mixed feelings about motherhood after the divorce. I wanted to raise my children and have them live with me, but I also wanted to experience what other single women have the opportunity to live out. I discovered tremendous anger about not having that freedom. Legally I was a single woman; but I did not *feel* single. I always had my two children in my life. Then I would feel guilty. Was I a horrible mother to feel this way? Did any other single mothers have these thoughts? It was almost impossible to combine a single-type lifestyle with motherhood, and I needed to have both components in my life.

After my marriage broke up, I wondered if I could ever have a successful, long-lasting relationship with a man. I questioned whether I was attractive, sexual, sensual, or intelligent. I needed to find answers to these questions, so I began to establish a life outside my mother role. I had to become confident as a woman as well as a mother.

It felt strange to bring new men into the house. Jennifer would back off from them even in conversation. I projected her feelings and felt even more guilty that perhaps she resented me for replacing her father with new men.

Dating and time alone away from my children became expensive. I always had unpaid bills. As a single parent, I either had to take the children with me or pay for a sitter to watch them. Often I traded off with other single-parent friends, and this was wonderful.

Sometimes I hated my children for preventing me from leading a completely single life. I wished they would disappear. My dreams became nightmares of longing for freedom, yet wanting a deep, close relationship with my children as their mother. Sometimes I chose to be totally there for my children during the evening or on the weekends. Often I would go to bed at nine o'clock and wake up early on a weekend morning to have a long, relaxing breakfast with my daughters. Other times I would get a sitter and go out dancing with a friend, stay out until early morning, and sleep late the next day. I am still working out the balance between being a mother and a single woman.

I was not in any hurry to establish another relationship with a man. When I did have my space away from my children, I often chose to be by myself. Sometimes I wanted the company of my sister, a friend, or a small group of close friends. Having very confused feelings about myself with men, I felt more comfortable and relaxed with women. It has taken me five years to begin to establish a healthy relationship with a man.

Slowly my life is coming together. After being in financial debt for five years, I am finally stabilizing our finances so that we can live a simple but happy life.

Looking back, I am glad I shared all I did with my children. I did not create a Superwoman or Supermother role model for Jennifer and Joanna. They know me for who I am: a survivor.

Study Questions

1. "It was not easy to attend graduate school five days a week, drive close to an hour each way, be a mother to a five-year-old and a one-year-old, take care of the house, shop and cook, be a friend, and also be a single woman. Often I felt like a switchboard operator working with too many wires—plugging them in and out, hoping that all the connections would be made." What is it about the single-parent role that seems to be bothering Lynn? The ambiguous expectations associated with the role (role ambiguity)? The conflicting expectations associated with the role (intrarole conflict)? Or the conflict between the expectations associated with the single-parent role and the expectations associated with the other roles that she must play (interrole conflict)? Maybe it is a combination of the three. On the basis of Lynn's comment, what would you guess are the biggest problems confronting single parents, and especially single mothers, in this society? Do you see any solutions to these problems?

2. Going through a divorce can take a toll on a person's sexual identity. A formerly married woman or man may begin to have doubts about her or his ability not only to make love but even to talk with and relate to members of the opposite sex (Hetherington, Cox, and Cox, 1976). Lynn, for example, says that it took her "five years to begin to establish a healthy relationship with a man." Interestingly enough, most people who divorce remarry within a few years (Furstenberg, 1980). What does this statistic suggest about the dynamics of courtship the second time around?

12

Divorce and Shared Parenting

CAST OF CHARACTERS

Harry, Jane's ex-husband; author of case
Jane, Harry's ex-wife
Matt, Harry and Jane's son
Diane, Harry's friend

HARRY IS A THIRTY-SIX-YEAR-OLD MAN who has been divorced for five years and who is sharing custody of his eight-year-old son with his former wife. As more and more men become committed to fathering and as more and more women become committed to careers, we can expect to see an increasing number of divorced couples choosing joint custody over the arrangement currently favored by judges, namely placing children, almost as a matter of course, with their mothers.

The fact that this case study is about joint custody makes it not only unusual but also revealing of one of the most common tasks confronting divorced parents—the redefinition of their co-parental relationship (Ahrons, 1979). Much of the case is devoted to Harry's telling us how being a single father—if only half-time—has taught him what it means to be a parent. He says, for instance, that he has learned he must anticipate his son's needs and that he has come to appreciate Matt more since he has gotten to know him better.

It would seem, if we are to believe Harry, that he has undergone a transformation *from* being someone who was emotionally distant and who was satisfied simply to help his wife with the baby *to* being a nurturant parent who goes so far as to quit his job and become self-employed in order that he can participate more fully in raising his son. In effect, Harry has become *feminized,* which is to say that he has adopted many of the traits that in our society are considered feminine, and he is exhibiting what sociologists call *situational adjustment* (Becker, 1964), which is to say that Harry has turned into the kind of person the situation demands.

The fact that Harry has become more sensitive not only to what it means to be a parent but also to what it means to be a woman is especially significant in light of what he says about why he and his wife broke up. Looking back on the events leading up to the divorce, he concludes that his wife's involvement in the women's movement served as a catalyst in the destruction of their marriage because it encouraged her to label his activities as sexist and chauvinistic. As he puts it, he became Jane's enemy: "The Man." It would be interesting to know how Jane would react to Harry if she were to meet him today for the first time. Has he perhaps become the kind of person she had wanted him to be?

Like Lynn, whose story precedes this case study, Harry found that his relationship with his child was one of the key factors in helping him cope with his divorce. Having Matt around "made the past connect with the present, and it even made the future seem less uncertain and scary." Since divorce generally results in decreased contact between fathers and their children, it is understandable that, as chaotic as divorce is for women, men more often complain that the breakup of their marriages makes them feel aimless and rootless (Hetherington, Cox, and Cox, 1976).

Harry

Harry F. Keshet

WHEN MY PARENTS SPLIT UP I was sixteen, I remember having a sinking feeling in my stomach whenever I told my friends about the divorce. I felt ashamed and confused. Why couldn't the two people I loved stay together? I made a vow that if I married it would be forever and I would have a real family that stayed together.

My own marriage ended in divorce after eight years.

During those eight years my wife and I had a son. Now I realize that I put him through some of what I went through as a boy. But there is a difference, too. My wife and I settled on a shared custody arrangement, and I stayed close to my boy despite the divorce. Over the last five years I have experienced the joys and pains of part-time parenting. During the school year my son, Matt, spends half the week living in my home and half the week living with his mother. We divide Matt's vacations, holidays and summers between our two households.

This arrangement grew from my desire to be close with my son and from some painful memories of my past. When my parents separated, my father visited only occasionally. We weren't very close. I blamed him.

When I separated, I feared that I, too, would lose my son's love and affection. Suddenly, I understood how my dad must have felt.

Finding a lawyer that would work for this half-time arrangement wasn't easy, though many lawyers gave lip service to father involvement. When I laid out my plan I ended up having to defend myself against the lawyer whom I sought to represent me. Most lawyers felt that my ex-wife should care for Matt and I should visit occasionally and pay the bills. Even some friends talked against "too much involvement" on my part. "How can you move him each week?" "It's not natural." "He'll suffer!"

For me, shared parenting seemed quite simple and obvious. I wanted to love and care for Matt and be part of his life as he grew up. I wanted him to know me as a real father, not just as a picture on the wall or a Santa Claus Daddy. Being a father meant being with Matt as much as possible. I couldn't accept the idea that the failure of our marriage meant I had to stop being an active and loving parent.

Being Married, Being a Father

Jane and I had met in college and we got married after I graduated. I was twenty-three and Jane was twenty-one. These were the sixties with the civil rights and antiwar movements sweeping across the nation. We joined in and worked for the changes we believed in.

There seemed to be very good reasons why our marriage should have lasted. We had similar backgrounds and had even grown up within two miles of each other. We were preparing for similar careers and often helped each other with our studies or our work problems. For us, a household meant sharing the chores. I more often cooked, shopped and did the laundry, while Jane more often cleaned, decorated and did the dishes. We both went to graduate school, worked and shared our earnings.

In hindsight, it is easy to see both our differences and our failures at learning to resolve them. I was the more distant emotionally; frequently, I didn't know when something was upsetting me or how to say what I felt. I avoided confrontations, then exploded. I liked quiet home things. Jane was more direct, more verbal, and she was quick to argue. She lived an active social life, was a joiner and enjoyed a large network of friends.

Matt was born after three years of marriage. It just seemed right to have a child. I was near the end of my studies, Jane had her graduate degree and was tired of working. We had some money saved and we both wanted a true family with children. After three months of vitamin E, queen bee jelly and temperature checks, Matt was conceived. We were excited, expectant parents, reading infant care books and taking natural childbirth classes at the local Y.

Matt's delivery seemed endless. Twenty hours of breathing, panting, yelling and pushing. Matt was fantastic with his long, chubby body and unbelievably big shoulders. Helping him get born, seeing him and holding him at birth filled me with wonder. I loved him immediately.

At first I wasn't too involved with caring for Matt. I felt that there wasn't much I could really do for him. Jane was breast feeding. They seemed inseparable, intense and interdependent. For over a year, Jane was engrossed with being a "good mother": she stopped working, stopped attending meetings, stopped going out and stopped her political activities. In contrast to Jane, I was the busy helper. I helped by changing Matt, bathing him, watching him, walking him, soothing him, playing with him. My energies also went into finishing graduate studies.

Breaking Up

The women's movement played a big role in changing both our marriage and my fathering activities. I believe that the women's movement has been and remains the most profound force shaping women and the relationship between the sexes. But I must say also that it acted as a catalyst in the breakup of our marriage. As an active participant, Jane found the impetus for forcing needed changes in our family lives. But she also found license to see all of her troubles, past, present and future, as stemming from sexism and male chauvinism. Whatever I did, from making breakfast to making love, she hastily labelled "sexist." Suddenly I became Jane's enemy. I was "The Man."

Breaking up was a painful time. We both said and did hurtful things to each other. I often felt bitter and reacted with feigned indifference to Jane's independence. Jane turned a deaf ear to my feelings and concerns. We became stones, hard and distant, rarely touching, opening up only to release sudden fury as our love and respect for each other dimmed.

During this time, I shared caring for Matt reluctantly. I imagined myself as a "super dad," working and caring for my kid. Many of our women friends praised me, while the men thought I was strange. I now realize, though I often felt ambivalent about my decision to share parenting, I felt closer to Matt than I had before. I knew him better and dealt with his changing needs and moods. I loved him more as I knew him more. In contrast, Jane and I grew more distant: we spent less time as a family with Matt. As our marriage fell apart, our battles took me away from Jane and toward our son. Matt became more important to me than Jane was.

We made a last-ditch effort to save the marriage: a new job and a new city. It failed. Instead of giving us both new energy, the move only showed me that we had little to build on. Our fights increased and I lost hope.

I felt very guilty and concerned about Matt. How was he taking our yelling and upsets? How could I help him when I was feeling so bad? I felt powerless to give him the kind of family life I wanted him to have. Was I hurting him in the same way that my dad had hurt me when he left? It made me cry.

Matt was three when Jane and I split up. Although Jane agreed to a shared custody arrangement, I still had my fears and questions. What did it mean to live apart from him? Would he want to be with me? How do you make an apartment feel like home? How do you make a child understand that you love him? What if the court declares that I was a bad person and gave him to Jane? How could I make lawyers and friends understand and help me? Besides dealing with the endless questioning, I encountered an unwelcome new reality.

I felt helpless, depressed and powerless. Doing the simplest things in my apartment or at work took great effort. My life suddenly seemed meaningless. I was living with strangers and not being with my family. I couldn't predict what would happen in the future. Everything just didn't seem "real"! My world was crumbling, and so was I.

To my surprise, taking care of Matt for part of each week helped me to get myself together. A three-year-old needs to be fed, bathed, played with, cared for, hugged and put to bed. This called for the basics, and the basics were just what I needed. He needed me, and I needed to be needed by my own child. Just having him around made the past connect with the present, and it even made the future seem less uncertain and scary.

The hardest times each week were taking Matt back to Jane's on Sunday mornings and picking him up again after day care on Wednesdays. When I took him to Jane it always felt as if he were leaving my life completely—as if he were suddenly going off to college at the age of three!

The hour before we'd have to leave was the hardest. Matt would get impatient. He'd put on all his winter clothes, talk about his mother and ask me over and over, was it time to go yet? Other times he'd want to stay with me and he'd cry as I got him ready to go. It wasn't any easier for me. Taking him back to Jane just reminded me of my failures, my losses and powerlessness. As if that weren't enough, Jane always wanted to chat. Had I paid the day-care bill? Did I know where the other red sock was? Would I like to hear about her new job? One time Matt ran to my car as I was leaving. He leaned on the car door and wept, "I don't want you to go. Stay here with me and Mom." I went home and stayed in bed for two days.

Finding an easy way to connect with Matt after not being with him took time and experience. When I first picked him up after day care I wanted to hug him a lot, talk with him about his day and discuss my plans for our time together. Matt wouldn't respond. He'd just sit and look out the window. I slowly learned that I couldn't be so intense. We needed a warm-up time. We'd go to a park and play ball, or I would push him on the swings. We'd go home and play a game of pick-up-sticks for a while. We needed something to bring us together slowly without talking about ourselves. I began to learn how to be close, and we became closer than we'd ever been. It helped that many things remained the same—bedtime continued to be as special as before. I read stories and sang, and Matt joined in with laughter as he always had done.

I also learned to be more in tune with Matt's feelings, to try to find out what his needs were and help him feel better. I began to trust my intuitions. I remember a time when Matt was miserable. He couldn't tell me what it was, but I could tell that he missed his mother. One phone call later all the tears and sadness had become smiles.

As a single parent I had to learn to be organized, a talent that I never possessed before. Jane had been a superb manager. She could orchestrate clothes, day care and entertainment with ease. Parenting, I found, was a lot more complicated than just being with Matt. I had to learn to fit together work, homemaking, child care and all the unanticipated challenges of being a parent. I began to plan and think about what was needed in advance. Going to the beach is a lot more fun when you don't forget to bring the kid's bucket and shovels and a change of clothes.

Relating with My Ex-wife

When we first separated, Jane and I argued frequently. Jane would call me to ask for what seemed like husbandly tasks. Would I come over and fix the sink? What was my opinion about her job offer? I didn't want to be her husband. I refused, and we both felt upset. I felt even more upset refusing Jane's requests for help with Matt. Could I bring Matt back later on Sunday? Would I watch him on Tuesday after school instead of Wednesday? My saying no made Jane angry and her anger upset me. Slowly we learned to look elsewhere before asking each other for help.

We also used to argue about holiday schedules. I doggedly defended myself against what I felt at the time were Jane's unfair demands. Now I see that Jane wanted Matt as much as I wanted him and that my anger had covered my loneliness and loss. Our separation took away the family feeling of the holidays, and I missed it.

A significant event that changed our future negotiations occurred when Matt's day-care teacher reported that he had difficulties at school on the days when he changed households. Jane suggested that we change the schedule.

I refused. We discussed, argued, stopped talking to each other and got nowhere. Finally, we agreed to meet with a child guidance professional. Our counselor observed Matt at our homes, in school and in the clinic. She recommended that he stay with Jane on the school days and with me on weekends and one afternoon during the school week. I didn't like it, but I accepted it, and to my delight, Matt quickly felt happier in school and with each of us.

With guidance we could accept that we each had different styles of parenting, and we could understand Matt's needs more easily. Clearly Matt was happier and doing well in each of our households when there was peace and clarity between Jane and me.

My work and social life have been greatly influenced by child rearing. Like the great number of women and increasingly large number of men who combine careers with parenting on their own, I have often found the work doesn't support my parenting efforts. My bosses were indifferent to my home responsibilities and did little to meet my requests for flexible work hours. When Matt is with me I don't work at night or on weekends. To have the time flexibility I want and need, I became self-employed. Parenting responsibilities were not the only factor in this career decision, but they made me really think about what I wanted and valued.

When I was newly separated, social life meant Matt and me spending most of our time together. We explored museums, playgrounds, the zoo, and beaches, and we visited friends. Although I carefully separated my dating and my parenting, I often wanted adult company. Later, I would invite a friend to accompany us on our activities, and Matt usually felt OK about this—as long as I didn't pay too much attention to my friend.

The real problems started when I developed a serious relationship with Diane. Matt became intensely jealous. When Diane was visiting, he would demand my attention, act grumpy, interrupt and refuse to play alone. It's a wonder that my relationship with Diane survived that endless time of Matt's painful testing. He seemed to be making a last-ditch effort at keeping alive the hope that Jane and I would someday get back together. The night before Diane and I were to leave for our first vacation together, Matt cried his sorrow out, and this dream was over.

With hindsight, I more clearly understand why caring for Matt on my own has been so painful. Five years of experience has been a good education. When I first separated, I had been afraid so much of the time because what I was doing was new. There were no models, and there's a lot of unexplored territory between the family and the single father.

Parenting Matt means a lot more to me now than it did eight years ago. It means watching the clock so I can be on time to meet him after school, tracking down doctors, and taking him to the dentist, swimming class and the eye clinic. It means I have to remember his likes and dislikes when we shop for food and try to fit them in with my own sense of what's good to eat. I have to remember to get to teachers' conferences, to find time to talk with the parents of his friends, to force myself to read about child development and decide what's "normal." And as with any other parent, being a single father includes putting up with the Cub Scouts and the Little League, doing the laundry and housework, and making sure Matt washes his hands, takes a bath and cleans up his room. It means getting him to play in his room (not mine), finding out why he missed school, why he's mad at his friends or at his mother, or at me. And I have to listen to the endless details of movies and TV programs, stories, fights, and the current batch of eight-year-old jokes, and to learn how, tactfully, to stop his ceaseless chatter about all things interesting and not so interesting.

Sometimes when he is not with me I still miss Matt and worry about him, but the fear I used to have is gone. We have connections. Matt is eight and has his own world. He takes my hand only when he wants it. But my hand is still within reach. Shared custody works for us.

Study Questions

1. If getting married involves the social construction of a marital identity—a sense of we-ness between husband and wife (Berger and Kellner, 1964)—then getting divorced must entail the destruction (or

at least the reshaping) of that identity. How is the social destruction of a marital identity illustrated in this case study? Cite specific passages from the case to support your points.

2. Compare the social structure (i.e., the power structure and the role structure) of divorced families in which child custody is awarded to the mother with the social structure of divorced families in which child custody is shared. Which of the two patterns is more compatible with the social structure of the United States as a whole? Why?

13

Widowhood and Remarriage

CAST OF CHARACTERS

Ruth, a widow at forty-two; later married to David
Lou, Ruth's deceased husband
Ann, Ruth and Lou's teenage daughter
David, a widower who becomes Ruth's second husband

DEATH. Just seeing the word is enough to panic some people. We know that we cannot escape death's clutches, but at least we can hope that it is not close by. Every now and then, however, death robs us of someone we love, and we are reminded that every relationship is vulnerable, that even the strongest ties can be destroyed.

Ruth's story is that of a middle-aged woman whose husband dies—leaving her, as she puts it, without anything to look forward to. It is a poignant tale of grief, courage, and rebirth and of how people often can be thwarted in spite of their good intentions.

The case begins with Ruth's describing how both her mother and a woman Ruth knew as a child reacted to the deaths of their husbands and how the members of her family were devastated when a cousin who had been like a brother to Ruth was killed in an auto accident. Each death came without warning—a fact that, in Ruth's mind, contributed most to the anguish of those left behind because there was no time to prepare, no time to get used to the idea that a loved one would soon be gone forever.

We are then told, however, that the situation was different when Ruth's husband, Lou, died. One day Lou's uncle, a doctor, asks Ruth to come to his office; upon arriving, she is calmly informed that Lou is dying of cancer and that he will probably not live long. Though Lou ends up dying a lot sooner than expected, two months later, Ruth says that she still considers herself fortunate to have known in advance.

Ironically, despite Ruth's strongly held beliefs about the importance of preparing for death, she and Lou's uncle decide not to tell Lou that he is dying. When a patient is not made aware of her or his impending death, a *closed awareness context* is said to exist. This is in contrast to an *open awareness context* (patient knows that she or he is dying), a *suspicion awareness context* (patient suspects that she or he is dying), and a *mutual pretense context* (patient knows that death is imminent but is allowed to pretend otherwise) (Glaser and Strauss, 1965). It is not uncommon for a family to choose a closed awareness context when one of its members is about to die. A lot of people assume that it is better for all concerned if the truth is avoided. Often, however, keeping the secret results in more harm than good—both to the one dying and to the family.

The simple fact is that the four awareness contexts are essentially four different cultural configurations. The relationship between culture and interaction dictates that the awareness context under which a family operates will significantly affect that family's behavior during a death watch. Thus, the decision to adopt a closed awareness context has significant ramifications, some of which are illustrated in Ruth's case (Glaser and Strauss, 1965).

For example, in choosing a closed awareness context, Ruth denies Lou the opportunity to *prepare himself* for death. Had he known he was dying, he might have decided to quit his job, or go on a cruise, or keep a diary. More important from Ruth's vantage point is that she denies her husband the chance to *prepare her* for his departure. In other words, not telling Lou cuts Ruth off from the person perhaps best qualified to comfort her. Not telling Lou also transforms the time Ruth has left with her husband into a deception, so that she experiences "unbearable strain" during the last two months because all of her "energy [goes] into keeping Lou from knowing."

Interestingly enough, Lou's uncle knew for almost two years that Lou's cancer was fatal, and he chose to hide this fact from both Ruth and Lou. Yet, nowhere in the case is there any mention that Ruth is bitter about this, which suggests that she wanted to know but not necessarily immediately. Perhaps, by maintaining a closed awareness context, she felt that she was giving Lou what Lou's uncle had given her. Still, when the end was near, Ruth was told, whereas Lou was not.

There is, of course, no way of knowing whether Ruth and Lou would have been better (or worse) off had they operated under a different awareness context. Ruth does confess, however, that knowing beforehand that she would soon be a widow was not enough to keep her from the pain that she remembers her mother experiencing. Relying on Valium to put her to sleep and on close friends and relations to keep her awake, Ruth discovers that losing a husband to cancer is very difficult to accept. We can only guess whether her preparations for the widow role would have been more successful if Lou had been told and if she had been told earlier by Lou's uncle.

About a year after Lou's death, Ruth starts dating, and about a year after that she meets a man who asks her to marry him. The man's name is David, and he has two sons from a previous marriage; his wife had died the year before, also of cancer. Though Ruth thinks David is a "lovable, wonderful" person, she is afraid at first to get too involved because she is not sure that she is ready for marriage again. But she eventually accepts his proposal, and the focus of her life (and the case study) shifts to the problems associated with forming a new family.

A *step family* originally denoted a family in which at least one partner replaced another who had died; *step* is derived from an Old English word meaning to bereave (Scanzoni and Scanzoni, 1981). Thus, it was not always appropriate to use the term when speaking of divorce and remarriage. Over time, however, it became more and more common to refer to any family that included a widowed *or* divorced spouse as a stepfamily and to identify the members of such a family by the prefix *step-* (e.g., stepmother, stepdaughter). Today, family scholars often use *reconstituted family* or *blended family* when they are talking about this arrangement because *reconstituting* and *blending* accurately describe the goals of many families falling into this category (Duberman, 1975; Roosevelt and Lofas, 1977).

Needless to say, it is one thing to want to combine two families and quite another actually to do it. Consider, for example, the problems that Ruth and David encounter when they try to merge their families. Ruth's daughter vehemently objects to her mother's marriage and says so to Ruth and David. This makes Ruth feel that she has to choose between being a mother and being a wife and leaves David puzzled as to what his proper role should be vis-à-vis his future stepdaughter. Ruth and David also find that since they both have "a world of unshared experience" from their previous marriages, they must learn to live with periodic pangs of jealousy and slips of the tongue (e.g., using the dead spouse's name by mistake).

In sum, while the words *reconstituting* and *blending* conjure up images of people mixing together like juice or cake ingredients, the members of a reconstituted, or blended, family never lose their memories and hence never cut themselves off completely from their past—even when death, rather than divorce, is the reason behind the new alliance.

Ruth

Mary Ellen Reese

RUTH WAS FORTY-TWO when her husband, Lou, died. He was forty-four and had been ill for a long time, but it wasn't until two months before his death that Ruth found out he had cancer, and that he was dying. "His uncle was a doctor and had known all along, for almost two years, what Lou had and that it was incurable. But he didn't tell me until almost the end, and Lou never knew."

Ruth's voice is soft and has a definite Boston lilt to it, the accent all America came to recognize when John F. Kennedy was president. But Ruth isn't part of the Irish majority in the city. She is one of the small, old Jewish minority, and was brought up in the suburb of Roxbury.

We met at a restaurant in Boston ("You have to eat seafood when you're here," Ruth said), and I think even without all the information we exchanged about how to identify each other I would have recognized Ruth. On the telephone she had talked intensely and warmly, in pauses and bursts—as if, having decided what she was going to say, there was no point in wasting time saying it.

She wasn't much over five feet tall, moved quickly, and had short, curly, dark red hair. The combination of an orderly mind and strong feelings, of warmth and control, that came through in our telephone conversation seemed to me to be reflected in what she wore: a severely tailored brown tweed suit with a soft, bright orange blouse.

Ruth was as curious about me as I was about her; during our first meeting it was a toss-up as to which of us asked more questions. She wasn't weighing whether or not she wanted to help me; she made up her mind almost at once that she did. Her curiosity sprang from personal interest.

One of Ruth's most striking characteristics is her acceptance of people—including herself—and of circumstances. She wants to understand, to get things clear, and once she does she doesn't alter the reality she sees. She's comfortable with things and people as they are.

Ruth enjoyed a secure childhood surrounded by a large family that was closely knit, although her parents came from widely different backgrounds. Her father had emigrated to this country from Eastern Europe as a child; her mother's family had lived in or near Roxbury for several generations.

Her parents also had sharply dissimilar personalities. Her father was quiet and serious. Her mother, Ruth said, was "spoiled and strong; in the twenties, as a young woman, she was a flapper who bobbed her hair and smoked. But they had a good marriage. They argued a lot, but there was passionate love between them. It was embarrassing sometimes. When we were little my sister and I would see them kissing and it would embarrass us."

Ruth feels there was nothing extraordinary in the way she grew up. No emphasis was put on religion in her household, but the traditional Jewish holidays were observed. "I've always had a respect for all religions, but I'm not religious myself," she said. "That's one of the good things about my family, they tolerate the widest range of religious views."

She took for granted her extended family and the involvement of so many people in each other's lives. She went to the local public schools, was a good student, and had planned to go on to college, but her father died when she was eighteen.

"My mother went to pieces when he died and just couldn't seem to come back from it," Ruth said. "So I felt responsible for her, and for my sister. Also I was worried about money. So I stayed home and took a job as secretary-bookkeeper for a local building company." Although she did not get a college degree, Ruth began taking courses at various universities in Boston. She has studied everything from poetry, her first love, to archeology, and still takes courses when she can find the time.

An unusual number of deaths have touched Ruth's life, the first when she was nine. But it was the circumstances surrounding that death rather than the event itself that had the greatest impact on her.

"When I was a child I used to go and stay on a farm, and I loved it," she said. "The summer I was nine the farmer died while I was there. I liked him. He was quiet and I didn't spend all that much time with him, but he used to explain things to me, and took me on the tractor with him sometimes. That day, it was about four o'clock, his wife and I were taking the empty milk cans back to the milking shed. We were walking down the road when a woman rushed up to us and blurted out, 'Rob's dead.'

"His wife went white and I thought she was going to faint. I remember I was terribly shocked. What shocked me most was the way the woman just blurted it out: 'Rob's dead.' No one prepared his wife. That was awful. She should have been prepared."

That incident must have had a strong effect on Ruth because she returned repeatedly to the importance of being given some warning, of being prepared for what was to come.

It worried her again a few years later, when a cousin who had been like a brother to her was killed in an automobile accident. "I loved him. It was a devastating experience, for me and all the family. I came home one day to find a hysterical scene. My mother, his mother, his sister—it was terrible how it had come without warning."

When Ruth's father died she had known Lou about a year. "We hadn't really gone out together, we just lived in the same neighborhood and knew each other. Then he went into the army and we started writing letters. It got so we were writing every week." Then Lou came home on leave just at the time Ruth's father died.

"Lou was basically a shy person. He didn't like big groups and having to meet a lot of people he didn't know. But he came to the house every day after my father died, and sat with us. I was very impressed with that. I knew how hard it was for him. The house was always full of our family and our friends, and my mother was taking my father's death very hard. But obviously he wanted to come. I was upset, too, and I was glad he was there.

"We were already friends, but it was after this that we began to fall in love." Four years later they were married. Twenty years after that, Lou was dead. "What can I tell you about those twenty years?" Ruth said. "We were happy. We had a wonderful marriage."

You can't quantify love or crawl inside a relationship; when one of a pair of lovers is dead you can't see them together and feel what passes between them. You're left with the words you're given. The words Ruth gave me were those of Edna St. Vincent Millay. "We see life the same way," Ruth said. "I can't tell you how often I reach for her poems. So often they say what I feel and can't say."

Like this, about how she felt when Lou died:

We were so wholly one I had not thought
That we could die apart. I had not thought
That I could move—and you be stiff and still!
That I could speak—and you perforce be dumb!
I think our heart-strings were, like warp and woof

In some firm fabric, woven in and out;
Your golden filaments in fair design
Across my duller fibre. And today
The shining strip is rent; the exquisite
Fine pattern is destroyed; part of your heart
Aches in my breast; part of my heart lies chilled
In the damp earth with you. I have been torn
In two, and suffer for the rest of me.
What is my life to me? And what am I
To life—a ship whose star has guttered out?*

"The day Lou's uncle told me Lou was dying, that was terrible. He said he wanted to see me, so I went over to his office. He was calm telling me about it, and I was calm while I was with him. But when I left I don't know how I drove the car. Somehow I got home, but I don't know how.

"We had agreed not to tell Lou, and of course neither of us thought it would come so soon. We thought it would take much longer. I'm so grateful I knew about it ahead of time, but I don't think I could have taken it for more than those two months."

As soon as she knew Lou was dying Ruth began to play a role, hiding her real feelings from the person closest to her. The knowledge that her husband was sure to die soon would have been burden enough, but the added need for what Ruth called "protecting him from the truth" put an almost unbearable strain on her.

Those last two months all Ruth's energy went into keeping Lou from knowing he was dying. "Everything I did and said was focused on that. I tried to keep things normal. The way they'd always been before I found out." But *she* knew, and it turned her world inside-out. "I didn't tell our daughter, Ann, either. I thought we had a lot of time. Eight months, or a year. There wasn't any point in making her go through months of misery, too. And anyway, it would make it easier to keep the truth from Lou if Ann didn't know either."

There wasn't much relief for Ruth. The knowledge that Lou was going to die did battle with his reassuring presence beside her. When he was there, the cancer was all a bad dream. When he was away from her, it was unbearably real. "When he wasn't around I was in agony. I couldn't eat. I couldn't sit still. Then the minute he

---

*From *Collected Poems*, Harper & Row. Copyright © 1921, 1948 by Edna St. Vincent Millay. Reprinted with the permission of Edna St. Vincent Millay's literary executor.

walked in I was fine. As soon as he would leave, it would start again, the agony. I would worry if he was late coming home from the office. Then I'd catch myself and say, 'It would be better for him if he died now.' "

The last ten days Lou's condition deteriorated quickly. "I remember someone called me from his office to tell me how horrible he looked. Sometimes I still wonder about that call. Do you suppose he thought I didn't know how Lou looked? But I thought we still had a lot longer to go. We didn't. When it came, it came quickly.

"He woke me up early in the morning. It was in December. He was very ill. I was frightened and called an ambulance. When we got to the hospital and the doctor told me that he was dying, that this was really the end, all I cared about was that he not suffer. I didn't want him to be in pain. I kept saying to the doctor, 'Don't do anything. Don't do anything. I don't want him ever to open his eyes again.' "

Lou died within a few hours, and then her pain began.

Ruth said, "You know how in battle sometimes a soldier will be severely wounded and not even know it for hours? He'll go right on fighting. The shock has numbed him. That's how it was for me. I was in shock, but it didn't last long. Not long enough."

After the numbness wore off Ruth had to fight a compulsion just to crawl back into bed, to huddle under the covers. She may not have wanted to face the day, but from the beginning she made a conscious effort to face the fact that her husband was dead. "A voice in my head kept repeating, 'The dialogue is over. The dialogue is over.' An inner voice said it again and again and again. 'The dialogue is over. There is nothing on the other end.'

"I never tried *not* to think about it," Ruth said. "It was the only thing I cared about, so I talked about it all the time, too." It was the same whether she was with people or not. "When I was alone I kept going over the same scenes. How it was just before he died. Over and over. I just let the scenes run. How he looked in the hospital: He looked so peaceful, as if he was sleeping peacefully. Talking to the doctor and saying, 'Don't do anything. I don't want him ever to open his eyes again.' "

Unlike the other widows,* Ruth had a strongly supportive

---

*Editor's Note: The "other widows" are the other widows in Mary Ellen Reese's study.

group around her when her husband died. "When I woke up early the morning after Lou died, my cousin was in the room with me. I felt as if I was at the center of a web with support flowing in to me from all sides," she said. "I'm sure it helped, just as I'm sure the Valium helped, but I can't imagine having any worse pain and living through it."

She had lost weight in the weeks before her husband's death and now it was difficult for her to eat at all. "There was a physical pain, too. It was all around my heart." But the things she remembers most vividly are constantly being tired and her determination to handle her loss better than her mother had handled hers.

"When my father died my mother was completely broken. She just sank into sadness. She became A Widow. She clung to her memories and did things like wear his bathrobe around the house. From the moment he died I had a feeling of great responsibility being thrust on me; now *I* was responsible for my mother. And at the beginning I resented it. I was eighteen and I felt I was too young.

"When Lou died I thought of what had happened with my mother, and I was determined that my daughter wouldn't feel the same about me. That I would be different." Although Ruth thought her life now was a "wasteland," the way she had felt toward her mother gave her a handle on a future she couldn't yet see.

It's ironic that Ruth, who felt so strongly the importance of having some warning about what was to come, hadn't been able to prepare her daughter for her father's death. "I hadn't told Ann because I thought we had so much time and I wanted to spare her. As it worked out, I told her the morning Lou died—on the way to the hospital in the car behind the ambulance."

Ann, who was thirteen, knew her father was ill, of course, but it had gone on a long time; it was just the way things were. Lou's uncle had told him, and the whole family, that it was a blood condition which was being controlled. So when Ruth told Ann her father was dying there just wasn't time to take it in.

"Ann's behavior didn't change after Lou died. People were constantly coming in and out bringing food and so on, and Ann was just fine. She was helpful and concerned about me, but she didn't show any signs of being particularly upset." Until after the funeral.

The procession of cars wound its way over several miles of

roads to the cemetery, where everyone gathered around the open grave. The coffin was put on a cradle above it while the words were said. Then it was slowly lowered into the ground as members of the family threw handfuls of dirt onto it.

"That's when Ann suddenly screamed. Until then she hadn't really realized her father was dead, and when she did, when she saw him being lowered into the grave, she let out a deep scream of pain."

Ruth isn't a religious person, but she does feel the Shiv'ah, the visitation period of the Jewish religion, was valuable. It helped her get through the stress of the first dreadful days. With people around she wasn't allowed to slide too deeply into herself. She talked constantly about Lou and replayed the last hours of his life over and over, but other people kept making demands on her attention. "They involved me in the plans that had to be made, and things that had to be done. They kept consulting me about details."

It was after that, when the flurry of activity tapered off, that she found it was too difficult to get up in the morning. "I hated the thought that I was awake. Sometimes I'd take half a Valium and fall back into bed. I just wanted to stay there. Not face the day."

Ruth felt emotionally rocky for months. "I hadn't bought any Hanukkah gifts, and about two weeks after Lou's death I went shopping with my cousin. I felt it was important, life had to go on. But I was like someone recovering from an illness, a convalescent." She knows they must have gathered as usual for Hanukkah, but doesn't remember anything about the day.

A few days later a neighbor invited Ruth and Ann for Christmas dinner with her family. "I *do* remember that," Ruth said. "There was a big, bright tree and lots of laughing. Somebody gave me a drink, and everybody was very friendly. We all sat down at one big table, and then they brought in the food. Everyone went 'Oh!' and 'Ah!' over the turkey—and I knew I was going to be sick. I rushed from the table and just made it to the bathroom. Ann took me home and I crawled into bed."

From the moment Lou died Ruth had been enveloped by her family, the rites of the Jewish faith, and the haze of Valium. Within six or eight weeks, although she was still in pain, she began to feel as much suffocated as supported. "I felt I wanted to get away from my support troops, away from the house, and out of myself. But I wasn't ready to commit myself to anything. I didn't know what I wanted, really, but then it found me."

Three months after Lou died a friend called and said she was going into the hospital to have surgery. The problem was that she was working as a volunteer on a research project at the university hospital and needed a replacement. "I was still fairly shaky, and I wasn't sure if I should do it, but she assured me it was only for a few weeks and it was part-time. So I did it.

"It was really good for me. The work was interesting—making short résumés of case histories for a long-term mental health project—and I was surrounded by new people who didn't know anything about me. I found after I'd been working for a few weeks I'd forget to take my Valium while I was there. So I gradually reduced them until I only took one at bedtime. Then I gave them up altogether."

When her friend was well enough to take back her volunteer job, Ruth was asked to join the salaried staff on the project, working on the cases, not just writing them up. "That was a big boost for my spirits, but I had some reservations." She was concerned about whether she was physically and emotionally strong enough to take on a full-time job so soon after Lou's death, and she was worried about making the necessary commitment. Moving into the professional category meant accepting new responsibilities to the project, and to the people she worked with.

She worried, too, about how she would react to getting close to the lives of the subjects of the study. "I saw all kinds of people trapped in tough life situations. Abused wives with unwanted babies about to be born. Mentally ill people who weren't receiving treatment—people with terrible problems. But it helped put my own in perspective."

Another thing that helped was the people with whom she worked. One of her colleagues was a woman in her middle fifties who had never married. "She was something. She had a lot of verve, and she had this positive attitude about life as a single woman. She made me look at my situation in a new light."

Another co-worker was a man, a dozen years younger than she, in the middle of a divorce and a complicated love affair. "We were both having a hard time and we were able to help each other. It was an ego boost to be able to help him, and it helped me to think of myself as a mature single person, not a widow.

"When he talked to me or asked my advice, it was *me* he was listening to, not half of us—Lou and me. It made me feel valuable on my own." Ruth didn't feel he was looking at her as a stock character: A Mother-Figure, a Happily Married Older Woman, or a Re-

cent Widow. She felt he turned to her because of who she was regardless of her status, background, or other relationships.

"There was a sympathy between us. A rapport. I know I was
able to help him and that made me feel good. It eased the pain I
was living with. It helped to think of someone else."

Ruth said repeatedly that when Lou died the future was a
wasteland. "I wasn't planning for the future, that didn't matter.
There wasn't any 'future.' There was money for Ann's education
and that was all that mattered. For the first time in my life I wasn't
looking ahead."

Ruth hadn't considered remarriage. "I had started a career.
Ann and I were comfortable. It just hadn't occurred to me. I remember the first time anyone mentioned remarriage to me. It was
about nine months after Lou died. My cousin's husband said, 'I'll
bet two, three years from now you'll be married again.' I was so
surprised. I remember I was flattered by the implied compliment,
but I didn't take the idea seriously at all."

It wasn't that she would have felt disloyal to Lou if she married
again; in fact that kind of thinking was completely alien to Ruth's
unblinking realism. "I realized almost at once that nothing, not
one single thing I did or said or thought, could change what Lou
and I had.

"I couldn't hurt him any more than I could help him. We had
what we had. Nothing could add to it or take away from it. It was
over. I've never felt any guilt for anything I did or said or didn't do
before he died. Or about my life since he died. Lou was dead. It
was over."

The end of the first year was a milestone for Ruth. "It took a
year. You go through everything in a year—all the anniversaries,
everything. And you just can't kid yourself." By the end of that
year a lot of things had changed. Lou had always been the strong
one, and she had been dependent. Now Ruth saw she was really
getting through this unbelievable thing that had happened, and
her confidence grew.

"I went out alone with a man for the first time a year after Lou
died. It was more than a year in terms of time—it was a symbolic
year, too. Anyway, whether it was because now it was 'allowed' by
the Jewish religion or whether it was because I was ready, I did
start going out with men."

Although she felt "socially uneasy" at the beginning, her first
date was a success. "We went to a Chinese restaurant and talked

about him. But it was relaxed and pleasant, and he asked me out again. It made me realize I wanted to see men again." Friends and relatives introduced her to a number of men, and only once, at the urging of a widowed friend, did she take the initiative.

"We went to an over-thirties singles party. I was appalled because here were all these lonely men and women not talking to each other. I felt like a social worker. I went right to work getting people to talk to each other. After all, that's why they were there. It wasn't fun, I thought of it as work."

Essentially, Ruth didn't feel pressured to meet men. "Ann was seeing a boy I didn't care for, and there were times I missed the strong discipline of Lou's influence on her, but we had settled into a good life together. Although we had some problems, we had good times, too."

The first time Ruth thought remarriage was an attractive idea was on a Sunday when she went out with a widower who had two young children. "It was about a year and a half after Lou died. I went to this man's house and the whole situation was so much in need of someone. The children, and the state of things, touched me.

"Suddenly all I wanted to do was clean the house and bake cookies. I couldn't believe my own reaction. It was *wifely.* It wasn't him, the man. It was the situation. I wanted to stay there and put things in order, when all the time I'd thought I was happy with just a career. The thought kept returning to me afterwards, and I was surprised at myself. Here I thought I was happy in my job, happy as a career woman, but I couldn't deny what I had felt."

Ruth met David exactly two years after Lou died. His wife, who also had cancer, had died the year before. "I knew immediately that he was the kind of person who would fit into my life but I didn't feel that I was ready for remarriage, and I was sure he wasn't." With that thought she was admitting that on some level she was considering a possible life with David.

"That first evening I spent telling him to come out of himself. To think of himself as a free and single man, not as a widower with the responsibility for three boys. I was giving him positive infusions because I felt I was farther along the path than he was."

David became serious quickly, but she was full of self-doubt. "Here was this lovable, wonderful man and I worried about everything. I worried that he couldn't feel what he said he felt so soon. I worried because he was so different from Lou. I worried about our children. For months it was just up and down. I would go out to his house and cook dinner for him and the boys. But I would be depressed and think, This isn't my life. What am I doing in this strange kitchen? And on the way home I'd cry."

At the same time, she felt it was a marvelous opportunity. The anticipation was fully conscious now, and she shared her anxieties with David. "We were very open with each other from the beginning and talked about everything. David only wanted to marry a widow. He felt she wouldn't be embittered about men or marriage or life.

"He was unsure about the continuing relationships in a divorce situation. The children still have a father, there is a relationship between the ex-husband and the wife, between all the members of both families and the children, between everybody and the wife. With a widow it's different. There may be just as many people, but it's less fraught.

"I agreed with him. I think there's a better chance for happiness if both people are widowed. You're more sensitive to each other's feelings." They agreed about most things, and still Ruth looked into the future, saw the difficulties that might lie ahead, and worried.

"It's so much harder the second time. You don't know the first time what marriage entails. Love is all," Ruth said.

That wasn't her only problem, nor her most serious. When it was clear that Ruth and David were considering marriage, her daughter, Ann, grew more and more difficult. Ruth told me about an incident which not only was distressing in itself but was quite remarkable in that it almost exactly paralleled one which involved Paula and her daughter.*

It has to be more than a coincidence that out of four widows who told me their life stories, the two with teen-age daughters had almost identical experiences. It points to the likelihood that this happens with agonizing frequency. And if that's the case, widows and divorcees would do well to brace themselves, and consider how to handle it. This is what happened between Ruth and Ann.

"Ann was very upset with me. She kept saying what was the matter with the life we had, and asking why I wasn't happy the way we were. It was terribly difficult. Then one night when David came over she was very wrought-up. We were in the living room and she

---

*Editor's Note: Paula is another widow in Mary Ellen Reese's study.

suddenly turned on him and said, 'Do you think I'm coming to live in your house?'

" 'Well I hope you'll want to,' David said.

" 'Do you think you'll be able to tell me what to do?' Ann said, and went angrily across the room. Then she picked up a cigarette and lit it. She came back to where David was sitting, held the cigarette out in front of him, and said, 'You know I smoke marijuana? My mother knows. Do you think you're going to stop me?'

" 'Well,' David said, 'I hope you won't because of the boys.'

"Ann started pacing back and forth across the room. 'I'm not going to stop. *You* can't tell me what to do.'

"It went on a long time, and Ann was getting more and more worked up," Ruth told me. "Then all of a sudden Ann sort of crumpled on the couch. I went and sat next to her. I didn't say anything, but I just felt I had to give her a sign of support. David may have needed me, too, but she needed me first. That's always been the case."

Ruth gave Ann support, but she didn't give up David. "Later that night, after David had left, Ann wasn't sorry. She kept saying, 'Why do you want to do this? We're happy in the house together.' She was angry and miserable—it was terribly painful to me. I was sorry to be doing that to her, to be hurting her. But I couldn't let that stop me.

"Ann was on her way out of my life and I knew it. It was self-preservation. I had the rest of my life to deal with. I couldn't give this up just because Ann felt that way now. I knew it would pass."

David's reaction after the confrontation was that he felt he should have been stronger and not allowed himself to be talked to that way by a young girl. " 'Children are children, they're not adults,' he said."

"I felt he might have handled it differently," Ruth said. "He might have said, 'We don't have to talk about that now,' or something. But he didn't get angry, and he tried to understand."

Interestingly, his boys never opposed the marriage, and there were no confrontations with them.

Ruth said, "I knew it was right for me. But it felt like standing at the edge of a pool when the water's cold or the board's too high. You think, Now I'll do it—and you don't. It took every ounce of strength I had—and I knew I was strong—before I finally took the plunge."

Something a friend said helped. "I had been agonizing for

weeks," Ruth told me, "and a friend said, 'Don't torture yourself. There's always divorce.' That gave me courage. I asked myself, Why do I feel as if I'm going to prison for life? It helped. I realized it was not irrevocable, after all." Once she got hold of that thought, things were easier.

"The first year was hard, though. We moved into David's house and that was probably a mistake. It would have been better if we had started out in a new house, one that was new for both of us. Then there was Ann. She wouldn't live with us. It was her last year in high school, and she stayed at her old school and lived with my cousin. We were ten miles apart and I used to drive over to see her. I missed her terribly and we'd both end up in tears. But the next year she went away to college and always came home to us. She still does."

Now Ruth and Ann reminisce a lot. "We try not to talk about the old times in front of David and the boys. But when we're alone we really go to it. I have a very open relationship with Ann. In fact there are times I wish she wouldn't tell me so much. She tells me more than I want to know."

The past hasn't entirely let Ruth go. "I dream a lot. Even now I'll have a dream about Lou. He's always alive and coming back after having been away. I always say the same thing in one set of words or another: 'Oh, I didn't think you were coming back.' They aren't comforting dreams. They're disturbing and puzzling."

Ruth is aware that David, too, has ghosts. "David and I are careful about each other's feelings," Ruth says. "The worst thing is making a slip and calling the other by the first one's name—my calling him Lou. That hurts. But we both understand, and it's harder on the one who makes the slip than on the one who hears it."

There is some jealousy about the past. An awareness that each has a world of unshared experiences. But the jealous feeling is fleeting. "We are both new people," Ruth says, "but we recognize each other's occasional pain."

Things still trigger that pain. "No particular thing. It's like dropping a pebble in a pond, the ripples go out in wider and wider circles. I still get hit by a ripple."

Ruth's realism is reflected in her philosophy: "I never saw Lou's death as an important event in the great scheme of things. It was a terrible blight that happened to someone I loved very much. But I never felt his death had any cosmic meaning. It was devastating to me, but I always recognized it didn't change the large world. I don't mean I sat around and thought about it in those terms at the time. I was in far too much pain. But I think that philosophy helped me."

Ruth is uncomfortable with the unexpected and the unexplained. "Occasionally I find myself feeling down. Sick to my stomach, and anxious. Afraid that something is going to happen. It's like having a heavy load to carry. Then suddenly I realize, 'Something is coming up.' Some date, some anniversary." The anniversary of Lou's death was particularly painful.

When those incidents occur she doesn't try to avoid them. She is able to throw a bright, clear light into the corners of her mind without fear of what she may find there. "I'd rather bring a thing up for consideration and then think about it," Ruth said. "I don't try to hide things from myself. What's the point?"

Ruth views life, if not with optimism, without disappointment or disillusion. Her outlook is positive. She accepts the world as it is, and is satisfied with it.

"I'm basically comfortable with the way nature works," she says. "Life goes on, and that's important if you believe life matters. You must do what you can with a situation. No matter what the pain is, it's worth going on."

When I asked her how she thought she had changed, Ruth said, "I think I'm a less serious person now. The worst has happened, and it changed me. I'm a different person. I didn't know it, but I started changing as soon as Lou died. He had been my whole life, everything. Then I began to discover myself.

"I can't compare that marriage to this one or that life to this one. I'm no more the person I used to be than David is Lou. I can say I like myself. And I'm happy."

Study Questions

1. What is the difference, sociologically speaking, between getting divorced and becoming widowed?

2. A family's balance between personal identity and group identity (between I-ness and we-ness) can be a critical factor in determining how well people in the family cope with traumatic family changes (Olson, Sprenkle, and Russell, 1979). Where on a continuum from I-ness to we-ness would you place Ruth's family soon after Lou's death? Is it a

family that emphasizes independence among its members, or is it a family that emphasizes interdependence? How does the family's location on this continuum affect Ruth's ability to cope with the death of her husband?

3. About a year and half after Lou dies, Ruth goes out on a date with a widower who has two children. When she gets to his house, she begins to act "wifely" because of "the situation" ("Suddenly all I wanted to do was clean the house and bake cookies"). What is this situation and why does it have such an effect? Do you think Ruth's reaction is typical? How can Ruth's statement be placed within a sociocultural context?

4. Describe the family group created by Ruth's marriage to David. What can you say about the family's culture, interaction pattern, role and power structure, and identity?

14

Growing Old

CAST OF CHARACTERS

Debbie, college student; author of case
Mom (Betty), Debbie's mother; Gram's daughter
Dad (Ralph), Debbie's father
Gram, Debbie's grandmother
Jimmy, Debbie's brother
Eddie and Joe, Gram's sons
Marian, Joe's wife

THIS IS THE STORY of a young woman's visit to the Wilmot Nursing Home to see her grandmother, who has recently had a stroke. It is a case you may find personally relevant not only because the interactions between the woman's immediate family and her grandmother are all too common but also because the case was written as a term paper for a college-level creative writing course. Carol P. Saul, the author, based the paper on an actual incident and chose to write in the third person, using the name "Debbie" to refer to herself.

I should explain precisely what I mean when I say that the story is all too common. Contrary to what many believe, only a very small minority—about five percent—of people sixty-five years of age and over live in nursing homes and other congregate facilities. In other words, the vast majority of the elderly live in family situations, with spouses or with relatives (U.S. Bureau of the Census, 1976). Thus, when I say that the interactions in the case are typical, I am not talking about Gram's living arrangement. Rather, what is common is the family's collective ambivalence about whether they owe Gram any more than they are giving her at present (apparently one visit per week), and what is also common is the pattern of communication that has emerged both within the family and between the family and the grandmother.

There is, for instance, the guilt that Debbie and her parents experience about having decided to place Gram in the nursing home after her stroke. Underlying this guilt is their sense that perhaps they should be doing more; perhaps they are not meeting their obligations to Gram. What is implied is the idea that their family, like any other social group, is a contractual system, which is to say that the individuals in it are joined by a norm of reciprocity: you help me and I'll help you (Gouldner, 1960). Thus, the question of whether or not they are doing enough for Gram rests upon their calculating what Gram has done for them and comparing the contributions on both sides to determine whether the arrangement is equitable.

Of course, there are any number of ways to calculate the exchange of goods and services in a group, and each way may result in a different answer to the question of who owes whom. For example, how much credit should Gram get for having borne and raised Debbie's mother? Could it not be argued that, given all the sacrifices a mother makes for a child, the least a child can do for a mother is to care for her when she can no longer care for herself? On the other hand, should children be asked to sacrifice their freedom and lifestyle for their parents simply because their parents chose to have children?

These and other questions are being debated in many households, as well as in Congress, and the fact that they are being asked at all points to some very important changes taking place in this country. In modern industrial nations like the United States, it is not uncommon for matters of health and welfare to be shifted from the family to the public sector. Thus, we have Social Security and Medicare, programs created to insure that the elderly would not be totally dependent either on their savings or on their children for subsistence and medical attention (Hess and Waring, 1978). However, people are beginning to wonder whether the country can afford these programs, and there are bills being introduced in Congress that would effectively reduce benefits for older Americans. Who will pick up the slack is a matter of no small concern to those in their later years, especially since recent studies suggest that many people today feel less obligated to support their aging parents (Yankelovich, Skelly, and White, 1977).

Finally, there is the way the family communicates with Gram. If you did not know how old Gram is, you would think that she is a baby. Debbie's parents hold a conversation with Debbie *about* Gram, yet Gram herself is in the room, and the few times that Debbie's mother addresses Gram, she resorts to baby talk.

When people communicate with an elderly woman or man, it is not uncommon for them to assume that the elder person cannot understand all the nuances of what is being said. This is especially true if, as is the case with Gram, the elder individual has suffered a stroke or has some other disability. But attributing incompetence to another may have the effect of *disconfirming* that person, that is, communicating that she or he is not there or does not exist (Watzlawick, Beavin, and Jackson, 1967). This is one of the most devastating experiences that a person can be subjected to and is an example of psychosocial violence (Laing, 1967). Gram is thus being abused—in a nonphysical sense—by her own family.

If anything makes Gram's plight personally meaningful, it is the fact that being old is one club that all of us can look forward to joining, provided we live long enough. So ask yourself as you read the case, how would *you* feel if you were Gram?

Gram

Carol P. Saul

IT WAS THE FIRST SUNDAY of my vacation. My mother and I were relaxing over a second cup of coffee chatting comfortably the way we
used to before I went away to college. My mother set her coffee
cup down and said, "Debbie, Dad and I are going to see Gram today." I didn't look up, and she hesitated. "I realize you don't get a
chance to come home very often and I hate to ask anything of you
when you're here, but—will you come with us?"

What she meant was that I had to go. After all, I was Gram's favorite granddaughter, and I hadn't seen her in more than six
months, ever since her stroke. Of course I loved Gram, and visiting
her had always been more of a pleasure than an obligation, but the
truth was that I was afraid to see her changed. Mom had writtten
me how Gram had fallen down the stairs when she had the stroke
and how her children had decided that letting her live alone was
too risky. While she was recovering in the hospital, Mom and my
uncles sold the big old house that Gram had maintained so long
for herself and reserved a place for her in one of the better, or so
they had been assured, nursing homes. Mom took her to stay at
our house for a while after the hospital had discharged her, and
then Gram had gone to live at the Home.

"Debbie?" My mother was waiting for an answer.

"Oh, I'll go," I said and, afraid that my answer had sounded too
grudging, I added hastily, "It's not that I don't want to see Gram or
anything, it's just that I—that I—."

"I know, Deb," my mother said gently, and a look of pain came
into her soft brown eyes. "But I know she'd love to see you again.
Your uncles don't even want to make the effort to visit." Her voice
was bitter. "Last week I told her that Eddie and Joe would be up to
see her soon, and she looked at me with that new blank expression
and asked me who Joe and Eddie were." She pursed her lips. "I
keep telling her every week that she has two sons, but they never
come to see her. It's no wonder she forgets." She stared past me
out the kitchen window. "She's gotten so old, so fast."

That chilled me. I was used to thinking about Gram as a strong, active, fiercely independent woman, with white hair combed neatly back into a nape bun, moving briskly about her house in a homemade apron. Gram cooked and baked and put up preserves from the berries in her garden. She let no one help her with the housework, yet the house always looked as if she had just gone over it with her ancient carpet sweeper, no matter when we popped in for a visit. And she still had time to fix huge family dinners for as many as could squeeze into her dining room.

"Has she changed much, Mom?" I asked.

"Oh, Deb!" she exclaimed softly. "If you saw her now, you'd never guess how tall and straight she used to be. She never goes for walks anymore because there's no one at the Home to take her. And she's not getting the care that she should, or anything." She shook her head. "And for what we're paying, too," she added.

"But it's Gram's money, isn't it?"

"Oh, sure, it's Gram's money." She pushed her cup and saucer away. "It's two lifetimes' worth of work, and at this rate it will be gone in five years. And she's not getting any pleasure out of it at all—remember how she and Grampa were going to use it to grow grapefruits?"

I nodded. The whole family always joked about the Florida citrus farm that Gram and Gramps would buy once they retired.

I reached across the table for Mom's cup and saucer and brought them to the sink. Above the rush of hot water I asked carefully, "Then why didn't you or Uncle Ed or Uncle Joe take Gram to live with you?"

There was a silence and my mother sighed. "It was the first thing we talked about, Deb. It just wouldn't work out. Ed has no room for her, you know that, with his five kids, and both Joe and Marian have their jobs. And the only time we have extra room is when you're at school. Besides I'd have to stay home with Gram all day. Really, Deb, it's much better for everyone concerned to have Gram in the Home." She got up decisively from the table and glanced at the new wall clock. "Daddy and Jimmy will be back soon. We'll have lunch and clean up, and we ought to be ready to leave about two." She looked at me and her face softened. "Try not to be too shocked, Deb," she said. "Just be prepared."

My father and Jimmy came home shortly afterward. They carried on most of the conversation over lunch; I said little and ate less. When we had finished, my mother asked Jimmy if he was coming with us to see Gram. "Aw," he mumbled and wriggled in his chair. "You don't have to if you don't want to, son," Dad told him gently and with relief Jimmy said, "Okay, then I won't go," and ran off to his room. My parents exchanged glances.

"He goes more than any other grandchild," my father apologized.

"I know, Daddy," I said irritably. "I already told Mom I'd go."

"It's just that it's very hard for him," he began.

"I know, Daddy, I know!" I interrupted a little angrily. I had heard it once; I was prepared now. They were building it up and at the same time trying to cushion me. It was almost as if they were trying to tell me about death for the first time, but they were afraid I'd cry. "Don't make such a big thing out of it, will you?" I got up from the table and started gathering up the plates. "It's all right, Deb," my mother said, half-rising from her chair. "I'll do the dishes."

"Sit down," I told her brusquely. "I'll do them." I threw the silver into the sink and turned the water on full force. Mom and Dad looked at each other and left the kitchen.

On the way to the Home, my parents talked quietly and I huddled in the back seat staring out the window at the bare trees. Gram's house had been surrounded by tall oaks, trees that Grampa had planted himself when they first bought the house. And there had been two gardens. A flower garden in front and a kitchen garden—Gram's pride and joy—in the back. Who, I thought glumly, owned the house now? They wouldn't bother with all the wonderful growing things; the plants and cuttings would probably wither and die from neglect.

My father pulled into a half-empty parking lot beside the sprawling red brick building. A huge plate glass window reflected the neatly clipped lawn, brown and dead now. "Wilmot Nursing Home" proclaimed a big black and gold sign. By now the pale winter sun had warmed the air to an exhilarating briskness, but no one was sitting in the lawnchairs or walking on the cement pathway to take advantage of the break in the weather. I nudged my father.

"It's so nice out," I said. "Why don't they bring the stronger ones outside?"

My father shook his head. "It's probably too difficult to move them, Deb. And anyway, they don't have enough attendants to take care of the patients inside." We had unconsciously lowered our voices, as if we were entering a hospital or a funeral home or some other place where old age and death continually hover.

Dad held open the glass doors for us. I peered down the wide corridor, feeling uncomfortable. My father steered me forward and to the right. "Look, Deb, the recreation room."

The smell of the place was so strong that I stepped back, trying to fight it off. It was a sickish sweetish conglomeration of aging flesh, urine, pine disinfectant, and the lingering perfume of visitors who had left long ago. I wanted to run. I longed for the fresh air outside and gripped my father's arm. "The smell," I whispered fiercely. He nodded, his nostrils drawn up. "I know. We've been coming here for months, and I still feel sick whenever that stink hits me."

We stood for a moment looking at the recreation room. Glass framed prints dotted the pale walls at precise intervals and, beneath them, the dull-faced residents sat in folding chairs. A few of them chatted together. Several of them looked up hungrily at us, and one old lady in a wheelchair beckoned to me with a clawlike hand. Two bored attendants exchanged laconic comments, and a nurse in a starched white cap wiped the face of a sweating, palsied old man. A few old people had visitors and, jealously guarding them in inescapable clusters of chairs, they leaned forward to grab onto every word. The visitors looked guilty and uncomfortable and miserably self-conscious. One chubby little boy was balanced on his grandma's lap, and while the wrinkled old lady talked fitfully with his parents, he stared with wideyed horror and fascination at the old people who watched him with envy and wonder.

My mother turned to us. "She's not here, obviously," she announced. "She's probably up in her room, as usual." We hurried down the corridor. A childlike wail cut through the air and I started. "What's that?" My father shrugged. "Some old man, probably, who's sick or lonely," he said. "You hear it once in a while."

I shuddered. The smell of disinfectant was getting stronger. Several old people labored down the corridor, grasping the long wooden rail along the wall. One man in a red bathrobe was shuffling along and muttering to himself, but passing nurses and attendants acted as if he weren't there.

As we reached the main desk, a middle-aged nurse looked up sharply from her record book and amended her glance with a thin-lipped smile. "Hello there," she said to my mother. "Come to see your ma?" My mother nodded. "She's doing fine," the nurse added.

"Oh, I'm glad to hear it," Mom smiled back.

Dad pressed the elevator button.

"Does she know Gram?" I asked, surprised.

"Don't be silly," my mother muttered. The elevator doors opened. "She doesn't know my mother from Adam. If Gram were dying she'd still say she's 'doing fine.' She tells everybody the same thing." The elevator swooped gently up to the second floor. "It's Room 220, Deb. Don't be shocked."

Doors were open along the beige corridor and I couldn't resist glancing into the rooms. The first room was darkened, and I caught a glimpse of a frail old woman lying fully clothed on her bed, head tilted toward the ceiling. Lying motionless, she could have been dead. In the next room a nurse was scolding a weeping old man while an orderly mopped at a puddle in front of the bed. I turned my head quickly to the other side of the corridor. In Room 216, two middle-aged ladies chattered at a thin old man in a wheelchair. There were two old ladies in Room 218; one was lying in bed babbling quietly, the other stared at the pink and red tile on the floor.

At the door of Room 220, we hesitated. My mother arranged her face in a bright cheery smile, grasped the doorknob and breezed in. "Hello, Mom!" she sang. My father followed her but I hung back, suddenly apprehensive. I wanted to whisper that I'd wait for them in the car, but Dad turned to me and said, "C'mon, Debbie," Then Mom said gaily to Gram. "Mom, Debbie came to see you today. Look, here she is," and I had no choice but to enter the room.

It was small, pale green and dim, even with the yellow and green curtains pushed all the way to the sides of the window. Flanking two neatly made beds with dark green institutional covers were two formica topped night tables. My father was standing by the closet door, and Mom was seated on the bed nearest the window, next to a small dark figure.

"Hi, Gram," I said softly.

Gram turned to me slowly and my stomach contracted. Her face was thin and pinched and covered with wrinkles. Her eyes, always bright and alert, were dulled. She looked wasted, shrunken. Her hands lay motionless in her lap, as neatly as if someone had arranged them. She stared at me and I stood in the doorway, unable to move.

"That's Debbie, Mom, my big girl," my mother said. A bright artificial smile seemed to paralyze the lower half of her face. "She's been away at school, you know. She's almost nineteen now. Hasn't she grown up?"

My father reached out and touched my stiff shoulder. "Go give Gram a kiss, Debbie," he prompted. I moved toward Gram and planted a kiss on her withered cheek. Around her hung an unfamiliar papery dry smell, and wisps of yellowed hair strayed from her bun. She kept staring at me. There was no recognition in her eyes.

"You know Debbie, Mom," my mother urged. She motioned for me to sit on the other side of Gram and leaned across her to tell me, "Well, at least she knows you're one of hers. Just talk nicely to her and smile and kiss her, and she'll be satisfied. We really can't expect anything more." I was shocked. How could she discuss Gram so casually when Gram was sitting right between us?

My father mistook my shocked silence for shyness. "Go on, Deb, talk to her," he directed. "Ask her how she is. Tell her about school, anything."

"Gram," I began. She turned to me politely.

An attendant wheeled a cart into the room. It was loaded with paper plates of cookies and dozens of tiny cups. "Juice or milk?" she droned.

"We'll have milk, I think. All right, Mom?" my mother asked. Gram nodded, and the attendant handed Gram a paper cup and a cookie and wheeled the cart out again. Gram held the cup in her trembling hands—they were as clawlike as those of the old lady downstairs—and sipped the milk. "Do they serve milk and cookies every day?" I asked.

My mother laughed shortly. "No dear," she said. "Only on Sundays, to impress the visitors." She patted Gram's hand and leaned over to open the drawer of Gram's night table. "Well, Mom," she said brightly, "and where did you put your dirty things this week? Let's see—ah yes, here's a bunch of them, right in with the clean ones. You know, dear," she said, extracting a few pairs of soiled pink cotton bloomers from the drawer and dropping them on the floor, "I wish you wouldn't mix the dirty things with the clean ones." An unmistakable odor came from the discarded clothes and I bit my lip. Gram used to be so meticulous that she would wash her hands even before she gardened.

"Well, that's the last of it, I think," Mom said, tossing a soiled lacy slip onto the pile. "And next week I'll bring them back to you, Mom, all nice and fresh." Gram was watching carefully as Mom gathered the dirty clothes into a plastic laundry bag. "Look how she's watching me, Debbie," my mother said. "They steal things left and right here. Look at her. She wants to make sure I'm not a crook." Gram gazed at my mother as if she hadn't heard what Mom had just said. I wanted to grab her and squeeze her tight until she protested, like she used to do, that I'd break her bones if I kept her in such a bear hug. But only her polite smile, I was sure, would answer me. I was a stranger to her, and my Gram was a stranger to me.

"Ralph," my mother was saying softly to my father. "Would you mind . . .?" He nodded and slipped out of the room, closing the door behind him. "I just want to change her," Mom explained to me. She bent and sniffed Gram's armpits. I winced; Gram didn't. "Mmm," my mother said and began to unbutton Gram's navy blue dress. "I think you should change your clothes a little more often, Mom." I lowered my eyes, too embarrassed to watch. I started to move off the bed and Mom said, "Oh, Deb, that's all right. It's just that Gram doesn't like being undressed if there is a man in the room. That's all."

I ventured, "Don't the nurses take care of Gram's clothes and stuff?"

"Don't be silly," she grunted. She pulled a pink lace slip over Gram's head. As she bent to unhook Gram's corset she said. "These attendants don't do anything for anyone unless you tip them very well, which I for one—here, Mom, here's a fresh bra for you—refuse to do. Aside from seeing that most of the patients get a bath once a week or so, and they skip the ones that give them any trouble, they just pass the cookies and juice and mop the floor and look busy when the relatives come. Mom, pick up your arms, dear, and let me get this slip over your head. And if you want any kind of care at all, Deb," she continued, "you have to hire a private nurse. Get me one of those dark dresses from the right-hand side of the closet, will you? That's fine, thanks." She slipped the dress over Gram's head, stood up and beamed at Gram. "There now, you're all fresh and clean. Isn't that better?" Gram nodded mechanically and smiled at no one in particular. "See, Deb, she understands, but she doesn't respond."

Then give her the courtesy, I wanted to shout, of not talking right through her. You treat her like a baby, that's bad enough, but then you act as if she's not even here. Mom patted my hand, unaware of my bursting emotions and said, "Talk to her, Debbie. I want to find the head nurse." She stood up and put her hands lightly on Gram's shoulders. "Mom, Deb wants to tell you about school. It's very interesting and she has a lot to talk to you about. I won't be gone long." She walked out of the room, and Gram and I were left alone.

We faced each other. I smiled at Gram experimentally and her polite smile popped back at me. "I like college," I blurted.

Gram nodded. "What a big girl you are," she said in the tone she used when I was seven and eight.

I swallowed. "It's very far away, you know. It's about 400 miles away." She was still nodding. "I live in a dormitory with lots of other girls."

"Momma lets you go so far away from home."

I was stymied. "Well, I go to school there. Mom knows. It's all right."

"Oh." She was nodding again, uncomprehendingly. Her eyes were mild, passive.

"I have tons of work," I plunged on, "especially in chem—chemistry, I mean. And I'm taking French, too. Next term I'll be taking lit—I mean, a literature course." I stopped. She was still watching me, but her eyes were cloudy again. "What a big girl you are."

I started again, slowly. She kept her eyes on me. I talked on about my roommate and professors and the boys I was dating. She never stopped me. She just sat, her wrinkled hands clasped in her lap, nodding and smiling until my throat became so constricted I stammered to a halt.

"And I missed you, Gram," I said. I threw my arms around her and hugged her fiercely. Slowly her hands came up from her lap and her arms went around me.

I didn't hear my parents come in until my father cleared his throat. I turned then and saw them and the spare-looking head nurse with them. I dropped my arms almost guiltily and took one of Gram's dry hands in mine. My mother turned to the nurse and pointed to the laundry bag leaning against the closet.

"You see," she said to the starched nurse, "I just found all these dirty things in her night table and I just took this dress off her back a minute ago. I wish that someone would make sure that she's changed at least every three days. She's really a very clean woman," she said, looking directly into the woman's small brown eyes, "and I know she doesn't enjoy being filthy. Could you see to it, please?"

The nurse cast a sour glance at the laundry and nodded. "I'll take care of it, ma'am. It's a shame isn't it, that they get so dirty when they get old, after they have been clean all their lives?" She leaned toward Gram. "Now, Mrs. Reed, you be good," she admonished, and turning on her white shoes, walked out the door. Dad said to me. "Mom asks someone every week to see that Gram is kept clean, and nothing ever happens. And nothing will happen, Betty," he turned to my mother, "until you face the facts and start tipping."

My mother picked up the laundry bag. "Oh, Ralph," she said tiredly, "leave me alone. If we had to start tipping everybody for every little thing we'd be out of money in no time flat. And I'll bet you she'd still be wearing dirty underwear." My father didn't answer. I moved closer to Gram and put my other arm around her as if to protect her—from what, I wasn't sure.

My father looked at his watch. "It's getting late," he reminded my mother. "I know," she said. She leaned over Gram and kissed her on the forehead. "Mom, we have to leave now," she said. "I'll be here next week with your clean laundry and some more things and," she lowered her voice, "don't let them take anything away from you."

She glanced at me. "Go on, Deb," she said, "Kiss Gram goodbye."

I threw my arms around Gram again and felt her hug me in return. I rested my cheek against hers for a minute, aware that the fresh smell of the clean clothes contrasted with the faint papery smell of her skin, and for a minute the old love came swooping back to me. Then Mom tapped me on the shoulder and said, "Debbie," in a voice choked with the precarious presence of tears, and I got up. "Be good, Mom," my mother said. Dad came over to the bed and when he bent down to kiss her, she grabbed his coatsleeve and said quickly, "I'll walk you to the door."

Gram took small, unsure steps, as if she had forgotten how to walk and I remembered how she used to stride along the street with me beside her scrabbling vainly to keep up. Now she leaned as heavily on me as she did on my father. When we reached the elevator she was almost out of breath, but she managed to give us each a squeeze. "Thank you for coming," she said, as if we had been visiting her in her own house.

"We'll be back next week," my mother promised, and then she looked at me. I nodded. "And Debbie will come too," she added. "Oh look, the elevator is here already. Goodbye, Mom," she called. As the doors closed, Gram raised her hand and tentatively waved goodbye.

We hurried past the big recreation room. I peeped in again. The visitors had departed; the little blond cherub was gone, too. Only the old people and the attendants were left. Somebody had switched on the television, but nobody was watching. We stepped out into the cold.

With typical winter perfidy, the sun had disappeared behind a bank of mottled grey clouds and the air was knife sharp. I inhaled deeply, relieved that the stench of the Home was out of my nostrils, and ran ahead to the car. I had a peculiar sense of freedom, of being let out of a cage, and I felt painfully sorry for all the poor old people whom we had left behind.

In the car, my mother turned to me. The brittle smile was gone from her face and she looked exhausted. "Well, Deb, what did you think?" I looked out at the street. "It's awful," I said flatly. "It's horrible and ugly and smelly and I can't understand," my voice rose, "how you can let Gram be so miserable!" My mother turned her head slightly so I couldn't look directly into her eyes. My father glanced away from the icy street long enough to give Mom a look of compassion.

"We know, Deb," he said mildly. "We know. But there's really nothing else to do."

"Did you see all those other people?" I persisted. I was speaking to the back of my mother's head now. "They're sick and crippled and much worse off than Gram. Didn't she manage all the way to the elevator?" I hesitated. They were going to tell me that I didn't understand. But I couldn't bear to think of Gram wasting her life away in that overpriced prison, and I was horrified to think that my parents could shrug off so lightly the responsibility of caring for Gram. "I think we should take Gram to live with us."

A silence enveloped us. My mother sighed. "Darling," she said patiently, "I've explained to you why it's impossible. We can't give her the care she's getting at—."

I interrupted her. "Oh come on, Mom! Don't tell me Gram's well off in that awful place."

"Debbie," my father said, "do you know what it would be like if we took Gram in? We'd all be nervous no matter how hard we'd try. We couldn't avoid the friction, Deb, can't you see?" He pulled into the driveway and the discussion was over.

My mother said something to me as we climbed the backstairs but I did not answer. I was too busy thinking about Gram's plight; it seemed incredibly selfish of the rest of the family to ignore it. I stumbled into my room, slammed the door, and flopped down on my bed. "It's so unfair," I said to myself. I thought of everything I had seen today. I couldn't let my Gram go through that. I would have to make my parents see that no sacrifice would be too great to have Gram in the house.

I lay back on the bed, planning. Oh, it would be hard at first, but we could manage. Mom was exaggerating. If she wanted to go shopping or something she could ask the neighbors to look in on Gram. They wouldn't mind. And then, of course, I'd be able to keep Gram company during the summer. I'd be willing to stay home with her; we could even go to the beach together. Gram and Grampa used to take Jimmy and me. The more immediate problem was arranging living space for Gram.

I slipped off the bed and surveyed my room. It might be a little crowded, but we could squeeze another bed between my bed and the closet. There would be enough closet space for Gram if I pushed my clothes over, and I could empty one of my drawers for her. She wouldn't need more; she always said clothes weren't important to her, that what mattered was her family. I felt immeasurably guilty about the fact that I had paid so little attention to what had happened.

"Maybe I should put my bed next to the closet," I mused. When I came home late after a date I wouldn't want to wake Gram by climbing all over the room to put my things away. And I realized, I would have to keep my room neater than it usually was. Disorder had always bothered Gram. My mind suddenly flashed back to the scene this afternoon of Mom foraging through Gram's night table to find her dirty laundry. It was so unbelievable; my Gram, who was always so meticulous.

What if she would do the same thing here? What if she couldn't remember which drawer was hers and hid her soiled things in one of my drawers? I shook my head to rid myself of the unpleasant thought. The only thing to do would be to mark off Gram's drawer so she would know which was hers and leave my things alone.

But she forgets easily now, I reminded myself. What could prevent her from forgetting which drawer belongs to her? Especially when she's tired and she wants to go to bed at night. . . .

Night. One of my favorite habits was to stay up far into the night, reading, listening to my little FM, writing poetry. And I liked to sleep late. I wouldn't be able to do any of that. Gram had always practiced early-to-bed-early-to-rise, and I'd be sure to disturb her if I wanted to stay up until three or four in the morning. Even if I didn't disturb her sleep I'd feel restricted by another person's presence, and what I loved about midnight and hours beyond was the serenity and freedom I felt then. Gram's puttering around in the early morning would wake me for sure, and I hated to be wakened before I wanted to get up. At least in the Home no one would disturb her sleep.

I slid the closet door shut. The Home was clean, they kept it very neat. Of course the smell was another matter, but then you could get used to almost anything. Hadn't I been able to adjust to the awful stink of the chem lab at school? Gram was all right at the Home. She had privacy, food, medical care if she needed it, and other old people near her if she wanted their company, which was more than we could offer her. It would be wrong to uproot her again and make her adjust to another new environment. Really, if the family would only visit her more, she would have everything.

I looked over my room once more and walked out, shutting the door behind me. "Mom," I would tell my mother when I got to the kitchen, "you really should speak to Uncle Joe and Uncle Ed about visiting Gram more often. They ought to feel some responsibility toward her, too. It's not right, not right at all."

Study Questions

1. You have probably heard the phrase "seeing is believing," which means that you are more inclined to believe something if you are a witness to it than if you merely hear about it secondhand. It is also true that "believing is seeing"; beliefs influence perceptions. How does this case study demonstrate that believing is seeing? Specifically, how do the family's beliefs about what it means to be old influence (a) the family's perception of Gram and (b) the family's perception of alternatives to nursing home care?

2. Any social interaction in which an individual is reduced in status or prestige is called a *status degradation ceremony* (Garfinkel, 1956). During such ceremonies, the individual is singled out and stigmatized (Goffman, 1963). Can we view Gram's interactions with the nursing home staff and with her family as a series of status degradation ceremonies? Why is Gram stigmatized?

3. After returning from visiting her grandmother, Debbie challenges her parents to take Gram out of the nursing home and care for her in their house. Her father replies: "Do you know what it would be like if we took Gram in? We'd all be nervous no matter how hard we'd try.

We couldn't avoid the friction." Why would there necessarily be friction in this family group if Gram moved in? While pondering the consequences of her suggestion, Debbie begins to see a number of problems that she had not thought of before. How would you sociologically analyze Debbie's second thoughts? Which sociological component (culture, interaction, structure, or identity) do you find the most useful in your analysis?

References

Ahrons, C. (1979) The binuclear family. *Alternative Lifestyles* 2(November):499–515.

Allen, C., and M. A. Straus (1980) Resources, power, and husband–wife violence. Pp. 188–208 in M. A. Straus and G. T. Hotaling (eds.), *The Social Causes of Husband–Wife Violence.* Minneapolis: University of Minnesota Press.

Allen, W. R. (1978) The search for applicable theories of black family life. *Journal of Marriage and the Family* 40(February):117–129.

Aries, P. (1962) *Centuries of Childhood: A Social History of Family Life.* New York: Knopf.

Aschenbrenner, J. (1978) Continuities and variations in black family structure. Pp. 181–200 in D. B. Shimkin, E. M. Shimkin, and D. A. Frate (eds.), *The Extended Family in Black Societies.* The Hague: Mouton.

Becker, H. (1963) *Outsiders: Studies in the Sociology of Deviance.* New York: Free Press.

———(1964) Personal change in adult life. *Sociometry* 27(March):40–53.

Bengston, V. L., and J. A. Kuypers (1971) Generational difference and the developmental stake. *Aging and Human Development* 2(November):249–260.

Berger, P., and H. Kellner (1964) Marriage and the construction of reality. *Diogenes* 46(summer):1–25.

———, and T. Luckmann (1966) *The Social Construction of Reality: A Treatise in the Sociology of Knowledge.* New York: Doubleday Anchor.

Bernard, J. (1972) *The Future of Marriage.* New York: World.

———, H. E. Buchanan, and W. M. Smith (1958) *Dating, Mating, and Marriage: A Documentary-Case Approach.* Cleveland: Howard Allen.

Bielby, W. T. (1980) More inequality: Christopher Jencks on the paths to success. *Contemporary Sociology* 9(November): 754–758.

Billingsley, A. (1968) *Black Families in White America.* Englewood Cliffs: Prentice-Hall.

Blau, P. (1964) *Exchange and Power in Social Life.* New York: Wiley.

Boss, P. (1980) Normative family stress: family boundary change across the life-span. *Family Relations* 29(October):445–450.

———— (1982) Family separation and boundary ambiguity. In O. Hultaker and J. Trost (eds.), *Families in Disaster.* Sweden: International University Library Press.

————, and J. Greenberg (1982) The measurement of family boundary ambiguity: a general variable in family stress theory. Paper presented at the annual meeting of the National Council on Family Relations, Milwaukee.

Bowen, M. (1960) The family as a unit of study and treatment. *American Journal of Orthopsychiatry* 31(January):40–60.

Chodorow, N. (1978) *The Reproduction of Mothering: Psychoanalysis and the Sociology of Gender.* Berkeley: University of California Press.

Cottle, T. J. (1974) *A Family Album: Portraits of Intimacy and Kinship.* New York: Harper & Row.

Cuber, J., and P. B. Harroff (1965) *Sex and the Significant Americans: A Study of Sexual Behavior among the Affluent.* Baltimore: Penguin.

Dakers, B. M. (1981) The postman and the public school teacher. Pp. 75–82 in C.V. Willie, *A New Look at Black Families* (2d ed.). New York: General Hall.

Davis, F. (1974) Stories and sociology. *Urban Life and Culture* 3(October):310–316.

Davis, M. (1973) *Intimate Relations.* New York: Free Press.

Dobash, R. E., and R. Dobash (1979) *Violence against Wives: A Case against Patriarchy.* New York: Free Press.

Duberman, L. (1975) *The Reconstituted Family.* Chicago: Nelson-Hall.

Durkheim, E. (1950) *The Rules of the Sociological Method.* New York: Free Press.

Emerson, R. M. (1962) Power–dependence relations. *American Sociological Review* 27(February):31–41.

Entwisle, D. R., and S. G. Doering (1981) *The First Birth: A Family Turning Point.* Baltimore: Johns Hopkins University Press.

Finkelhor, D., R. J. Gelles, G. T. Hotaling, and M. A. Straus (eds.) (1983) *The Dark Side of Families: Current Family Violence Research.* Beverly Hills: Sage.

Fisch, R. (1977) Sometimes it's better for the right hand not to know what the left hand is doing. Pp. 199–210 in P. Papp (ed.), *Family Therapy: Full Length Case Studies.* New York: Gardner.

Foreman, P. B. (1948) The theory of case studies. *Social Forces* 26(May):408–419.

Frazier, E. F. (1939) *The Negro Family in the United States*. Chicago: University of Chicago Press.

Furstenberg, F. (ed.) (1980) Special issue on remarriage. *Journal of Family Issues* 1(December):443–571.

Gail, L. (1981) Surviving, with a little help from my daughters. Pp. 226–230 in R. Friedland and C. Kort (eds.), *The Mothers' Book: Shared Experiences*. Boston: Houghton Mifflin.

Garfinkel, H. (1956) Conditions of successful degradation ceremonies. *American Journal of Sociology* 61(March):420–424.

——— (1967) *Studies in Ethnomethodology*. Englewood Cliffs: Prentice-Hall.

Garrett, W. R. (1982) *Seasons of Marriage and Family Life*. New York: Holt, Rinehart & Winston.

Gelles, R. (1974) *The Violent Home: A Study of Physical Aggression between Husbands and Wives*. Beverly Hills: Sage.

——— (1976) Abused wives: why do they stay? *Journal of Marriage and the Family* 38(November):659–668.

Glaser, B. G., and A. L. Strauss (1965) *Awareness of Dying*. Chicago: Aldine.

Goffman, E. (1959) *The Presentation of Self in Everyday Life*. New York: Doubleday Anchor.

——— (1963) *Stigma: Notes on the Management of Spoiled Identity*. Englewood Cliffs: Prentice-Hall.

Goode, W. J. (1960) A theory of role strain. *American Sociological Review* 25(August):483–496.

——— (1971) Force and violence in the family. *Journal of Marriage and the Family* 33(November):624–636.

——— (1982) *The Family* (2d ed.). Englewood Cliffs: Prentice-Hall.

Gouldner, A. W. (1960) The norm of reciprocity: a preliminary statement. *American Sociological Reveiw* 25(April):161–178.

Greenberg, J. B. (1980) Single parenting: the one-man band. *Dimensions* 9(October):39–42.

Haley, J. (1963) *Strategies of Psychotherapy*. New York: Grune & Stratton.

Helmbold, F. W. (1976) *Tracing Your Ancestry*. Birmingham: Oxmoor House.

Hess, B., and J. Waring (1978) Parent and child in later life: rethinking the relationship. Pp. 241–273 in R. Lerner and G. Spanier (eds.), *Child Influences on Marital and Family Interaction: A Life-span Perspective*. New York: Academic.

Hess, R. D., and G. Handel (1959) *Family Worlds*. Chicago: University of Chicago Press.

Hetherington, E. M., M. Cox, and R. Cox (1976) Divorced fathers. *Family Coordinator* 25(October):417–428.

Holloman, R. E., and F. E. Lewis (1978) The "Clan": case study of a black extended family in Chicago. Pp. 201–238 in D. B. Shimkin, E. M. Shimkin, and D. A. Frate (eds.), *The Extended Family in Black Societies.* The Hague: Mouton.

Jaffe, S. S., and J. Viertel (1979) *Becoming Parents: Preparing for the Emotional Changes of First-time Parenthood.* New York: Atheneum.

Jencks, C. (1980) Structural versus individual explanations of inequality: where do we go from here? *Contemporary Sociology* 9(November):762–767.

Kalmuss, D., and M. A. Straus (1982) Wife's marital dependency and wife abuse. *Journal of Marriage and the Family* 44(May):277–286.

Kanter, R. M. (1972a) *Commitment and Community.* Cambridge: Harvard University Press.

——— (1972b) Getting it all together: some group issues in communes. *American Journal of Orthopsychiatry* 42(July):632–643.

Kantor, D., and W. Lehr (1975) *Inside the Family.* San Francisco: Jossey-Bass.

Keshet, H. F. (1981) A father speaks. Pp. xv–xxiii in K. M. Rosenthal and H. F. Keshet, *Fathers without Partners: A Study of Fathers and the Family after Marital Separation.* Totowa: Rowman and Littlefield.

Komarovsky, M. (1973) Cultural contradictions and sex roles: the masculine case. *American Journal of Sociology* 78(January):873–884.

Kuhn, A. (1974) *The Logic of Social Systems.* San Francisco: Jossey-Bass.

Laing, R. D. (1967) *The Politics of Experience.* New York: Pantheon.

———, H. Phillipson, and A. R. Lee (1966) *Interpersonal Perception.* New York: Springer.

LaRossa, R. (1977) *Conflict and Power in Marriage: Expecting the First Child.* Beverly Hills: Sage.

———, L. A. Bennett, and R. J. Gelles (1981) Ethical dilemmas in qualitative family research. *Journal of Marriage and the Family* 43(May):303–313.

———, and M. Mulligan LaRossa (1981) *Transition to Parenthood: How Infants Change Families.* Beverly Hills: Sage.

Lehtinen, M. W. (1977) Sociological family analysis. *Teaching Sociology* 4(April):307–314.

LeMasters, E. E. (1970) *Parents in Modern America.* Homewood: Dorsey.

——— (1975) *Blue-Collar Aristocrats: Life-styles at a Working-Class Tavern.* Madison: University of Wisconsin Press.

Lichtman, A. (1978) *Your Family History.* New York: Random House Vintage.

Marks, S. R. (1977) Multiple roles and role strain: some notes on human energy, time, and commitment. *American Sociological Review* 42(December):921–936.

Martin, E. P., and J. M. Martin (1978) *The Black Extended Family*. Chicago: University of Chicago Press.

Marx, K. (1938) *Critique of the Gotha Programme* (ed. C. P. Dutt). New York: International Publishers.

Mathis, A. (1978) Contrasting approaches to the study of black families. *Journal of Marriage and the Family* 40(November): 667–676.

McAdoo, H. P. (1978) Factors related to stability in upwardly mobile black families. *Journal of Marriage and the Family* 40(November):761–776.

McClendon, M. J. (1980) The missing link in the process of getting ahead. *Contemporary Sociology* 9(November):758–762.

Merton, R. K. (1957) The role set: problems in sociological theory. *British Journal of Sociology* 8(June):106–120.

Mills, C. W. (1959) *The Sociological Imagination*. New York: Oxford University Press.

Minuchin, S. (1974) *Families and Family Therapy*. Cambridge: Harvard University Press.

Moynihan, D. P. (1965) *The Negro Family: The Case for National Action*. Washington, D.C.: U.S. Department of Labor, Office of Planning and Research.

Nye, F. I., with H. M. Bahr, S. J. Bahr, J. E. Carlson, V. Gecas, S. McLaughlin, and W. L. Slocum (1976) *Role Structure and Analysis of the Family*. Beverly Hills: Sage.

Olson, D. H., D. H. Sprenkle, and C. Russell (1979) Circumplex model of marital and family systems: I. Cohesion and adaptability dimensions, family types, and clinical applications. *Family Process* 18(March):3–28.

Piotrkowski, C. S. (1979) *Work and the Family System: A Naturalistic Study of Working-Class and Lower-Middle-Class Families*. New York: Free Press.

Rainwater, L. (1966) Some aspects of lower class sexual behavior. *Journal of Social Issues* 22(April):96–108.

Raush, H. L., W. A. Barry, R. K. Hertel, and M. A. Swain (1974) *Communication, Conflict, and Marriage*. San Francisco: Jossey-Bass.

Reese, M. E. (1979) *Moving On: Overcoming the Crisis of Widowhood*. New York: Wyden Books/PEI Books.

Reiss, D. (1981) *The Family's Construction of Reality*. Cambridge: Harvard University Press.

Reiss, I. L. (1980) *Family Systems in America* (3d ed.). New York: Holt, Rinehart & Winston.

Rogers, C. R. (1972) *Becoming Partners: Marriage and Its Alternatives*. New York: Delacorte.

Roosevelt, R., and J. Lofas (1977) *Living in Step: A Remarriage Manual for Parents and Children.* New York: McGraw-Hill.

Rosenblatt, P. C. (1981) Ethnographic case studies. Pp. 194–225 in M. B. Brewer and B. E. Collins (eds.), *Scientific Inquiry and the Social Sciences.* San Francisco: Jossey-Bass.

———, and S. L. Titus (1976) Together and apart in the family. *Humanitas* 12(November):367–379.

Rossi, A. S. (1968) Transition to parenthood. *Journal of Marriage and the Family* 30(February):26–39.

——— (1977) A biosocial perspective on parenting. *Daedalus* 106(spring):1–31.

Rubin, Z. (1970) Measurement of romantic love. *Journal of Personality and Social Psychology* 2(October):265–273.

——— (1973) *Liking and Loving: An Introduction to Social Psychology.* New York: Holt, Rinehart & Winston.

Ruesch, J., and G. Bateson (1951) *Communication: The Social Matrix of Psychiatry.* New York: Norton.

Safa, H. I. (1971) The matrifocal family in the black ghetto: sign of pathology or pattern of survival? Pp. 35–59 in C. O. Crawford (ed.), *Health and the Family: A Medical-Sociological Analysis.* New York: Macmillan.

Saul, C. P. (1974) Coming home. Pp. 60–70 in S. Saul, *Aging: An Album of People Growing Old.* New York: Wiley.

Scanzoni, J. (1971) *The Black Family in Modern Society.* Boston: Allyn & Bacon.

———, and M. Szinovacz (1980) *Family Decision-making: A Developmental Sex Role Model.* Beverly Hills: Sage.

Scanzoni, L. D., and J. Scanzoni (1981) *Men, Women, and Change.* New York: McGraw-Hill.

Schiller, B. R. (1970) Stratified opportunities: the essence of the vicious circle. *American Journal of Sociology* 76(November): 426–442.

Schur, E. M. (1971) *Labelling Deviant Behavior: Its Sociological Implications.* New York: Harper & Row.

Schutz, A. (1967) *Collected Papers I: The Problems of Social Reality.* The Hague: Nijhoff.

Scott, M. B., and S. M. Lyman (1968) Accounts. *American Sociological Review* 33(February):46–62.

Sheehy, G. (1974) *Passages: Predictable Crises of Adult Life.* New York: Dutton.

Shimkin, D. B., E. M. Shimkin, and D. A. Frate (eds.) (1978) *The Extended Family in Black Societies.* The Hague: Mouton.

Sieber, S. D. (1974) Toward a theory of role accumulation. *American Sociological Review* 39(August):567–578.

Somerville, R. M. (1964) *Family Insights through the Short Story: A Guide for Teachers and Workshop Leaders.* New York: Columbia University Press.

Sommerville, J. (1982) *The Rise and Fall of Childhood.* Beverly Hills: Sage.

Sprey, J. (1969) The family as a system in conflict. *Journal of Marriage and the Family* 31(November):699–706.

——— (1979) Conflict theory and the study of marriage and the family. Pp. 130–159 in W. R. Burr, R. Hill, F. I. Nye, and I. L. Reiss (eds.), *Contemporary Theories about the Family II: General Theories/Theoretical Orientations.* New York: Free Press.

Staples, R. (1971) Toward a sociology of the black family: a theoretical and methodological assessment. *Journal of Marriage and the Family* 33(February):119–138.

Straus, M. (1974) Leveling, civility, and violence in the family. *Journal of Marriage and the Family* 36(February):13–29.

——— (1979) Measuring intrafamily conflict and violence: the conflict tactics (CT) scales. *Journal of Marriage and the Family* 41(February):75–88.

———, R. J. Gelles, and S. K. Steinmetz (1980) *Behind Closed Doors: Violence in the American Family.* New York: Doubleday Anchor.

———, and G. Hotaling (eds.) (1980) *The Social Causes of Husband–Wife Violence.* Minneapolis: University of Minnesota Press.

Thibaut, J. W., and H. H. Kelley (1959) *The Social Psychology of Groups.* New York: Wiley.

Turner, R. (1962) Role-taking: process versus conformity. Pp. 20–40 in A. Rose (ed.), *Human Behavior and Social Processes.* Boston: Houghton Mifflin.

U.S. Bureau of the Census (1976) *Demographic Aspects of Aging and the Older Population in the United States.* CPR Special Studies Series, P. 23, No. 59.

Valentine, B. (1978) *Hustling and Other Hard Work: Lifestyles in the Ghetto.* New York: Free Press.

Valentine, C. (1978) Introduction. Pp. 1–10 in B. Valentine, *Hustling and Other Hard Work: Lifestyles in the Ghetto.* New York: Free Press.

Waller, W., and R. Hill (1951) *The Family: A Dynamic Interpretation.* New York: Dryden.

Watzlawick, P., J. Beavin, and D. D. Jackson (1967) *Pragmatics of Human Communication: A Study of Interactional Patterns, Pathologies, and Paradoxes.* New York: Norton.

———, J. Weakland, and R. Fisch (1974) *Change: Principles of Problem Formation and Problem Resolution.* New York: Norton.

Weber, M. (1947) *The Theory of Social and Economic Organization* (ed. T. Parsons). New York: Oxford University Press.

Weigert, A. J. (1981) *Sociology of Everyday Life.* New York: Longman.

Weiss, M. (1974) *Living Together: A Year in the Life of a City Commune.* New York: McGraw-Hill.

Weiss, R. S. (1966) Alternative approaches in the study of complex situations. *Human Organization* 25(fall):198–206.

Wilkes, P. (1975) *Trying Out the Dream: A Year in the Life of an American Family.* Philadelphia: Lippincott.

Willie, C. V. (1981) *A New Look at Black Families* (2d ed.). New York: General Hall.

Wiseman, J. P. (1970) *Stations of the Lost: The Treatment of Skid Row Alcoholics.* Englewood Cliffs: Prentice-Hall.

———, and M. S. Aron (1970) The case study: the family. Pp. 73–82 in *Field Projects for Sociology Students.* Cambridge: Schenkman.

Yankelovich, Skelly, and White, Inc. (1977) *Raising Children in a Changing Society.* Minneapolis: General Mills.

Zerubavel, E. (1979a) *Patterns of Time in Hospital Life.* Chicago: University of Chicago Press.

——— (1979b) Private time and public time: the temporal structure of social accessibility and professional commitments. *Social Forces* 58(September):38–58.

Name Index

Subject Index